AGAINST THE CURRENT

AGAINST THE CURRENT

Father Tom Oddo and the New American Catholic

TYLER BIEBER

Unencumbered Press

AGAINST THE CURRENT published by:
Unencumbered Press
Spokane, WA

ISBN: 979-8-9865664-5-0

Cover design by Luis F. Ramos
Interior design by Luis F. Ramos
Edited by Alexa V. Schmidt

For permissions, inquiries, or additional rights requests, please contact the publisher at marketing@unencumberedpress.com.

To Mom,
I love you.

Great are the myths … I too delight in them.
Great are Adam and Eve … I too look back and accept them;
Great the risen and fallen nations, and their poets, women, sages,
inventors, rulers, warriors and priests.

Walt Whitman,
Leaves of Grass (1855)

a purpose of human life, no matter who is controlling it, is to love whoever is around to be loved.

Kurt Vonnegut,
The Sirens of Titan (1959)

Table of Contents

Part Three: Camelot
1986–1989

Part Four: This Is Death
1989–present

Prologue

Sunday
October 29, 1989
Portland, Oregon

Norman Countryman had a premonition. Something about the way the air felt, heavy and foreboding, made him tremble. He wasn't afraid, but fear still lurked around the corner. A crisp chill from the previous night hung over the city, the first to drop below freezing that fall. By the afternoon, temperatures inched into the 50s. The day was perfect for those eagerly awaiting Halloween, and the coming days of All Saints and All Souls, but it felt strangely charged to him.

Despite this feeling of dread leaching at the edges, Norman left home to fulfill an obligation to his tenant. On any other Sunday, he might have spent the day in instead of running errands, but this errand served a larger purpose. The tenant had requested he remove a wrecked car from the house they were renting on Calvert Street, near the Kenton neighborhood of northwest Portland, that Norman had owned for many years. He was storing the car in the yard for use in rebuilding a race car he had constructed a year prior. Amateur stock car racing had become his pastime, a "diversion" from staying in and watching TV, then his "only other hobby." Joining Countryman was his son Jeremie. Norman was forty-one, Jeremie was eighteen, a few months away from his high school graduation.

They planned to push the car, an old Chevy Nova, onto a trailer and haul it two and a half miles to a storage unit on North Vancouver Avenue. The trip would take about ten minutes without traffic, mostly on North Columbia Boulevard—a long, four-lane, east–west roadway stretching from the Port of Portland to the recently-opened I-205 interchange and Glenn Jackson Bridge. Norman and Jeremie left the house in Kenton around 3:30 p.m.

At 3:42, as their truck drove eastward, Jeremie was looking in the rearview mirror when he saw the locking pin holding the rig together fail. The hitch slipped out and the trailer detached from the truck. He watched as the trailer ran into oncoming traffic before it collided with a Toyota Corolla in the westbound lane. A second later, the Nova rolled off and hit a second truck driving alongside the Toyota.

Jeremie yelled, "Stop! You lost the trailer!" and Norman hit the brakes. Both jumped out and ran to the scene immediately behind them, first to the other truck. They helped the driver and passenger out, shaken but unhurt, before all four moved toward the crumpled Toyota. As they approached the wreck, Jeremie saw the driver's body convulse, then go still. The man had been internally decapitated by the steering wheel. Norman, growing frantic and running around in search of a phone, completely broke down, screaming for help against the sound of passing cars.

Portland Police, then an ambulance, made their way to the crash. Responding medics began using the jaws of life, carving open the Corolla to retrieve the driver's body. As the police proceeded with their survey of the wreck, the Countrymans looking on, *The Oregonian*'s photojournalist Brent Wojahn arrived. He took a photo of the Corolla pulled to the side of the road with the doors flayed open and the roof torn upward like a sardine can. No human remains are visible in the image, but it can still be described as graphic.

The officers did not inform Norman the driver was dead; they didn't have to. The Countrymans watched the body exit the Corolla on a stretcher. No citations were issued, but they stayed at the scene for over two hours, aware their day wasn't through. After the site was cleared, they still had to transport the Nova to the storage unit, and proceeded with great remorse to load the car back onto the trailer to complete their errand.

Meanwhile, word spread from the accident back to the University of Portland—a short drive in the opposite direction, mere minutes from the house on Calvert Street—that the driver was Father Tom Oddo. His car had become just as recognizable as his Sicilian tan, or the light in his office window in West Hall, glowing late into the night. Those in the UP orbit traveling on Columbia Boulevard would've known the worst had transpired as they passed. Word spread through the dorms, the library, and the new university computer lab. A freshman working in the lab that night said the person who told him was on the verge of tears.

Patti Brown, a food service worker in the University of Portland's Bauccio Commons, saw a TV news report showing the crash that afternoon. A brief flash of the wreck horrified her as she prepared for evening meals. Hired in 1979, Brown was an integral part of the commons, making meaningful connections with students dining there. Father Tom was a regular at Bauccio, breaking tradition to break bread with students. The news of his sudden passing left her in shock, leveled by a cosmic gut punch like so many others.

Most of the university's Holy Cross Order learned of his death over dinner. The normally cordial and happy gathering of religious brothers suddenly became quiet and morose. Across UP, some students cried, but most were unable to react, paralyzed in their grief. By 10:30 p.m., the Sunday Evening Mass was packed as the campus community searched for meaning in the face of calamity.

Norman woke to a report on a local radio station, blaring through his alarm clock: The driver of the Corolla was identified as Father Tom, a Holy Cross priest and the seventeenth president of the University of Portland. The news was catastrophic. Immediately, Norman felt the crush of realization sweep over him: Tom was a national, even international figure; then, in an instant, he was gone. It would take Norman months before he could bring himself to visit the campus, much less begin the grieving process for himself. Monday classes were canceled, leaving students to wander the campus in mourning.

The Oregonian's headline CRASH KILLS UP PRESIDENT ran on October 30. The story by Don Hamilton included an inset staff picture of Father Tom and details of the crash alongside a postcard-sized version of Brent Wojahn's photo. Over the next week, numerous letters to *The Oregonian* decried what readers considered a lack of editorial standards for running the image of a death scene on its front page. Though the paper made no official response to the criticism, the October 30 issue is no longer available to the public through its online archive and may now only be found in surviving printed copies. Don Hamilton cited numerous community and Holy Cross leaders' remembrances of Father Tom, including Auxiliary Bishop of Portland Father Paul Waldschmidt, a former UP president himself, who called Tom "a great priest and a great leader." Archbishop William Levada, meanwhile, was notably "out of town … and unavailable for comment."

The news spread around the world within forty-eight hours. A prayer request to the Holy Cross superior general in Rome appeared the day following the crash. *The New York Times* ran an obituary on Tuesday, October 31, while local papers covered the story of his funeral services, a sharply choreographed spectacle of events despite no advance planning, owing greatly to the competencies of their organizers. As Father Tom was laid to rest, and the remembrances continued in print and sermons into November, the question of his legacy became a major topic of conversation. To many students, he was the president who made himself available, who showed up to events and ate alongside them, who still taught theology courses, and who made an effort to connect in ways that no other campus administrator or executive had before him. He became a friendly face on the Bluff, the cliffside UP stands on. Even those who didn't know he was president knew Father Tom.

At his death, Tom was forty-five—recently adopting gray streaks in his hair; he had been just thirty-eight at the time of his appointment, making him the same age as many students' parents. But because of his youth, he was seen as a vibrant and capable administrator who delivered real results to his campus. His magnetism was obvious. One student described him as "John Kennedyesque" to the university's student-run newspaper, *The Beacon*, not the first of many who made the connection between Tom and the Camelot era of American history, both during his life and following his death. He was easy to talk to and easy on the eyes, a conversationalist who was eager to meet people, which made people excited to meet him. To many, Father Tom was their friend, and some *still* consider him one.

For those that knew him prior to his term at UP, though, he represented something greater than an accomplished university administrator and educator. He was a new kind of priest, a gay man living and ministering in a world set loose from tradition by the Second Vatican Council. A world that, throughout the course of his life saw the Civil Rights Movement, the creation of Title IX, and the desegregation of schools, the horror and the shame of the Vietnam War, Watergate, Iran-Contra, the AIDS crisis, and the ongoing child sex abuse scandal in the church. As national secretary of a group called DignityUSA in the 1970s, he is a nearly-forgotten progenitor of the modern gay rights movement, even though his name appears frequently throughout the modern socio-political history of the United States. His life was rich and full, his mission clear, despite his youth, despite the suddenness of his death. How his life transcended into myth in the same way as John F. Kennedy is also clear, slipping the bonds of reality into the cloud of memory, which kept churning in the form of vigils and memorials for years after his death.

Today, one runs into Father Tom's footprint several times on the UP campus, and his building accomplishments even more so. A student scholarship and memorial plaza both carry his name. And beyond the Bluff, his presence is still felt among those he met and those he taught, those who worked and organized with him, and those who loved him. The memory of the man has become fused with the memory of a critical moment in the struggle for LGBTQ+ rights, reverberating through the ages with every small step forward in the march toward equality.

But for all of the grief and remembrances, and the ripples he made in the waters of American history, it is easy to lose sight of the kind of person he was—and, by extension, the age in which he lived. To properly remember him, to give him the credit or the criticism he is due, requires a deeper look than an obituary or a homily. It requires time and distance, a long period of reflection without which we are blind to hindsight, and without which we can forget the humanity of those we've lost. Now more than ever, Tom's story deserves to be told.

Part One: Hail Mary, Full of Grace

1944–1982

Hail, Mary, full of grace,
the Lord is with thee.
Blessed art thou amongst women
and blessed is the fruit of thy womb, Jesus.
Holy Mary, Mother of God,
pray for us sinners,
now and at the hour of our death.
Amen.

Hail Mary Prayer

Chapter 1

Queens

The Oddos[1] are one of millions of families whose American story began at Ellis Island. Tom's father Dominick Oddo was the son of Gesualdo Oddo, a barber and later realtor, and Mary Oddo, a housewife. Dominick, his brother Vincent, and their parents had lived for many years on Broad Street, their names appearing on state census records from 1925. Gesualdo, listed in the 1920 US census as "Harry Oddo," emigrated when he was sixteen from Italy with ten dollars to his name. His wife, Mary, had also emigrated from Italy, when she was twenty. Both had crossed the Atlantic in the shadow of war and uncertain futures in Europe. The two had met and married in New York, starting a family within blocks of a relentless and roaring Wall Street.

As he grew to adulthood Dominick aspired to help people, eventually training to become a physician at Georgetown University's School of Medicine. He graduated with his MD in June 1938, and soon after turned to the armed forces for work. He enlisted in the army in 1940, prior to the attack on Pearl Harbor and US involvement in World War II. Once American troops began to engage the enemy, Dominick shipped out to help treat the wounded and dying. When he enlisted, he was single, with his mother Mary listed as next-of-kin, then residing at a two-story brick townhouse on Utopia Parkway in Flushing, Queens.

Sometime after his enlistment, between 1942–1943, he met and married Catherine Arthen, the daughter of Jacob Arthen, a telegrapher, and Magdalena Arthen, a housewife. Catherine came from a devout Catholic household and received first Communion when she was six. Since her childhood, she'd been active in church life, and in 1939—before she was

1. Pronounced "Oh-DOE."

twenty-one—graduated from the Mary Immaculate Hospital School of Nursing in Jamaica, Queens. An August 1939 news item reported on a sudden death and possible poisoning at Mary Immaculate of an informant in an "abortion racket" case, citing Dr. Dominick Oddo as "house surgeon." It's highly probable Catherine and Dominick met at the hospital, or through a mutual connection there. Both Tom's parents had healing and service to others woven into their stories, traits that would become necessary for Catherine shortly after marrying her soldier-doctor.

Thomas Charles Oddo, their only son, was born on June 12, 1944, in Long Island, six days after American GIs stormed the beaches of Normandy. The day was overcast and humid, a drizzle of rain falling throughout the city. It is not known whether Dominick was present at the birth, and it is unlikely considering his proximity to the Allied Forces' advance that year.

New York had evolved quickly from the Oz-like world which his ancestors had experienced. Tom was born into a city rushing toward the future: Mayor Fiorello LaGuardia opened the 1939 World's Fair at Flushing Meadows Park, just minutes away from Tom's childhood home. The fair, billed as a vision of the "World of Tomorrow," offered a look into what life would be like once transformed by the emerging technology of the age. As the Radio Corporation of America's pavilion carried the opening ceremony and speech by President Roosevelt on early television sets, NBC inaugurated its own television service within New York City. Nylon fabric and toy viewfinders made their debuts at the fair. General Motors promoted a car-centered model city called "Futurama," while Westinghouse introduced "Elektro the Moto-Man," a seven-foot robot that could speak, move, even smoke cigarettes.

While life in New York still hustled and bustled through the war, Dominick's world a thousand miles away was markedly different. An article from December 1944, shortly before the disastrous Battle of the Bulge, reports a Private Clifford E. Tewell resting in an army hospital in England after being struck by fragments from a German artillery shell along the River Metz. The article quoted one "First Lieutenant Dominick C. Oddo of Flushing, Long Island" saying "Pvt. Tewell is recovering rapidly and will soon begin our rehabilitation program." Dominick was listed as a ward surgeon, giving some hint to the work he performed. Back home, Tom was still in diapers. His mother, Catherine, beset by worry, prayed the Rosary nightly with him from the earliest days of his infanthood, a tradition that would last all of Tom's life. Upon Dominick's return, he did his best to rejoin the medical community and regain some sense of normalcy.

Growing up, Tom saw changes all around him, outside his door and across the nation: the rapidly reshaping New York skyline and the explosion of Robert Moses's highways; the ticker tape parades of V-E Day; the boom of tourism to the city from all nations; the vicious war in Korea; the pinging of Sputnik over the world; and the fiery debates on race and equality which accelerated with Rosa Parks's refusal to move in 1955, and the West Harlem police beating of Hinton Johnson in 1957. But these topics were largely immaterial compared to the everyday things Tom busied himself with: schoolwork, who was dating whom in the orbit of Holy Cross High School, and playing basketball every afternoon with his cousin Ed.

Tom and Ed Oddo were inseparable. Ed's father, Dominick's brother, was a cab driver living in the Bronx, and the families spent a considerable amount of time together despite living in different parts of the city. Ed and Tom received their first communion together, and afterward celebrated with a big Italian dinner at a restaurant across from the church. Throughout their school years, they found themselves involved in many of the same activities. In multiple yearbooks, *E. Oddo* and *T. Oddo* appear next to or near each other in group shots of clubs and teams. One could assume they were brothers seeing how close they were, and they stayed that way through adulthood. Afternoons were spent in Tom's backyard shooting hoops, or singing doo-wop music and recording their voices over the tracks. Then, after Ed would go home, they would find themselves talking on the phone for hours at night, much to Dominick's frustration at the mounting bill and the boys' non-stop yammering. The fact that Ed was a Yankees fan and Tom an aggrieved Dodgers fan only made for longer chats over the phone.

Ed, looking back, says that Tom genuinely loved people, and loved the connections he made with everyone he met. He became popular for his kindness, framed by a toothy smile and a buzz cut, and got Ed into parties and friend groups. He made the opposite of an Irish Goodbye whenever Ed wanted to leave a party; they had to budget at least fifteen minutes for Tom to be able to say goodbye to everyone, such was the regularity of the episode. They dated together, taking girls out on double dates. Tom dated two girls while at Holy Cross. The second, nearing their graduation, wanted to get serious and settle down. But with eyes already set on the priesthood, he broke things off before they could.

"He wanted to live the life of a non-priest," Ed says now, explaining Tom's wish to experience life as an ordinary person, a member of the laity, so that he could best serve people confessing their sins or recounting their troubles. He thinks that Tom largely succeeded in that goal. Even as he became a popular figure at Holy Cross, busying himself with the work of student leadership and preparation for a future in the priesthood, he never lost sight of his friends.

In the 1959–1960 yearbook, his junior year, he appeared with Ed in photos of announcers for WHCHS, the school radio station. They also appeared in the section for the school photography club, the Photo Tradesmen Guild. Tom's father, Dominick, appears on the staff page in that same yearbook as the School Physician, a role he maintained for several years before and after Tom's enrollment. Also included was a profile on Dominick in the Health and Physical Education section. The write-up mentions how Dr. Oddo, as a city-approved physician, would hold meetings with students needing special medical attention and perform general physical examinations for all students entering Holy Cross's interscholastic sports program. Among these was the administration of a brand new service, the Heaf skin test for tuberculosis.

While Tom and Ed attended Holy Cross, Dominick also volunteered his time as the Team Physician for the school's sports teams, and one photo of him on the grounds of the school's football stadium reads: "Dr. Oddo kneels in the sideline quagmire at the Thanksgiving game." Dominick had made a name for himself in local medical circles, rising to multiple positions of leadership in professional associations, including president of the American Academy of General Practice–Queens Chapter and co-treasurer of the Queens County Medical Society.

Within its pages showing the variety of student activities at Holy Cross, the 1959–1960 yearbook includes a photo of Tom with Brother Matthew Gara, CSC, head of the Religious Studies Department, going over a script for the January 20 morning religious bulletin. The caption for the photo reads "This shot was taken one minute before Tom's familiar voice ranged throughout the school … " Tom's hand is on the microphone, awaiting the announcement chime. In another shot of all the morning announcers, Ed holds the microphone while Tom stands next to him, in a suit and Christmas sweater. Tom looks like the typical American teenager that the country had professed would be the leader of the free world within the next generation: tall, trim, smartly dressed, and proper. In those days, Tom's adherence to order paired with his outgoingness, propelling him to early success among his peers.

Senior year, 1960/61, was a banner year for Tom at Holy Cross. Beyond his continued work at WHCHS and in the Photo Tradesmen Guild—where he, Ed, and two other students are credited for much of that year's yearbook photography—he also appears in group shots for the Holy Cross Mission Unit, the staff of *The Lance* student newspaper, and intramural basketball. He was also in the cast of a student production, "The Reluctant Romeo," as a member of the Dramatics Club with Ed. His presence throughout the school's culture can be felt on each page, with many of the published photos coming directly from his camera, from his own perspective. Wherever he wasn't already participating in school activities, Tom would be snapping pictures and recounting the memories later in the darkroom.

By 1961, he appeared far less in yearbook shots; now lead Yearbook Photographer, he was the one taking them. Despite his obligations to *The Lance* and his own preparation for religious training, he still made time to perform in another show, Thornton Wilder's "The Matchmaker," and continued helping with the morning religious bulletin. The 1960–1961 yearbook itself is a remarkable document. Created in tribute to the inauguration of the first Catholic president of the United States, John F. Kennedy, the cover is adorned with a presidential seal over a left-set cross. The first pages are awash in red, with a white silhouette of Abraham Lincoln and the words:

> A NEW NATION
> CONCEIVED IN LIBERTY,
> AND DEDICATED TO THE PROPOSITION
> THAT *ALL* MEN ARE CREATED
> *EQUAL.*

The next pages, a mixture of red, white, and blue text with an image of the Statue of Liberty, capture the star-spangled mood of the times within the American church:

> The
> CATHOLIC CHURCH IN AMERICA
> Basking in the glow of
> LIBERTY'S TORCH
> Aims at the development of a
> TRULY FREE AMERICAN,
> Strong in the love of his

> CREATOR
> Virile in his attachment to his
> COUNTRY,
> A God-centered patriot,
> Morally responsible,
> Physically sound,
> And possessing the
> Highest degree of
> Political and social
> INTEGRITY
> A truly
> CHRISTIAN
> And
> AMERICAN
> Product of
> CATHOLIC
> EDUCATION
> For DEMOCRACY

Other pages include quotes from Kennedy's inauguration speech and alternating drawings of priests, a soldier with a rifle, and a graduating Holy Cross student. The contrast between priests in their vestments and Cold Warriors in fatigues belied the future that lay ahead for many of Tom's peers. His cohort couldn't know what lay ahead for them—the scare of the Cuban Missile Crisis, the institution of the draft, injury and death in the jungles of Vietnam—but Tom had a clear vision laid out for himself.

Since he was ten years old he had wanted to be a priest, and had never seen another future for himself beyond it. His time at Holy Cross had only further cemented his desire to be like his school elders, the Holy Cross brothers. In an autobiographical sketch written by Tom many years later, he recalled his attraction to the brotherhood and why he chose to pursue it:

> I remember my great admiration for the brothers, particularly their intense and generous investment in the lives of young people, their commitment to service, their family spirit. But like many, I put these thoughts on hold for a while, following my parents' counsel to let some time pass within a general college setting.

The Congregation of Holy Cross (signified by the suffix CSC after priests' names) is a religious congregation within the Catholic church whose primary mission is to educate others on the faith, and by extension knowledge, of the wider world. Tom would've had congregational options available to him through college and seminary, but he was always drawn to the tradition he'd been raised in, to eventually join the ranks of Holy Cross educators he grew up around.

With both of their sights set on college, Ed assumed they'd both go to the same school again. But Dominick, while less ecstatic about Tom's career path than Catherine, was determined to provide his son the best education possible. A guidance counselor at Holy Cross suggested that, if they could afford it, they should send Tom to the University of Notre Dame, an institutional centerpoint of both the Holy Cross brotherhood and American Catholic higher education. And so, that year Tom was Notre Dame bound, while Ed chose Siena College in California.

Despite a distance of over 2,000 miles, they wrote letters to each other regularly. What could be said in a phone call was different from what they could write to one another. Nowadays, Ed tells me there were only two people in college that he kept in contact with this way: his wife of more than fifty years, and Tom—his surrogate brother from Queens.

Chapter 2

Indiana

This chapter (and a few others in Part One) deal with the minutiae of Catholicism, details that may not be familiar to you. I've tried my best throughout this book to write about religion in the easiest way possible without ignoring your intelligence, so that you can fully understand the context of Tom's work and service. It's the way he would've wanted it.

Catherine's joy at Tom's matriculation to Notre Dame quickly turned to horror: Tom would spend his first year in a "forced triple [apartment] in the attic of Breen–Phillips Hall." The building was known among students as "Stalag B-P," a riff on the 1953 POW film *Stalag 17*, and because of the hall's strict rector with Germanic roots. Despite this reputation, when Tom arrived, the hall and the rest of Notre Dame were engaging in a "radical 'experiment' … the elimination of mandatory study times and evening 'lights out.'" Though liberal and freeing, this did not dissuade Tom from his studies or extracurriculars. A math major at first, he switched to philosophy, the subject required by seminaries at the time, after fall 1961.

That first year at Notre Dame, Tom joined the university swim team. While not the most accomplished swimmer, he quickly established himself as a team player. He appears each year in team photos, beaming beside his fellow swimmers. As early as the 1961/62 season, he's listed as a "numeral winner," a rank under the varsity "monogram winners" for the team. Regardless of wins, he was a vigorous athlete, regularly competing in the 500-yard freestyle, trying hard but never quite reaching a varsity letter.

While swimming provided Tom both healthy competition and a place of solace, he quickly became active in other areas of campus life. Tom's 1962 freshman photo is a group shot with the label "Watch the Camera."

The boys in the shot are either lined up on the stairs in the background, or either slouching or sitting on the hillside in the foreground. Tom stands on the hill, in another sweater with his hand in his pocket. His pose reflects his rising to the occasion: That year, he was elected spiritual commissioner for the sophomore class, and became involved in the Hall Chairman's Council.

Fall 1963 was already the start of an eventful academic year as students prepared for Thanksgiving Break. The November 12 Religious Bulletin included notes on varying attendance and engagement at campus Masses, recent comments by Pope Paul VI on Catholicism in America, and a one pager from a "Fr. Baker" entitled "Are You in the Swim?" Baker began his write-up by describing how unfulfilling life may appear to the average Notre Dame student:

> It's no wonder the Christian life is so dull and unchallenging. It holds out no satisfying value. It's a complex of empty rituals. And the ideal of goodness is looked-upon as a hangover from childhood—an ancestral code of taboos. Not only is such a way of life dull but the hypocrisy of it all completely revolts you.

Baker then challenges the reader:

> Honestly, have you ever let yourself experience the dynamic alchemy of the Christian life? Have you ever lived, for a day, this profound mystery? Have you dug your teeth into its ageless challenge? Since "coming of age" have you jumped into the swim of your Baptism and experienced in every pore and nerve-end the Christian paradox—that you must die to live?
>
> As long as you sit snugly and smugly on the outside of the Baptismal pool, the Christian life will most certainly remain dull, flat, ritualistic and mechanical. And you're so right—you are in every sense a hypocrite because a Christian means living this mystery in your own flesh and blood today—1963—on this campus. Its fierce dynamics don't consist in wearing a medal, saying a Hail Mary before a test, or standing inside a certain building for 38 minutes every Sunday morning.

He ends with the following postscript, something Tom no doubt would've found joy in: "P.S. It's impossible to experience the joy of swimming if you never throw yourself in the water." Such engagement with the mystery of his faith was the animus that made Tom move, the desire to swim in the waters of God and often against the current of the world, a current that would become a riptide in a matter of days.

On Friday, November 22, campus was quiet. The skies were gray. Those milling about South Bend were preparing for the Saturday football game, a non-conference match against the University of Iowa Hawkeyes, as both teams wound down their seasons. That afternoon, at 1:40 p.m., anyone watching CBS would've seen *As the World Turns* interrupted by the voice of Walter Cronkite, reporting that President Kennedy had been seriously wounded in a shooting in Dallas, Texas. Within minutes, NBC and ABC joined the coverage, with some frenzied newsmen reporting that President Kennedy was dead. Radio stations would also start pre-empting scheduled programming and commercial breaks in favor of wall-to-wall coverage of the event—the first such event in the history of American television news.

Students talked amongst themselves. Tom would've heard the whispers too. In the hallways, rumors spawned rumors which begat more rumors. Some classes were canceled abruptly. Others, like Dr. John Meagher's 3:00 p.m. Shakespeare class went ahead as scheduled. Meagher, a wunderkind of Notre Dame who graduated with two PhDs in the 1950s, walked into his classroom without a word, without greeting his students. He started his lecture without preface, without acknowledging what had transpired in Dallas. The students, juniors like Tom, one by one started taking notes, as was their habit. Meagher spoke on *King Lear*, as another alumnus Jack O'Connell remembered years later:

> Meagher continued talking about the tragedy of Lear and the jealousies and murders and backstabbings and—slowly looking up to the ceiling with his arms outstretched—concluded with Cordelia's words from the end of Act IV, "No cause, no cause." Then he walked out of the room.

Cordelia delivers the line as a dying King Lear seeks reconciliation with his daughter, estranged after he ignored her and sought favor with her sisters. As Lear remarks that she has a reason to hate him, to continue holding a grudge, she says simply, "No cause, no cause." Meagher's delivery of the line, in contrast, suggested he believed the violence of the president's murder to be without cause, without meaning. Senselessness was a communal feeling, as Tom must've felt. Two days later, as some students watched on TV, Lee Harvey Oswald was murdered by Jack Ruby in a Dallas police garage. A period of national mourning not seen since the assassination of Abraham Lincoln descended upon the country.

The death of President Kennedy, felt profoundly among the Catholic faithful, shuttered the South Bend campus. Notre Dame officials canceled the Iowa game. It would never be played, out of respect for Kennedy. We can't be sure what Tom's exact thoughts were on the assassination, the moment, the feeling, or that timeless phenomenon of recalling exactly where you were when "*it* happened," but we can be certain it led to some profound moments of prayer, and private searches for meaning.

During his junior year, still in the search, Tom inched closer and closer toward the priesthood. He registered for Latin classes held in Moreau Seminary, a tight-knit community on the Notre Dame campus. While there, Tom acted as an information agent for seminarians sequestered from the news of the world. Whenever Tom arrived, he would report the latest.

In December, Tom was selected as chairman of the President's Reception Committee for Notre Dame's Junior Weekend, planned for March 1964. His performance in helping execute the event may have helped him prevail in a close election for the presidency of the Notre Dame Hall Presidents' Council in May, defeating a student government peer and past class president. In the May 1, 1964 edition of *The Scholastic*, Notre Dame's student newspaper, the report on Tom's victory mentioned that he "expressed the belief that next year the Council will assume a more dynamic and important role on the campus, increasing its activities on the hall level." Tom didn't waste any time delivering on that promise.

Two weeks later, *The Scholastic* ran the following story under the headline "Don't Choose the Mug":

> Last Sunday afternoon a few strollers on the main quad were shocked to find three or four racing bicycles bearing down on them. These unfortunate pedestrians just happened to be in the way of the Hall Presidents' Council's first annual Bike Race.
>
> Tom Oddo, president of the Hall Presidents' Council, cautioned the contestants, "Remember, you're only racing for beer mugs. If it comes to a choice between a beer mug and running someone down, don't choose the mug."

The story described the route of the race, a course that hit half a dozen buildings across the campus, traversed in four or five minutes by the racers who met Tom at the finish line. That same month, Tom was awarding trophies again, this time for hall displays—the best since the contest began, in his estimation—at halftime of the Homecoming football game.

In fall, never the slacker, Tom began his term as a student senator, and quickly became involved in campus life issues. In September, the Senate's Student Affairs Commission initiated a program run by a subgroup, the Religious Committee, to better include the three-percent Protestant student population in local churches, on- and off-campus. The Committee, led by Father Lloyd Teske, CSC—Notre Dame's assistant vice president of student affairs and university chaplain—was advised by Tom and fellow Senator Mike Wilsey. The committee opened its membership to all residential halls, with members chosen by hall rectors, Teske, and Father Ted Hesburgh, CSC, the university president. This early instance of ecumenicalism was something Tom would build upon throughout his life, and would become a driving force of his ministry.

As senator, Tom voted on an updated speaker policy for the university, following the appearance of the segregationist Governor George Wallace earlier in the year. He was also involved in the formation of the Stay Hall system, a residential life experiment that gave students the option of living in the same halls through their graduation, breaking with the custom of class-specific halls. The idea was first developed by a committee which eventually added Tom to its ranks. While much doubt existed about its implementation—which would relocate some freshmen and equal divisions of sophomores, juniors, and seniors amongst three residential halls—a Senate vote to approve or reject the proposed four-year plan was scheduled for February 1965. Committee members campaigned vigorously for the plan, and when the votes were tallied all but four senators voted in favor. Despite initial difficulty getting traction, the plan went into effect that year.

Decades later, Tom would note that a Student Government retreat at Moreau Seminary—a long weekend held inside the building, a window into the lives of the brothers studying there—convinced him to formally pursue the priesthood. Tom approached his hall chaplain after the retreat to seek his professional guidance, and soon was meeting with the campus Holy Cross vocation director. Tom's educational track matched the track of seminarians so closely that he was able to matriculate into a Novitiate immediately after graduation, a seamless transition from academic study to religious apprenticeship. Finally, he was "in the swim."

His last term as an undergraduate, spring 1965, Tom was recognized for his work. In March, Notre Dame announced the first recipients of the new President's Medallion, the highest non-credentialed honor bestowed upon its students, which replaced a previous honor—the Who's Who Award. After a process involving 137 nominations and interviews with forty-three finalists, Tom and twenty-four of his senior peers were chosen. Of his selection process and criteria, Father Ted Hesburgh said the recipients should have "distinction within that order in which students can achieve distinction, and excellence in the various forms in which it is achieved on this campus," referring to academics, good character, moral responsibility, and leadership in student activities. Tom charmed the Medallion Board in his interview, and he fit the bill perfectly.

Nearing graduation, Tom was ready to enter his year of Novitiate, the first step on the road to priestly vows. His work would be completed at Sacred Heart Novitiate in Jordan, Minnesota, a suburb of the Twin Cities eight hours away from South Bend. And while many years of study lay ahead of him, he had already deeply reflected on his faith, and the state of modern Catholicism. As he prepared to enter the work as a college graduate and priest-in-waiting, the church he served had seen a radical reawakening, a mini-revolution which began overseas and was landing on America's shores. And Tom joyously welcomed its arrival.

Chapter 3

The New American Catholic

Thousands of miles from South Bend, Indiana, the future of the church and Tom's career path had been debated and discussed by priests from around the world, determined to start a new chapter in Catholicism. When Tom was eighteen, in his first year at Notre Dame, Pope John XXIII opened the Second Vatican Council, the first ecumenical council of its kind in nearly a century. To open such a council was, in the words of the pontiff, an attempt to find "new enthusiasm, a new joy and serenity of mind in the unreserved acceptance by all of the entire Christian faith." In the years following the council, a common metaphor to describe its impact was one of throwing open the doors of the church to let in fresh air, and fresh faces.

For Tom, the council and its declarations made a deep impression. In many ways, he grew up with it: Vatican II was first announced in January 1959, in the early months of John XXIII's papacy. Planning for the Council stretched through Tom's later teen years, with discussions trickling down from the cardinals to the clergy. By the Council's end in 1965, after the death of Pope John XXIII and the election of Pope Paul VI to finish the job, multiple commissions within the Council had offered their insight on major issues of faith and theology reconsidered for the modern world. These determinations and declarations came when Tom was in his early twenties, well into his religious training.

Vatican II, the council's short name, was felt in all corners of the church. Catholic religious life, long a home of high church charisma and the trappings of ancient custom, suddenly began to reflect the world around it. The Council ushered in an era of ecumenicalism and interfaith dialogue, anchored by an embrace of the "Universal Call to Holiness," the idea that *all* Christians are called to God, not just the Catholics. It directed the usage of local vernacular in the recitation of Mass, replacing the old Latin, which many generations grew up hearing from the pulpit, with language most people in their community could understand. Priests would now face the congregants as they recited the words, and the laity could receive their own Communion of bread and wine. Other statements made by the Council's commissions declared and restated major positions of the church, including the primacy of liturgy, a condemnation of anti-Semitism and mass destruction in war, recognition of other Christian denominations with a call for outreach and reiterating the importance of Mary, Mother of Jesus and the faith, to church life. The effects of these changes rippled across the church, and appeared in Tom's writing at Notre Dame.

In early June 1965, the senior graduating class attended their Last Visit to Sacred Heart Church, a tradition at Notre Dame for students on their way to the priesthood. Tom's booklet from the event is marked up with notes for a speech he delivered that morning. Within the notes, mirroring the program of the event, Tom ruminated on Mary. Brainstorming on the topic, he makes several comments, some crossed out in the process:

> No Mother Image—crutch type of thing
> Such might seem sissy
> Be 100% what we are to be

Another referred to her as the "director" of the church, directing the people to Christ. The next reminds us she stayed with her son until the very end. Neither comment is particularly charged, although both are subjective. Far bolder were the following lines:

> Nothing divine about her—
> She is <u>HUMAN</u> +
> therein lies her
> greatness.
>
> Mother of <u>Christ</u>
> Mother of Christ's earthly body to whom the
> Church looks to [*sic*] for direction
> She teaches only <u>love</u>.
>
> *She is the mother of Christ + so she is the
> Mother of all those who are part of Christ

In looped cursive over five pages, Tom poured his heart out to Mary. Trying to get the speech right, he crossed out whole sections and moved others with the long addition of an arrow uprooting the text, setting the words farther down to allow a new thought, a new epiphany to fill the blanks. To him, Mary was the embodiment of pure, maternal love on Earth. Remembering the nightly rosary growing up, he no doubt thought of his own mother Catherine as he wrote.

Tom began by saying, “It might be good for us to think for a moment of the personal meaning Mary should have for each of us[,] the college educated student ready to meet the world.” But rather than expound on what Mary meant to him personally, Tom spoke about what she meant for the world, for every Catholic but also every Christian, in the renewed discussion of her importance at Vatican II:

> It seems to me that the vibrant discussion over Mar[i]ology today is one of the best indications of the health of our times. For no longer can we be satisfied with Mary as a childlike mother-image, surrounded with a devotion that is tinged with superstition and lack of conscious understanding of what we are doing + why we are doing it. Instead, we must ask “What does ‘Son, there is your mother’ really say to us[?]”

He referenced John 19:27, where Jesus calls Mary a mother of a disciple from the cross, and the global implications of that quiet declaration:

> She is the mother of Christ and so is the mother of all those who are part of Christ. She gives us not our own life but the life which all of us must share, the life of Christ, a life of love.

In closing, Tom had a unique take on the graduation speech, thinking aloud about the future:

> As we leave here today, the most important task we have ahead is to become another Christ <u>through</u> the life we are living in the world—doctor, engineer, businessman. Mary literally brought that life of Christ to us, and she did this only by being what she was supposed to be, the perfect mother. We honor her not because she was divine—for her greatness really lies in the fact that she was human. Rather we honor her because she did what we must do—carry Christ to the world, no matter what the cost.

Tom's relation of becoming "another Christ through the life we are living in the world," with a sample of white-collar jobs held disproportionately by white men made the speech relatable to the newly graduated college students set loose on the professional class of the 1960s. But the line also meant that the graduates should make real-world application of Christ's teachings in their careers, in whatever sector they worked. Compared to Mary whose burden included giving birth to Jesus in the worst circumstances (and later watching him die), all because God told her so, the weight of faith was much lighter for Notre Dame graduates. Through just their work, they could "carry Christ to the world." I think Tom had a lot of self-reflection in that line.

One question that remained unresolved in the post-Vatican II world was the question of priestly celibacy. Before the Council, discussion of topics like marriage for priests and the rescinding of the celibacy rule had risen to the forefront in Rome. John XXIII himself believed, as Robert Anello wrote for *US Catholic Historian*, celibacy "was not an immutable Church law but a discipline which he could by his own signature rescind." Anello cites the 1964 ordination of a Lutheran minister, married with children, to the priesthood in Germany as a major point of contention in the church during the Council's deliberations.

When the Council finally produced a document on priestly life, *Presbyterorum Ordinis*[2] in fall 1965, it was approved mere weeks before the close of Vatican II. Despite "5,600 suggested modifications (including over 1,300 regarding celibacy)," after five years of continuous consideration and reconsideration, the document was approved by the assembled bishops 2,390 to four. It left open the questions of priestly celibacy and marriage.

Tom would take his own simple vows of celibacy, poverty, and obedience once he finished his Novitiate, as required by the Congregation of Holy Cross. Novitiate is a time of intense prayer and reflection on religious life, a period of contemplation meant to help priestly aspirants in the same way basic training helps the armed forces weed out recruits until only those who are capable of surviving war remain. Afterward, there would be a taking of vows. *Solemn vows* are the ones that usually involve public declarations of the vow, then surrendering all money and property to the church, committing to a contemplative life (usually within a monastery). By and large, they are only revocable by the Pope, and when you say them you commit to them until death. The Holy Cross brothers and many other Catholic orders take *simple vows*, which are any other type

2. Subtitled "Decree on the Ministry and Life of Priests."

of vow taken either in public or in private, and they are not always permanent. Nevertheless, they are promises made to God. These would've weighed just as heavily on Tom's mind as the developments in the larger church when he graduated Notre Dame.

His year of Novitiate (1965/66), despite the liberal reforms of the church, was a strict and largely cloistered existence. Sacred Heart Novitiate required its residents to live mostly in silence, and Tom struggled with the contemplation expected of him, missing the days at Holy Cross and Notre Dame filled with social interaction and his friends. But he still found a way to smuggle books in and, with time, made the most of his Midwest interlude. It was preparation for the great contemplation he'd encounter the rest of his life.

Meanwhile, a gap in theological direction was felt across the church as priests continued to advocate for optional celibacy and the right to marry through the early years of Paul VI's papacy. These advocates, who Tom no doubt read about and saw on TV while in Indiana, grew so loud in their calls that Paul VI crafted his own solution, the encyclical letter *Sacerdotalis Caelibatus*[3] in 1967.

The letter left open the possibility for married men to enter the priesthood, but closed the conversation about celibacy, noting it was a mainstay of the Western Church. Reactions to Paul VI's attempt were largely critical, and may have led to a decline in ordinations starting in 1968. A gulf was developing between younger and older priests, those who largely believed in optional celibacy and those who defended the tradition: 61 percent of priests under thirty-five according to the National Opinion Research Center (1970) approved of the idea. Anello also noted the link that existed between discussions of celibacy and homosexuality within the priesthood, which may have impacted the number of priestly aspirants as well.

That same year, 1968, NBC aired a documentary titled *The New American Catholic*. The hour-long special presented a major culture shift occurring in Catholic congregations across the US to millions of viewers. B-roll footage of parishes that once reveled in the conservative hierarchy of the past now showed scenes that resembled a rowdy college campus, with guitars, singing, marches, prayer requests, and qualities that would conjure the image of a liberal Methodist, or even Unitarian Universalist[4] gathering. Against the backdrop of riots in LA and other cities, the deaths of Martin Luther King, Jr. and Robert F. Kennedy (within days of the

3. *On the Celibacy of the Priest.*
4. A liberal religion that worships without a specific creed. Formed after the merger of the American Unitarian and Christian Universalist churches.

broadcast), and catastrophe in Vietnam, the images of Catholics singing *Kumbaya* while holding hands and surrounded by balloons proved a joyful if stark difference. Throughout the special, congregants and priests alike praised "the changes" made by Vatican II, saying they improved their church experience and inspired non-Catholics to attend, many for the first time. Others came back into the fold because of it.

This combination of direct, emotive, and welcoming theologies advocating for love and acceptance washed over American Catholicism, and some of the faithful began to drown in it. The seeds of the reaction to Vatican II, which accelerated following the death of Paul VI in 1978, were rooted in its antithetical mission of throwing open the doors of one of the most secretive and mysterious organizations in world history. Once open, those doors were impossible to close.

Several debates were put to rest with the 1971 Synod of Bishops on the Ministerial Priesthood, who voted against the ordination of married ministers and reaffirmed the importance of celibacy to the priesthood. While these issues continued to be debated throughout the decade, they decreased in prominence. The Synod was one of many direct and indirect reactions to Vatican II that would reshape the church landscape; a landscape Tom would soon navigate.

Chapter 4

"The Maturing Years"

From his Novitiate, Tom entered the next stage of his professional and spiritual development. Writer Christopher Boehme, in an article on Tom for the fall 1989 issue of *Portland* magazine included a timeline of his life with various segments labeled for their themes. Boehme calls the period of 1961–1982 "The Maturing Years." This title is especially fitting for the years 1965–1971.

After his year at Sacred Heart, Tom enrolled in a masters of professional theology program at Notre Dame that included study at Holy Cross College, a seminary in Washington, DC. While there, he also briefly studied at the Catholic University of America. He became a fixture of the Catholic University pool, swimming laps each day, and playing handball when he wasn't. As part of his seminary education, he was required to teach at least six hours a week at a "federal reform school." Of this experience Boehme writes, "Oddo is so popular there that he puts in a minimum of 12 to 18 hours a week," and his popularity didn't stop at the classroom door: His meticulous notes became a high-value commodity among his fellow seminarians.

Among these seminarians was Edward Malloy. Originally from Washington, DC, Malloy had attended Notre Dame and graduated with a bachelors and masters in English while Tom completed his undergraduate work. Until seminary, they had always passed each other while treading the same waters. Most people, including Tom, know Malloy as "Monk."

Tom and Monk met in an Ordination class in 1968. Soon after, they both served as assistant rectors in the same residence hall, and quickly became friends. As they worked, taught, and learned together, they discussed Vatican II, the shifting sands of their religious world, and their respective places in it. For Tom, his goal was always to be a priest and an educator, Monk remembers, to one day be like the Holy Cross brothers he knew in high school, and the priests he'd looked up to at Notre Dame.

An incident in Maryland in late summer 1969 would further connect the two seminarians. They had been vacationing at Deer Lake, Maryland, close to Holy Cross College, with several other deacons and priests. Seven of them piled into a station wagon to drive back to South Bend in order to attend a training. Tom was driving while Monk sat in the back seat. The weather was awful, and torrential rain made their route even more treacherous.

Somewhere in the Allegheny Mountains, the road narrowed to a one-lane bridge over a dark, swollen river. As Tom drove downhill toward the bridge, where the road curved at almost ninety degrees, he felt the car start to fishtail. In a split-second decision, Tom sped up and turned the wheel hard to the right to avoid drifting off the road and into the river below. The left side of the car smacked into the guardrail of the bridge, which kept it from drifting farther. Monk wasn't seriously hurt, but Tom had a broken wrist, cuts, and abrasions. A priest traveling with them, Father Jim Sullivan, CSC, was bleeding from a cut after his head hit the windshield. Monk said Sullivan "had already survived two surgeries for brain tumors," and medical attention was needed quickly.

Monk broke open his door and ran out of the car to get help. Minutes later, a semi-truck driving the opposite direction bore down on them. Monk stood in the road, waving his arms, praying the driver would see him. The truck stopped at the last second, five yards from the car, and the driver hopped out to see what had happened. Monk then ran to a nearby farmhouse, whose owners had heard the car skid and crash, and lent him their phone. According to Monk, the weather was so terrible it took twenty-five minutes for the first police car to arrive, and forty-five for the first ambulance. Tom and fellow seminarian Jack Lahey would spend several days recuperating in a local hospital. For years after, he would be apologetic about the incident to Monk. But to Monk, Tom probably saved his life: "I am a confirmed non-swimmer," he writes in his memoirs. Reflecting on it today, he thinks it's unlikely he would've survived if the car had tumbled into the river. It was a surprisingly close brush with death for the crew.

Shaken up but undeterred, Tom marched on toward his final vows. Several decades later, Father Patrick Sullivan, CSC would recount Tom's experiences in the DC area, remembering the impact he had on those he worked with: "Tom was a Big Brother for ghetto youth and a census-taker for Catholic parishes in the nation's capitol. He surveyed and tallied the hardship and stigma of welfare mothers and corner boys in Baltimore's inner city."

While his path had diverged from DC, the destination remained the same. He was picked to serve as assistant to the chaplain at St. Mary's Church and graduated with his master's. In April 1970, Tom and Monk were ordained together in Sacred Heart Church, the place Tom had addressed his fellow seniors. In the weeks and months after, Tom would be active in the religious life of South Bend, performing marriages and delivering homilies—often for nuns professing their final vows. Keeping his momentum, with Harvard in his sights, he prepared to pursue his doctoral degree.

Monk would take a similar path. Shortly after ordination, he was accepted into a doctoral program at Vanderbilt University in Nashville, Tennessee. From there, he would graduate in 1975 and begin a whirlwind career in Catholic higher education. He remained close with Tom throughout, keeping in touch and watching his peer's trajectory from a distance. Their friendship, born from the stressors of seminary and the assumption of final vows, would evolve into a professional allyship in future years. But it was in those maturing years that their paths became interwoven, through shared experience and study where both men explored their futures together. And during those years, it's possible Tom first learned of a new support group called Dignity, the organization with which he would find his voice for social action.

Chapter 5

Dignity

In early 1969, Father Pat Nidorf was facing a problem at his San Diego parish: congregants who confessed their homosexuality, but had nowhere to turn for help and no one to counsel them. The notion of homosexuality was, in the American popular consensus following World War II, a mental disorder akin to psychopathy. For Father Pat, the resources of the church weren't up to the challenge.

Two years before, CBS aired *The Homosexuals*, a now-infamous Mike Wallace documentary featuring numerous gay men, along with Gore Vidal, Columbia University Professor Albert Goldman, and psychiatrists Charles Socarides and Irving Bieber[5]. Socarides believed homosexuality was a disorder while Bieber believed it was an acquired trait, but also pathological. Later in the special, a gay man is interviewed with his wife and two children. A highlight of his interview is the observation that, despite his sexuality, he felt gay men were too narcissistic to form a long-term, romantic relationship. The ending note of *The Homosexuals*, a short epilogue delivered by Wallace, captured the moment of gay America prior to Stonewall, Harvey Milk, and the liberation movement:

> The dilemma of the homosexual: told by the medical profession he is sick; by the law that he's a criminal; shunned by employers; rejected by heterosexual society. Incapable of a fulfilling relationship with a woman, or for that matter with a man. At the center of his life he remains anonymous. A displaced person. An outsider.

5. No known relation to the author.

Tom may have distinctly felt those last lines as he entered the priesthood, knowing his sexuality would preclude him from other professions, but could remain undisclosed in the clergy. Meanwhile, as the threat of police harassment, public embarrassment, and legal jeopardy continued nationwide, pockets of queer people had turned to creating support groups within their own circles. But for queer people in the Catholic Church, few circles existed, and where they did, their reach was strictly local, within cities and within parishes. Nidorf thought he could start something similar in San Diego. A few months before bricks flew at Stonewall, Dignity had its first meeting. Nidorf never imagined the group growing beyond his parish, but it soon did: transforming from a counseling meeting to a general support group, and opening its first satellite chapter in Los Angeles within a year.

Ask them now, and only some who knew Tom will mention he was gay. Some will say it was a major part of his personality. Some don't bring it up at all, either out of respect for his priestly vows or because they never knew themselves. Some, perhaps, have other feelings entirely. But Tom's decision to speak out on behalf of gays—a term used, because of the times, to refer to all queer people[6]—was fueled by more than empathy for those in his congregation. Tom sought real change in the church because it was his church, and he believed he could do something to make it happen. But it is unclear just how open he was about his personal connection to the struggle. At least one article in the *St. Louis Post-Dispatch* said, at the time, Tom was not a "professed gay," only one who empathized with and gravitated toward the struggle of gay Catholics. As he grew older, though, his sexuality became less of a secret and more of a motivating force.

Sometime in fall 1972, a young man named Paul Diederich walked into the Newman Catholic Center in Amherst, Massachusetts. He had moved to Boston in 1969, after two years of navy service, and had found a job as a customs house broker from *The Boston Globe* classifieds. But without a church, he still felt without a community to call his own. Paul's profile in the LGBTQ Religious Archives recounts how, upon visiting the center—which catered to Boston's colleges and universities—one Sunday, he listened to a homily about "neglected minorities" and homosexuals in particular. The homilist was Tom, and Paul was enraptured by his words. They met later that day, exchanging greetings and finding commonality in

6 This blanket use of *gay rights* reflected the sentiments of the age, but did not reflect the realities of transgender and genderqueer Christians. Whether Tom ministered about trans issues is unknown, although his message was one of inclusion for all people into the church. It is likely gender identity was a topic he spoke on at one time or another.

the message of acceptance by the church. Paul then suggested Tom and the center organize a "homophile forum," a weekly group for the faithful to discuss issues related to homosexuality. From this conversation came the beginnings of Dignity/Boston, and the roots of a relationship that would change both mens' lives.

In activist circles, Tom and Paul were soon an item of quiet discussion. Although the two did not share public affection, they shared a love of God and each other. Wherever one went, the other was sure to follow. Conference hotel room assignments would always pair the two, and those that knew them recall how protective Tom was of Paul, and Paul equally so of Tom. Their relationship appears to have been romantic and long-term, but without public recognition or acknowledgment. Such disclosure would've meant professional hardship for both partners. But this did not deter them from working together. By early 1973, Tom was first mentioned in print as a chaplain of Dignity/Boston, a chapter whose mailing address was a private residence in Worcester. Paul served as chapter president.

As Tom and Paul grew the Dignity operation in Boston, Tom also began a brief flirtation with local politics. In February 1973, he testified in support of bills to prohibit discrimination due to "sexual preference" in employment and public accommodation that were under consideration by the Massachusetts House Committee on Commerce and Labor. In those hearings, a boisterous State Representative made his opinions clear:

> Sponsor of the two bills ... Rep. Barney Frank, D-Boston, called homosexuals a "hidden minority."
>
> "What difference does it make," Frank added, "What a bank teller's or mailman's sexual preference is. Either these people are going to be employed or they are going to be on welfare. That's one choice this committee is being forced to make."

In his remarks, Tom spoke about the many congregants he'd counseled who experienced targeted discrimination in both areas. He, like Nidorf, felt powerless to do anything. "What can I do as a religious counselor, what can I say to these people?" he asked the legislators. "I see and feel with them the pain of what this is doing [but] I'm unable to change these restrictions. Only you can do that."

In an Associated Press story on the hearings, Tom is described as "a pastora[l] counselor to the homosexual community in Boston." It was because of this role that he had already met another person testifying that morning: Elaine Noble, moderator of a talk radio show on WBUR, "The Gay Way." Noble, and fellow committee speaker Robert Dow, president of the Homophile Union of Boston, were queer leaders in the city and welcomed Tom to their fight. Their three names often appeared together or within a column of each other in the pages of *Gay Community News*, a major gay publication of the age.

In June, Tom wrote a letter to the editor of the *Fitchburg Sentinel* (now the *Sentinel & Enterprise*) commending State Senator Robert Hall for bringing companion versions of the House anti-discrimination bills to the Senate floor for votes. Despite losing overwhelmingly, Tom applauded Senator Hall's "great courage and leadership." His letter further expressed his concerns in detail:

> Each day in counseling my clients present me with examples of unjust discrimination against them in the areas of housing, employment, and insurance. These are part of the pains they are feeling, part of the reason they seek out a priest-counselor and ask some very serious questions about justice and love. I see what this discrimination has done and is doing to my clients, and I seek to heal where I can, to understand and support. But I have great difficulty in offering spiritual help when each day they continue to face these examples of injustice, many of which are carried out in the name of religion (but certainly not Christ's).

Serving as chaplain to the growing network of Dignity chapters across the US meant Tom became an accessible figure for news outlets to contact when they sought the opinion of clergy who worked with gay people—an exceedingly rare breed of priest in the early 1970s. His first real national news exposure came a month after his *Fitchburg Sentinel* letter, when the *Boston Globe* ran a multi-page feature as part of a larger series on Catholicism.

"The Homosexual, the Catholic Church and Dignity" was the third story in the series by Kay Longcope, the first openly queer reporter at the outlet. On the front page of the story, which ran in the *Globe Magazine*, a photo portrait of Tom appears with a slight smile, the camera placed so close it appears uncomfortable, causing an effect similar to a Richard Avedon portrait. The photo caption is a quotation from Tom: "Most gays throw away the church because of the guilt drilled into them." Longcope's story, in parallel, began with anecdotes of gay Catholics who felt unwanted and cast out by the church. To their collective pain, Tom could only empathize. "It's a real hangup," he said to Longcope. "Either they sublimate their guilt by dropping the whole structure imposed on them, or they try not to express themselves sexually."

The article made a note that, for gay Catholics, the problem of rejection was worse than in Protestant denominations, where congregants weren't required to confess their sins to their ministers. Tom not only believed that he and gay Catholics shouldn't feel excluded from living full lives, but that priests should help:

> "As priests for gays, we have to be different from the old church," maintains Fr. Oddo, who serves as chaplain to the Boston group.
>
> "Some gays may conceive of Dignity as a support group not to have sex, but we encourage them to be full persons," he said.

The article was sure to mention the things Dignity wasn't: It was neither a group in competition with Protestant and Catholic congregations, nor a "pseudo swinger group" focused solely on finding sex partners. It was, in fact, a group that opened doors but kept the line of Catholicity:

> Though members of other faiths are welcome, Catholicism is not minimized. Neither is sexuality played up.
>
> "We don't emphasize gayness in the liturgy," declared Fr. Oddo, who celebrates Mass for the group. "We are careful to stay away from primary identification with the sexual."

Tom's efforts at St. Clement's Archdiocesan Eucharistic Shrine on Boylston Street, and the efforts of the Homophile Forum group at St. Clement's, produced a Dignity chapter with monthly meetings drawing upwards of sixty to seventy attendees from three states. It was clear a demand existed for this kind of group, and Dignity was sorely needed in the church.

The article mentioned the efforts of other priests who ministered to LGBTQ+ people outside of the Dignity network. Besides Tom, it also profiled Father Paul Shanley, another priest active in the Boston area at that time, who was sanctioned by Cardinal Humberto Sousa Medeiros, the city's archbishop, to make gay ministry his full-time work. Shanley is the second priest with a photo profile and lengthy quotations in Longcope's article. Throughout Tom's ministry in Boston and while associated with Dignity, they would invariably appear in the same stories, and as speakers at the same events.

Prior to Tom's and Shanley's orbits traversing, the latter had privately developed a reputation of grievous misconduct. As early as 1961, Shanley had sexually abused young boys within his care. This continued throughout the 1960s, without any action by the church or local law enforcement. In the late 1970s, Shanley attended a conference on sexuality on behalf of the Archdiocese of Boston. While there, he vocally defended the value of relationships between men and boys. Soon after, other attendees of the conference would form NAMBLA, the North American Man/Boy Love Association; Shanley was never involved in it, but his free admission of these beliefs would've eliminated any doubt of his activities. His crimes were eventually divulged to the public when he was arrested for child rape in 2002. He was laicized in 2004, and served twelve years in prison. He died in 2020, three years after his release, while he was still on supervised probation.

It may be easy to assume Tom's connection to the man collectively referred to as the "street priest" by their close association in historic news columns, but whatever closeness they had was incidental. They moved in the same circles, but always acted independent of one another. Shanley never appears in Tom's speeches or writings (except to note his attendance at events), and their styles were drastically different. Activist Brian McNaught recalls how they were both "Type-A personalities;" where Shanley was a brash disruptor, Tom was a patrician strategist, carefully choosing his words and his battles. Tom is not known to have associated with Shanley's ministry where documented abuse occurred. And requests for information to both the FBI and the Survivors Network of those Abused by Priests (SNAP) produced nothing on Tom. Regardless, they forever remain connected in the archives of the *Boston Globe*, *Gay Community News*, and other papers in the Boston metropolitan area.

A deeper question persists around what, if anything, Tom knew about Shanley. The 2001–2002 Spotlight investigation conducted by *The Boston Globe* uncovered evidence of the child sex abuse endemic among the city's clergy, including the disclosure of Shanley's crimes. But in the 1970s, his reputation for crossing lines with congregants was known, at least among some of his fellow activists. From the public record, we can only confirm that Tom—if he knew—did nothing about it. Whether this was because of a fidelity to Holy Cross brotherhood or an actual lack of knowledge or evidence is up for discussion. I choose not to speculate based on the documents I've reviewed.[7]

In late August 1973, Dignity held its first national convention in Los Angeles. Three-hundred attendees filled the Hollywood Holiday Inn ballroom to formally organize the network of twelve chapters under the theme "The Spirit Is Calling Us." Father Nidorf was a special guest of honor. A board of officers was voted in by the membership: Paul Diederich was elected president, and John E. Hart as treasurer. Tom, meanwhile, became the first national secretary of the new organization, DignityUSA. His role, primarily based in communications, chapter development, and member outreach, was crucial in those early days. As he and Diederich were both Massachusetts based, the Dignity office was set up in Boston.

In December, the Dignity/Boston chapter celebrated its first anniversary. It was an emotional, hopeful, and joyful event attracting what *Gay Community News* described as a "wide age range which is so obviously lacking at the bars. Little old ladies with babushkas, denimed youths, lovey dovey lesbian couples and coat-and-tied businessmen all sang and prayed together." At the event, Tom delivered a sermon which called on those assembled to "find [their] own way of living out the Gospel." For Tom, Dignity's mission was intrinsically linked to the Gospel:

> DIGNITY doesn't make too much sense as a "cause" alone. Sure we seek freedom for people, an end to oppression. We hope to help people to grow to be themselves. We hope to help a Church understand and even a society understand. But I think we're saying more. We are saying that DIGNITY has something to do with life, Christian life, resurrection life.

The latter he expounded on in detail:

> Resurrection isn't just sexual freedom. Resurrection isn't just an end of discrimination or a Church finally saying "God bless you." All of these are, of course, very important. But there is something more. Resurrection means a new life in Jesus, a plunging into his way of life and really believing that when we're with him there is light and hope and brothers and sisters as one.

7. In an April 2025 correspondence with Ray Struble, Brian McNaught's husband (also a Dignity activist), he assured me that the Dignity/Boston community, including Tom, did not know of Paul Shanley's crimes. It was not until Shanley's arrest in 2002 that many former friends and colleagues learned of his indiscretions.

Then, everyone joined hands in a circle, praying together. Tom led a prayer for "those who [didn't] understand" their plight. *Gay Community News* called the moment a "natural high." But not all was friendly within the group, as some members vocalized their criticism of Catholicism's patriarchy, and openly discussed the question of women becoming priests. Tom suggested that, rather than strike out for such radical changes, the church would destroy their group if "too many rules [were] broken," an insightful statement considering how Tom approached his own activism. Paul Diederich, perhaps more directly, said the reason women couldn't become priests was "because we're Catholic."

Despite this break in festivities, the triumph of Dignity was palpable. In four short years, this little group had grown from a church basement meeting to a national organization with real political and cultural influence. And Tom's leadership meant it was on a path of clear growth. The January 1974 edition of Dignity's self-titled newsletter lists fifteen active chapters with a national office four blocks down the street from St. Clement's, where he worked. A skim of *Dignity*, the organization's newsletter, shows a wealth of content, from anonymous notes and letters to the editor, poetry, and a front-page editorial whose opening line is its thesis: "Oral and anal copulation seem to be the primary goal in life for many Gays—a never-ending quest for a fleeting moment that has nothing but memories. There has to be a higher goal than that." What was once a simple, typed mimeograph shared between disparate groups was now a full-fledged publication for gay Catholics, and by extension gay America.

That month, frequent Dignity patron Father John J. McNeill, SJ had been put on notice by Rome. An associate professor of moral theology at Woodstock College, McNeill became synonymous with the gay Catholic rights movement and delivered an address at Dignity's first conference in Los Angeles. The Vatican Congregation for the Doctrine of the Faith, a group whose purpose is to promulgate Catholic doctrine and root out heresy, contacted McNeill's religious superiors to request an investigation into his beliefs on homosexuality. The investigation was a private, internal affair handled by the Jesuits, McNeill's order. The story in *NC News* cited Tom for contextual pieces on Dignity. Toward the end of the write-up, Tom mentions a letter that was sent to all religious orders around the country after the formation of Dignity's national organization, to little response. All the same, Tom reported, bishops were largely aware of Dignity's work. Whether they acknowledged it was another question.

In March 1974, a fifteen-page booklet titled *Principles to Guide Confessors in Questions of Homosexuality* was created by the US-based Committee on Pastoral Research and Practices. A church publication on pastoral care to gay people, it reaffirmed traditional teachings on the subject, including the observation that homosexual acts—i.e., sex—were "grave transgression[s] of the goals of human sexuality and of human personality." Tom and Paul Shanley both spoke out against the booklet, against the wisdom of the American bishops, as Kay Longcope reported on it for the *Boston Globe*:

> "The document completely ignores the broader dimension of the need of the gay community for pastoral concern and care," Fr. Oddo [said]
>
> [He] further stated the guidelines are "no answer" to a request made last December by Dignity's 1000 members that US bishops "expand your apostolate to us."

The letter sent by Dignity was quoted at length in the article, asking for the bishop's "leadership … love and concern" in the group's pursuit of justice. These guidelines, effectively, served as a tart response to that letter. Tom believed the church had acted in bad faith:

> In issuing the guidelines, the bishops "didn't do much research or seek any kind of consultation from their own theologians who are now suggesting more humane approaches to inclusion of homosexuals in the church," Fr. Oddo said.
>
> He pointed out that an article in the Feb. 15 issue of *Commonweal*, a prestigious weekly Catholic Journal, supported Dignity's position that "it is the call of Catholic homosexuals to affirm their sexual orientation in faith, to regard themselves as equal members of the believing community, and to express their sexuality in a manner consonant with Christ's teaching of love."

Here too, Paul Shanley is heavily featured. Another cited is Father John McNeill, who was still under investigation on order from Rome.

In May, Tom participated in the fourth annual "Gay Rites of Spring" at University of Massachusetts–Amherst. The event, a three-day festival culminating in a dance at the UMass ballroom, drew a stark contrast with other campuses in New England. An article reporting on the event mentions the recent legal battle between the University of New Hampshire Gay Student Organization and Governor Meldrim Thomson, Jr., a conservative Republican who sought to ban the group from campus. With similar battles in other states, the event drew a regional attendance.

Tom's part came on day two, with a Saturday workshop entitled "Religion and Gays." Tom is featured in a photo from the event, misidentified as "Rev. Robert Oddo." His hair is still long, and he looks more like a preppy Jesus Freak than a priest, wearing a collared shirt, patterned slacks, Oxford shoes, and a large crucifix necklace. He sits at the center of a semicircle while attendees listen, arms folded and legs crossed. Some form of this workshop would reappear throughout Tom's life, where he'd deconstruct theology and human sexuality. He also began to hold public lectures and workshops for groups outside the gay Catholic orbit, with the motive of introducing them to the gay community and related issues in a safe, non-judgmental environment. That same month, Tom gave a talk to North Shore Parents Without Partners, one of several groups in Massachusetts that would come to know the long-haired priest.

His work wasn't lost on domestic church leaders. Likely seeking to expand on the efforts of *Principles to Guide Confessors in Questions of Homosexuality*, the church tried again on the question of how to minister to gay people. In early June, Father Daniel Pilarczyk, a former rector of St. Gregory Seminary in Ohio and future archbishop of Cincinnati, gave a talk on "Church Policy and Gay Ministry" at a four-day conference on the topic in Dayton, Ohio. Tom and others (including Paul Shanley) presented in tandem. Pilarczyk's talk distinguished between "homosexual[s] pure and simple," those who were same-sex attracted but did not act on those attractions, and "practicing homosexual[s]," those that did act on their attractions. Pilarczyk then outlined four "principles" he believed should become the standard for gay ministry, which the Dayton *Journal Herald* reproduced in summary:

> - Being a homosexual pure and simple is not sinful and implies no guilt, because all sin implies free choice and the homosexual has not chosen his condition and so is not responsible for it.
>
> - Homosexual acts are per se sinful. The Judaeo-Christian tradition holds that homosexualit[y] is contrary to human sexuality. Human acts are objectively moral evil.
>
> - The church is a teaching community, and one of its major responsibilities is to teach morality, so there must be no doubt possible on

> where the church stands on fundamental moral questions such as homosexuality.
>
> - The church exists in order to reconcile, not in order to condemn. Its main function is to bring men back into union with God through Christ. "Compassion and healing are what the church is all about."

In closing, Pilarczyk compared gay Catholics to divorced ones, whose problems were not of their own making and whose "prospects of legitimate sexual fulfillment are slim if not non-existent." Pilarczyk added that, "The church must offer help to the weak, but without condoning sin. The church must reject moral evil, but without closing doors to those involved in moral evil."

Dr. Franklin Kameny also spoke at the event, after Pilarczyk. The president of the Washington, DC chapter of the Mattachine Society, an early gay rights organization founded in 1950, he was blunt in his response:

> Your compassion is patronizing, degrading and dehumanizing. Your position is unchristian, anti-christian and a disgrace to Christianity in the name of Christ. The position you're taking is driving countless thousands of people out of your church and, as great as their loss may be, and it is great, your loss is greater.

Kameny believed that leaders like Pilarczyk were making the church unwelcoming to gay parishioners, and that their flawed understanding of this group directly led to an exodus of church members. In this exodus, Tom saw the continuing need for Dignity, which offered the premise that they too were worthy of sharing in Christ's love and the glory of the Gospel. His response was also captured by the *Journal Herald*:

> [Dignity] is "not waiting for a clearly-defined theology of sexuality," he said, but is ministering to gays …
>
> … [Dignity] has a dual theory and approach, he said, "reaching out to gay people themselves, helping them to learn the dignity already in gay life," and balancing that, "reaching out to the church, trying to teach the dignity of gay people so it can better minister to gay people."

Although Tom made it clear that Dignity was neither a dating service nor a radical political group, he also didn't back down from the challenges his organization and its membership faced:

> Dignity is "not waiting for the church to say it's OK to receive the Eucharist," Father Oddo said, "We don't wait for the institutional church to catch up in its theology to where the people are. We will assist the church by going ahead and doing it."

His comments reflected a major point of contention between the church and Dignity: the offering of Communion to gay parishioners. In direct circumvention of church doctrine, Dignity's Mass services had given Communion to all attendees, regardless of sexuality or relationship status. The topic is still controversial today, but Tom believed it was one of the least controversial steps a church could take; indeed, that it was necessary for a healthy church. And despite the harsh criticism of "Church Policy and Gay Ministry," *Dignity* called the conference in Dayton "an important step in the continuing open consideration of the pastoral needs of gay Catholics."

A few weeks after the Dayton conference, Tom and other members of Dignity marched in New York City's 1974 Gay Pride Parade, an early version of an event that now attracts over four million attendees annually. A photo of Tom holding a sign with a large heart emblem appeared on page 33 of the July 1 *New York Times.* Though they would've seen the *Times* everywhere when they lived on Utopia Parkway in Queens, Dominick and Catherine Oddo had moved to Florida by 1974, and it's unlikely they saw Tom's photo.

A few weeks later, Tom participated in the New England Clergy Institute, a gathering of about one hundred priests from across the region in Easton, Massachusetts. Largely focused on the topic of gay ministry, the event came shortly after the Sacred Congregation of Catholic Education published *A Guide to Formation in Priestly Celibacy.* The guide was a direct follow-up to the church's multiple attempts at establishing a last word on celibacy in the priesthood. Apart from promoting the sacredness and benefit of celibacy, it also took the stance that narcissism and homosexuality were "immature tendencies" one should overcome to attain sexual maturity. Tom's remarks at the Institute reflected his thoughts on this guide and other statements made by the church that year.

He stated, firmly, that priests were an essential piece in helping gay Catholics connect with God, that "The ministry has a special role in overcoming the alienation of gay people and communicating to them God's unconditional acceptance." But he made distinctions. "[A priest] in expressing God's acceptance does not have to affirm every type of homosexual lifestyle." A media press release detailed what he meant:

> Father Oddo said that there are irresponsible homosexual relationships just as there are irresponsible heterosexual ones. "However," he said, "there are life styles within the gay community where a genuine and deep sense of love exists and I feel that they are very beautiful and sacred."
>
> A priest should counsel the gay person "to make sex a more integrated human expression—that is, a personal loving act, rather than a simple bodily urge."

As Tom called recent efforts by bishops across the United States to advise on gay ministry a "disaster," he declared that:

> the Catholic Church needs a new theology covering the whole [realm] of sexuality. "Rather than view sex as simply a mechanical or biological process as the old theology seemingly does, we need a theology that views sex as a responsible human expression."

Yet even Tom, a happy warrior through each battle, knew enough to be practical. "We cannot wait for a new and total theology to replace the old one," he said. "We must plung[e] ahead and rely upon our own understanding and experience counseling gay people." He knew a kinder way existed, one that focused on reforming church culture over custom, and that it could work within modern Catholicism. In Dignity Masses, there were true love and palpable connection with God among devoted parishioners, an energy that Tom believed could only strengthen the church in the long-term. Week after week offering Communion to gay Catholics and their allies, he felt compelled to do more, to support his spiritual community through direct action.

Chapter 6

Happy Warrior

The first notable clash between Dignity and the church occurred in the summer of 1974. Brian McNaught was a twenty-five year old writer for the *Michigan Catholic*, the Detroit Archdiocese newspaper, and caused a stir among local clergymen and journalists. It began with a trip to cover the four-day Bergamo Conference, the gathering of gay Catholics in Dayton, Ohio where Father Pilarczyk presented his theories on homosexuality as Tom, Paul Shanley, and others spoke in opposition. McNaught met Shanley and Jeannine Gramick there, but had already known Tom over phone conversations regarding Dignity—in his spare time, Brian was co-founder and chapter president of Dignity/Detroit. Over the conference, he and Tom developed a friendship that would prove vital in the coming weeks. Returning from Dayton, Brian wrote a column inspired by Paul Shanley's words entitled "Gay/Straight, Love is the Goal." In it he argued that homosexuality, as many Dignity speakers declared, was not a sin, no more than left-handedness! The piece was an open challenge to church orthodoxy, printed in a Diocesan publication. It caused an immediate backlash among advertisers and subscribers to the *Michigan Catholic*, one of the oldest newspapers in the state, and put McNaught in the media spotlight.

A week later, he agreed to an interview with the *Detroit News* to defend the controversial column. His employer (who knew of his sexuality, as did his coworkers) was aware of the interview, and he gave Tom, Paul Diederich, and his family advance warning—to be ready for whatever backlash might come from it. He didn't come out in the interview, but still stated emphatically, "My sexuality and expression of it does not deprive me of my spirituality and my Kingdom of Heaven." Shortly after the interview was published, McNaught's column was dropped by the *Michigan*

Catholic. He wasn't fired, but he would no longer have a regular assignment at the paper. National publications picked up McNaught's story, a combination of personal interest and a civil rights item on a gay person fit for print. In August, McNaught filed a complaint with the Detroit Human Rights Commission, a new body under the recently enacted City Charter, which had quietly banned discrimination on the basis of "sexual orientation" among other groups. The Detroit Newspaper Guild also investigated his case, as the union's contract with the *Michigan Catholic* prohibited discrimination due to political activity, which McNaught posited was his work in Dignity. But it was his subsequent hunger strike, a widely-publicized fast, that spurred allies among the gay Christian community to converge in Detroit. Throughout it all, McNaught kept Tom updated, and he offered Dignity's support in turn.

For twenty-four days McNaught went without solid food, and for seventeen he only had water. With his story now reporting on both coasts, a demonstration in support of McNaught was scheduled for Labor Day. A Solidarity Mass, a concelebration featuring representatives from seven Dignity chapters, was held in Most Holy Trinity Catholic Church. Tom assisted Monsignor Clement Kern, the pastor at Holy Trinity, and others in the service as the principal celebrant. Shanley gave the Homily. At the beginning of his address, a group of counter protestors from the far-right Catholic group Breakthrough, known for violence against clergy, stood in front of the altar with a banner reading "A MORAL WRONG CAN NEVER BE A CIVIL RIGHT." Their interruption was quickly drowned out by a spontaneous rendition of the hymn "They'll Know We Are Christians (By Our Love)" from the attendees, over 250 in total. Detroit Police were called in, and the counterprotestors quickly removed. Shanley completed his homily, followed by comments by Monsignor Kern "expressing the sentiments of the diocesan priests present" for the event.

After the service, about one hundred attendees marched ten blocks from Holy Trinity to the Archdiocese, most carrying signs and banners with curiously pointed slogans, like "WRITE ON, BRIAN," "GOD IS GAY," and "I'M GAY AND JESUS IS MY LOVER." Outside the Archdiocese Chancery, a rally was held with multiple speakers: Shanley, Dignity President Paul Diederich, and Sister Jeannine Gramick SL, a Catholic sister and fellow Notre Dame alum who had co-founded Dignity/Baltimore and Dignity/Washington DC.

They were soon joined by Brian McNaught himself, speaking through the pangs of his hunger. He quoted a passage from Ezekiel, condemning the shepherds of Israel for not looking after their whole flock, turning his message out to the "Shepherds of Detroit" and their treatment of gay members in their respective flocks. When the rally concluded, Dignity/Detroit hosted an indoor picnic inside Most Holy Trinity. Through it all, journalists from *The New York Times*, *San Francisco Chronicle*, *Chicago Tribune*, *National Catholic Reporter*, and others had followed the group for stories running that week.

Tom wrote of the event's success in *Dignity*. A multi-page letter describing the event and its highlights, including the incursion by Breakthrough, ran in the newsletter's September edition. He made note of the demonstration's commitment to the faith: "We were again impressed with the deep religious spirit of the protest—certainly with its commitment to non-violence and moreover with its firm Gospel roots." He also talked about the event's significance in Dignity's history, and that of the larger gay Catholic rights movement:

> All were agreed that the day was an important one for DIGNITY as well as for Brian. We had chosen in this instance to dramatically and prayerfully confront our Church with its infidelity to the Gospel. As in New York and Worcester, the Church must be told that it can no longer continue its inadequate and unjust stance on the issue of gay civil rights, since to do so places it i[n] clear opposition to its Gospel mission.

So significant was the protest that McNaught received a letter of support from Fathers Thomas Gumbleton and Joseph Imesch, both Detroit bishops. They wrote that the church had "a serious obligation to root out structures and attitudes that discriminate against the homosexual as a person" and pledged to help educate the clergy on gay issues. In light of this pronouncement, McNaught ended his fast, but it wouldn't save his job. Shortly after the demonstration, he was fired by the *Michigan Catholic*. A resulting lawsuit for wrongful termination was settled out of court. In the end, there was a sense of hurt mixed with subdued hope for reconciliation in the church among gay Catholics.

In a September 1974 front page editorial, *Dignity* lamented this "first formal confrontation," and added, "We pray [this] does not end in alienation between DIGNITY and the church. We ask our brothers and sisters in DIGNITY to remember Christ's command to forgive the wrongs done them seventy times seven." At the same time, the editorial remarked how Dignity's mission relied on "forming a family within and between our groups," referencing the need for continued engagement with the larger church, especially for those members unable to express themselves and experience the fullness of their faith.

Besides his efforts at expanding DignityUSA's membership and advocating for gay Catholics wherever the need arose, Tom found other areas to become active in the political sphere without becoming overtly political himself. In the 1970s, there was no official rule or custom barring priests from being politically active, or even holding political office. While Tom was Dignity's national secretary, Fathers Robert Drinan and Robert John Cornell both served in the US House of Representatives. Drinan, a Jesuit priest, was a liberal Democrat and a prominent supporter of abortion rights, and in 1973 he introduced a resolution seeking to impeach President Richard Nixon for his secret and illegal bombing of Cambodia. A lightning rod in the chamber, Drinan's stances continually irked the church. Cornell, meanwhile, a Norbertine who took more moderate stances, became nationally known as the first Democrat to win his district in thirty years. Both would depart elected office when Pope Paul VI ordered priests to cease political activity in 1980. While seeking office was never a goal of Tom's, he made sure to help others where he could.

One particular instance made history: the campaign of Elaine Noble, one of Tom's activist friends in Boston. She was considering a run for a seat in the Massachusetts House of Representatives in the 1974 elections, following successive hearings for anti-discrimination bills that were debated, then eventually left for dead. Noble wanted to become part of the process—to make change from the inside. She ran a moderate campaign that did not emphasize her sexuality. Nevertheless, she received relentless harassment for it, ranging from hate mail to shooting out her car and house windows. Despite receiving no response from the Boston Police Department, she refused to be intimidated and would not withdraw from the race.

In a bitter primary fight, Noble faced four other Democratic candidates. Though openly lesbian, she instead distinguished herself with a strong stance for desegregated school busing. The topic was a major flashpoint in Boston politics in the 1970s: Starting with the June 1974 decision of Judge W. Arthur Gerrity, Jr. in *Morgan v. Hennigan* to mandate Boston schools desegregate, riots at city high schools would lead to more than 130 injuries that academic year. Civic leaders including State Senator William Bulger and City Councilor Louise Day Hicks had used white supremacist backlash under the veneer of Boston Irish pride to fuel the flames of local outrage, creating an increasingly hostile political climate to those in favor of desegregation. Noble was undeterred, even as the political situation in Boston became increasingly dangerous.

Nearing the primary election, one of Noble's challengers explicitly made her sexuality an issue. At a "Candidates Night" event, Helene C. Johnson appeared with her husband and children in a show of her family-friendly presentation. Noble, without a husband, brought her Welsh terrier Dylan as her male companion. "Dylan's five years old," she said to the crowd, "he won't make much noise, and he has one attribute my opponent hasn't yet claimed for her husband—Dylan is housebroken." Things became far more serious when a local priest, likely in support of Johnson's campaign, circulated a letter threatening anyone voting for Noble or supporting her campaign with excommunication two weeks before election day, a bold statement to a largely Catholic city.

Tom came to Noble's aid. On Harvard stationary, he wrote a letter detailing what an upstanding citizen she was, a child of God even though she was openly lesbian, indeed because of it. While not an outright political endorsement, it nevertheless served as a personal endorsement—a vouch—that was quickly passed to a church elder named Mrs. Mullen, described as "the maven of Newbury Street." She spent those following two weeks walking the neighborhoods of Boston showing the letter to everyone she could. When she ran into the original edicting priest on Commonwealth Avenue, she stuck the letter in his face. "What do you think of this, Father?" she asked intently. When he wouldn't answer, she couldn't help but dig in. "When we first came over from County Cork, we used to sleep six or seven lassies in the bed! What do you think of *that*, Father?"

Noble would end up winning the primary with 48.6 percent of the vote to Johnson's 34.8 percent, the rest split between the other candidates. In actual terms, it was a 169 vote margin, a slim but historic victory. As the Democratic nominee, Noble was the presumptive favorite in November, and she won the general election with 59 percent of the vote against her independent challenger, Joseph Cimino. Noble was the first openly gay person elected to a state legislature in the United States, three years before the election of Harvey Milk to the San Francisco Board of Supervisors. She would eventually win re-election, serving two full terms, then unsuccessfully run for US Senate in 1978, coming in fifth in the Democratic primary to Paul Tsongas. More than forty riots would erupt across the city in the two years following her original victory related to busing and school desegregation. Yet Noble won her seat in the eleventh hour, largely thanks to Tom. While he no doubt continued to support her privately, and attended Dignity-related events as a presenter with her throughout her tenure, it is unlikely he acted as a public booster for her 1976 re-election or 1978 Senate campaigns. He would not make any other major endorsements of public officials before Paul VI's politics edict in 1980.

Tom's efforts made big strides for gay Catholics across the US, and his work soon attracted international attention. In April 1975, the Australian gay Catholic group Acceptance coordinated a three-day convention and Mass in Sydney, where representatives from the Protestant Metropolitan Community Church and Jewish group Chutzpah attended as observers. The *Sydney Morning Herald*, in its coverage of the event, noted that three to five priests would be participating but did not release their names, all hailing from parishes outside the Sydney Archdiocese. The article contrasted the necessary anonymity of Australian priests with American ones:

> Priests associated with Acceptance are reluctant to be named for fear of ecclesiastical censure. It is not so in America, where a priest, Father Tom Oddo, is national secretary of Dignity, an American Catholic homosexual movement which claims 15,000 members and with which Acceptance is affiliated.

Still, his work *had* caused some consternation among church leadership. *The Boston Globe* recounted how Tom's testimony on anti-discrimination bills in fall 1974 included an observation that Cardinal Medeiros, Archbishop of Boston, did not believe "any minority should be discriminated against." Many frenzied calls by worried Catholics were then made to the Archdiocese to clarify what the young priest meant as he spoke to lawmakers, and whether Cardinal Medeiros was condoning a gay lifestyle. It was an episode marked by Tom's youthful energy and the church's moderating reluctance; Tom was making an overture that was not his to make.

The response from church leadership, however, was not outwardly condemning. There was some attempt at dialogue, at mutual understanding, that year. By then, Brian McNaught had assumed the role of Dignity's National Chairperson for Social Action, and used his position to pull together a meeting between Dignity officers and the Liaison Committee of the National Conference of Catholic Bishops (NCCB). The Committee, led by Bishop Father Warren Boudreaux—then serving in the Diocese of Beaumont, Texas—sought a meeting after stirrings of concern among the conference about gay issues. Tom, Paul Diederich, and others met with the Committee members for an hour and a half to review a presentation Boudreaux would present to the larger Conference. Within the final document was an outline of Dignity's mission and a call for priests to, as Dignity summarized, "condemn discrimination, support civil rights and assist Dignity in [their] pastoral outreach to gays and lesbians." The growth and sustained momentum of the organization had started to change minds, if incrementally, about the church's approach to gay Catholics.

Soon after, *Dignity* announced the organization's Second Annual National Convention, to be held on Labor Day Weekend 1975, in Boston. Shanley, Father McNeill, Sister Gramick, and other regular names among gay Catholic advocacy groups were slated as speakers, with the "Honorable Rep. Elaine Noble" featured as a special guest. In the same issue, an open letter by McNaught to *Dignity* readers provided a different announcement: the formation of an ad-hoc group called Catholics for Gay Rights, which the convention speakers, Tom, and several other notable figures were members of. The group sought to demonstrate peacefully during the annual meeting of the NCCB, and to deliver a petition signed by "bishops and theologians, politicians and Church leaders" from multiple denominations pledging to end discrimination against gay Catholics. McNaught reminded readers that the church declared 1975 a year of reconciliation, and that their efforts would not be in vain: "The bishops are waiting and watching .... something other than the game on television."

The 1975 convention was attended by over 300 people representing chapters from across the country, including Puerto Rico. DignityUSA as a national organization had grown to 15,000 members and counting, adding new chapters each year. The event was documented by *The New York Times* in a short story titled "Homosexual Rights Backed by Parley." Featured in speaking roles and leading workshops were the usual suspects: Tom; Shanley; Brian McNaught, who spoke on his work with the NCCB and plugged Catholics for Gay Rights; Sister Jeannine Gramick, who spoke out against the church's historical treatment of women, "plucking blatant misogyny right from the scrolls," and Dr. John Boswell, described by *Gay Community News* as "Boston's gay historian."

Boswell was a young, gay, promising Medieval philologist who, like Tom, was completing a PhD at Harvard. He had drifted into Dignity's orbit and began to appear on speaker rosters that year. In his talk, he asked for "rational understanding" of the church in its apparent misunderstanding of Scripture with regard to gay people in general. He presented a theory that the idealization of homosexuality in Greek and Roman cultures led to early Christian communities lashing out at what they believed were excesses not permitted by God, but that such misunderstandings could be resolved.

At the US Conference of Bishops meeting in November, the theme of reconciliation hung in the air. In addition to considering Dignity's approach to gay ministry, days before the conference Bishop Michael J. McAuliffe of Jefferson City, Missouri, called for the Conference to establish an "office of women's concerns," to reevaluate the church's positions on women in leadership and decision-making roles. To some, the subtext of Father McAuliffe's argument was a call for women priests, an unthinkable proposition to most. They had particular disagreements with Dignity as well.

Joseph A. Breig, a prolific writer for Catholic publications, issued his criticism of the group and Tom's approach in the *Pittsburgh Catholic*:

> Homosexuals, Father Oddo said, have been driven from religion by "discrimination and ignorance in the Church." If that be so, the situation calls for correction. Christ came to call sinners to repentance and redemption. He founded the Church to carry on that work through time and space.
>
> Members of "Dignity," however, must shun the modern movement which seems to aim at justifying homosexual behavior as being blameless—not to say admirable ....
>
> There can be no spiritual progress without honest facing of one's sinfulness, and honest repentance and determination for reform.

The risk to tradition and custom was palpable, but the risks created by inaction were even greater. A bridge was desperately needed to reach gay Catholics. At the Conference, Bishop Boudreaux offered Dignity's contribution for consideration. As he addressed the assembly, Boudreaux noted that the bishops' support of civil rights protections for gay people did not equate to a theological condoning of gay lifestyles.

Meanwhile Tom and hundreds of others participated in a water fast, delivering their petition on the rights of gay Catholics signed by thousands more, in a "national day of reconciliation" with the larger church. Another of Dignity's requests for the bishops involved the larger question of homosexuality and its relationship with the faith itself: to establish "a committee of theologians, social scientists and homosexual persons 'to study the question of homosexuality on all fronts and its implications for church and society.'" Bishop Joseph Bernardin, Archbishop of Cincinnati, said the matter would most likely be decided by the NCCB's standing committee on pastoral research and practices. It was a minor win for Dignity, amid much headwind. While no immediate action was taken, their requests were heard and referred out to a committee for further study. In the same meetings, the ordination of women was not only discussed but soundly condemned, despite Bishop McAuliffe's efforts at improving female representation (but never ordination) within the church.

Dignity's biggest piece of advocacy was yet to come: the creation of a booklet meant for "Catholics at large who want to learn more about homosexuality and [for] gay Catholics who are attempting to integrate their sexual orientation with their religious beliefs and practices." Tom, Gramick, and Father Robert Nugent, another Dignity-affiliated priest, authored *Homosexual Catholics: A Primer for Discussion.* The twenty-page publication had Dignity's Statement of Position and Purpose printed inside the cover, with an introduction that included one theologian's observation that homosexuality would become the issue of the 1970s as birth control had been in the 1960s. Outlined in a question/answer format both thoughtful and easy to read, the booklet served in some ways as a direct response to the NCCB's *Principles to Guide Confessors,* but for two audiences not exclusive to the clergy: gay Catholics wishing to live the fullness of their faith, and those in the larger Catholic community who "harbor many fears, myths and prejudices" due to a lack of education.

Homosexual Catholics, through its trio of authors, addressed the words and guidance of Scripture while taking apart major arguments of the church's hierarchy. The first question posed by the booklet, "Can a person be a practicing Catholic and an active homosexual?" set the tone with its answer:

> In recent years there has been a growing insistence on the part of many people that the Church re-think its classical position on homosexuality and homosexual relationships. Theologians, philosophers, psychologists and pastors of many denominations, including the Catholic Church, are beginning to believe and state openly that, under certain conditions, a homosexual can express her/his sexuality (including genital sex) in a way that does not necessarily separate him/her from either the Christian community or the love of God which includes (for some) full participation in the Eucharist by the reception of Holy Communion.

The Eucharist was an especially important part of the conversation. Traditionally, receiving Communion—the body of Christ—requires the offering of a wafer from priest to parishioner. By this design, gay Catholics who are actively sexual or in a non-heterosexual relationship are excluded from both sides of the sacred process. But to Tom, the Eucharist was something meant for everyone.

Ed remembers Tom's visits to California, staying with Ed and his family whenever he was in town for a conference or Dignity event. Each time, Tom—never *Father* Tom to Ed's family—would pull the loaf of bread out of the fridge, take a slice and tear it apart to make his own wafers. He'd give the Eucharist over the kitchen table, with grape juice for the wine. Ed's kids loved it, and looked forward to the little ceremony each time he'd visit.

Diane Sidorowicz, an electrical engineer at Polaroid, first attended a Dignity Mass in November 1975, shortly before *Homosexual Catholics* was published. Prior to that evening, she had regularly attended her local parish's Mass, but felt increasingly outcast in the pews. When she walked into St. Clement's on Boylston Street, her whole perception of church seemed to change. She was greeted by a man who asked her name, and guided her to the right room. Inside, she found people chatting and laughing, so different from her prior experience of church that she was convinced she was in the wrong place. When Tom's liturgy moved her, she felt called to stay, and kept coming back to Dignity Mass. She eventually became a leader in the organization while it was headquartered in Boston. Something she remembered specifically about Tom, recalling her own years in Dignity, was his approach to the Eucharist: "that anyone could do Communion," starting with one man and one woman. Diane soon found herself participating in the Eucharist at Dignity/Boston, distributing the host as Tom looked on, a remarkable development in the history of the American church.

Tom's experience in Dignity leadership reached its peak with a conference in San Diego. "Gay Ministry: A Workshop for Priests in the San Diego Roman Catholic Diocese" was an event open to clergy, laypeople, and counselors working with gay patients. Prior to the June 1976 event, Tom asked Pat McArron, a Dignity member, to establish a formal chapter in San Diego, the place where the organization began, but which still did not have a formal chapter. Also referred to as "Homosexuality and the Church Today," it was the first major event hosted by Dignity/San Diego, attracting more than sixty attendees from across these vocations. In McArron's words, it was a "huge success." The Cardijn Center, located next door to the Old Town Community Church, was packed with attendees to various panels, a short film presentation, and Tom's keynote address. Photos of the day show an energized crowd gathering for a meal after the event at Rheinlander Haus in La Jolla Shores. Through them all, Tom is beaming—feeling at home, among his people, among his extended family of Catholic brothers.

The year would bring more to celebrate in November, when the NCCB, now Dignity's primary foil, published *To Live in Christ Jesus: A Pastoral Reflection on the Moral Life.* A fifty-two page pastoral letter issued by the NCCB's Ad-Hoc Committee on Moral Values in Society, it spoke to various topics of contemporary American life in the context of Catholic teachings and beliefs. Part One dealt with the committee's "Principles of the Moral Life," while Part Two dealt with the application of those principles on topics as varied as abortion, marriage, society writ large, and the role of women in it. In the section on "Children," *To Live in Christ Jesus* makes a striking note:

> Some persons find themselves through no fault of their own to have a homosexual orientation. Homosexuals, like everyone else, should not suffer from prejudice against their basic human rights. They have a right to respect, friendship and justice. They should have an active role in the Christian community. Homosexual activity, however, as distinguished from homosexual orientation, is morally wrong. Like heterosexual persons, homosexuals are called to give witness to chastity, avoiding, with God's grace, behavior which is wrong for them, just as nonmarital sexual relations are wrong for heterosexuals. Nonetheless, because heterosexuals can usually look forward to marriage, and homosexuals, while their orientation continues, might not, the Christian community should provide them a special degree of pastoral understanding and care.

While not a full-throated endorsement of their complete acceptance, this passage both spoke directly to gay Catholics, and to their rights. It spoke about gay people as a part of the larger Catholic community—worthy of the same rights, and deserving of pastoral resources for their care—nearly fifty years ago. Such an accomplishment would've been inconceivable, if not impossible without DignityUSA's efforts, or without Tom.

Chapter 7

The Monk and The Activist

As Tom entered the last years of his doctoral study at Harvard, 1976–1979, he prepared for his PhD program's final requirement: a dissertation and defense. For his topic, Tom chose to analyze the styles and theological substance of two major figures in recent Catholic history: Father Daniel Berrigan, SJ and Father Thomas Merton, OSCO. Taken as a whole, the dissertation is an interesting study of Catholic leftism at the height of its power, highlighting the impact of social justice movements in particular. But at its core, it is a thorough analysis of two men who, on paper, appear to be at polar opposites of the same faith. Tom argues that without such dichotomy, Catholicism would be rudderless.

It is remarkable that Fathers Berrigan and Merton ever met. The two lived dramatically different lives, yet had surprising theological kinship as Tom later recognized. Merton was "The Monk," the contemplative Trappist who lived most of his life in a small apartment at Abbey of Our Lady of Gethsemani in Kentucky, writing more than fifty books over three decades. Berrigan was "The Activist," becoming a national name for pouring animal blood and napalm on Selective Service records with his brother Phillip, a Josephite priest, and others opposed to the Vietnam War. Both used their respective perches to advocate for peace.

Despite their different approaches to their collective faith, they were friends and colleagues who exchanged dozens of letters throughout the 1960s. It was shortly after Berrigan was sentenced to three years in prison for his protest action that Merton suddenly died in Thailand while at a monastic conference, under mysterious circumstances. No foul play was determined by the local authorities, but theories regarding his demise still abound. With Merton dead and Berrigan incarcerated, two major voices against the war went silent. But in the short time they both ministered to the world, Tom had been captivated by their work.

In his dissertation, *The Monk and The Activist: A Comparative Study of the Spirituality of Thomas Merton and Daniel Berrigan*, Tom drew connections between the two that suggested their styles, "Catholic Activism" and "Monasticism," relied on each other, and that one was ineffectual without the other:

> over and above the theological appeals for integration that Merton and Berrigan suggest, there are crucial practical and theological reasons why action and contemplation demand each other, why love of neighbor and love of God must go hand in hand for one seeking to live as a Christian.

Beyond a thesis statement, Tom understood the balance between the active and the contemplative and the need for both to achieve the "fullness of Christian life and Christian community." More than that, he saw himself in them:

> I suggest that there can be no worship or love of God unless it arises in the heart of one who actively seeks the well-being of all creation. And, on the other hand, there can be no Christian action unless it remains rooted in the "agape of God," unless it is a response to God's love received and nourished in contemplation.

It is unclear when precisely Tom wrote these words. What is certain is that they were inspired by the continued efforts of the Vatican to clarify church policy on homosexuality through the end of the seventies. While *To Live in Christ Jesus* had introduced a kinder, more accepting message to American parishes, the official line from Rome was starkly different.

In late December 1975, the Sacred Congregation for the Doctrine of the Faith issued *Persona Humana: Declaration on Certain Questions Concerning Sexual Ethics* from the Vatican. The letter addressed several topics, including homosexuality and masturbation, under the banner of "sexual ethics." It was an extensive document, definitive in its categorization of homosexuality, and whether it was acceptable within the church:

> some people conclude that their [sexual] tendency is so natural that it justifies in their case homosexual relations within a sincere communion of life and love analogous to marriage, in so far as such homosexuals feel incapable of enduring a solitary life.

> In the pastoral field, these homosexuals must certainly be treated with understanding and sustained in the hope of overcoming their personal difficulties and their inability to fit into society. Their culpability will be judged with prudence. But no pastoral method can be employed which would give moral justification to these acts on the grounds that they would be consonant with the condition of such people. For according to the objective moral order, homosexual relations are acts which lack an essential and indispensable finality. In Sacred Scripture they are condemned as a serious depravity and even presented as the sad consequence of rejecting God.

Persona Humana, signed by Pope Paul VI, closed any door toward an increasing acceptance of gay Catholics, and it fueled a reflexive wave that broke against Dignity's bow. It was the Vatican's first direct statement on the issue, which comprised less than three total paragraphs of text. In those lines, the doctrinaires had declared, with the Pope's assent, that "every genital act must be within the framework of marriage," that homosexuality was "intrinsically disordered," and that chastity was an acceptable alternative—one worthy of appreciation. Dignity was quick to respond.

Persona Humana was released to the public on January 15. The next day, *The Boston Globe* reported on Dignity's renewed call for a church committee of experts on homosexuality and its implications for society. Tom is quoted as Dignity's National Secretary and "chaplain of the 200-member Boston chapter," a laudable accomplishment for a chapter less than five years old. He was clear in his dissent with the Vatican's assessment of homosexuality, much less its pastoral approach to gay Catholics:

> Fr. Oddo said that to speak of homosexuality that way "is to neglect current biological and psychological data on homosexuality and the life experience of gay people who find their sexual orientation not a disordered curse but a God-given gift.
>
> "It is intrinsically good when it is expressed in an ethically responsible, unselfish and Christian manner, as all sexuality must be," the priest said.

Despite this effort, a committee of experts never transpired. Archbishop Bernardin of Cincinnati suggested that the response from Catholic America would be more subdued than the backlash that accompanied *Humanae Vitae*, the 1968 encyclical which reaffirmed the church's ban on birth control. It was becoming clearer and clearer that permanent change in church custom on gays was still far from reach.

A 1976 article "Hate the Sin But Love the Sinner. Sin? What Sin??" in *The Linacre Quarterly*, the journal of the Catholic Medical Association, explored the conundrum in detail. The article, one chapter of a larger manuscript by John F. Russell, cited Tom, Shanley, Father McNeill, Sister Gramick, and others within Dignity's circles as national leaders in the fight for gay Catholic rights. Tom's remarks from the 1974 New England Clergy Institute are highlighted. But Russell's article was less about the progress made by these religious revolutionaries, and more about the impossible position in which they had put the larger church:

> Yet, what is the Church to do? Can she really change her traditional position on the morality of the homosexual act without having to revise her entire moral structure regarding all sexual practices. One affects the other ... If the church accepts the homosexual act without moral stigma, is there really any substantial Church defense left that would prevent the chain reaction of the toppling dominoes on matters of sex outside marriage, sex intentionally non-procreative, and finally, abortion?

To traditionalists in the church, Tom, Digntiy, and their ilk were dangerous, all potential threats to the larger fabric of Catholicism. Russell asked readers just how dangerous they were:

> Is the forceful outspoken questioning of magisterium by church members—priests, nuns, brothers, laity—just a symptom of the times or is it a small sign of revolt in the Church that, if left unattended, will eventually spark the fuse to explode other issues regarding doctrine and authority, some quiet now and poised below the surface but also some seething?

Tom would not have called himself a revolutionary, or a radical. Many who knew him now say he would've disavowed such epithets without much thought. Tom always saw his work in the context of spreading the Gospel, no matter how powerful—or familiar—those he dissented with were. And his methods, far from violent or aggressive, were instead passionate affairs that almost always involved educating the church on the lives of gay people. A protest in August 1976, for example, had Tom overseeing the distribution of 20,000 printed leaflets at the International Eucharistic Congress, held at the University of Pennsylvania. The aim was to "sensitize" attendees to Dignity's mission and goals, and to the plight of gay Catholics in general. Their mission was reform through collective action, which included educating the public, and these efforts had quick effect.

In 1977, the Catholic Theological Society of America launched a study of sexual orientation and church doctrine that would later be published as a report entitled *Human Sexuality: New Directions in American Catholic Thought*. The study deduced that homosexuals were either imperfect or should be judged on their relational significance, particularly to heterosexual people. More importantly, the study suggested large-scale dissatisfaction between Catholic theologians and church leadership on the topic of gay rights. These conclusions drew the ire of the NCCB and the Vatican, who published a lengthy rebuttal outlining the perceived errors in *New Directions*, as the study became known.

A "Quotes from Readers" section in *The Boston Globe* that year includes a contribution from Tom, shortly after he completed his term as Dignity's National Secretary, which suggests his own struggle had grown larger than the fight for acceptance within the church: "We in religion speak about Christ's call to 'loosen the fetters of injustice.' It is time we put such words into action toward the gay community. Ending oppression is the very challenge to the Gospel."

He had also appeared in a film produced by Dignity in 1977, *Being Both Gay and Catholic*. The seventeen-minute short includes testimony from Dignity members, footage from a protest action in New York in favor of public employment protections for gays, and clips of Paul Diederich and Tom after Dignity's participation in a festival-type event—possibly New York City's Pride in June that year. A few weeks prior, Miami-Dade County had repealed a gay anti-discrimination ordinance by public vote after a relentless campaign by Christian singer Anita Bryant. The campaign became so nasty that Bryant would lose her vaunted contract with the Florida Citrus Commission and a deal with the Singer Corporation to host a variety show. The parade in New York, and dozens of others across the country, went ahead despite the vote outcome in Florida, which left some activists seething for more demonstrations, and more direct action.

Tom's appearance in the film is anything but seething. His comments, off-the-cuff, delivered in rolled-up sleeves in a subtle, Long Island accent through a toothy grin, are transcribed here in full:

> Hi, I'm Tom Oddo, National Secretary of Dignity, and I wanted to share with you a little bit of the excitement that we feel of what's happening in Dignity across the country. We are a national organization of gay and

> concerned Catholics who are really seeking to show and express Christ's love to all people regardless of their sexual preference, and we now have chapters in about forty cities of our country, with many people in all of our states and also foreign countries. Lots of great things are happening. Our organization centers around three particular concerns: The religious concern, social and educational [concerns]. We've been gathering in these chapters to celebrate Eucharist and the real pursuit of the religious dimensions of our lives; also gathering to educate both gay and straight people that, for a long time a gay person growing up has felt the incompatibility of their both being gay and Catholic, but we're trying to help people both the church and gay Catholics themselves to understand that's not necessarily the case. That gay people can be both close to God and live the fullness of their Catholic religion, and also live fully their sexual orientation as gay people. We understand that gay people are gay and even look upon that as God having created them as gay, and therefore feel they, like all other people, are called to live their sexuality in a responsible and uplifting way. We've received some very official and happy support from the various officials of the Catholic Church and a number of the dioceses across the country, really letting us happen and, kind of, sharing with us in a supporting way our pastoral work. So we share that excitement with you and ask you to be a part of us in that great movement of both living the fullness of religion and one's sexuality. Thank you.

As he finished his doctorate at Harvard, Tom's name appeared less and less in print. He kept busy with his work at St. Clement's, his ministering to Dignity/Boston and the larger national organization, and he gave public lectures on faith and sexuality under titles like "Sexuality and Christian Morality." He also taught courses at Stonehill College, first hired in 1974 to the faculty of the small Holy Cross institution's religious studies department. And he eventually ended his romantic partnership with Paul Diederich. Though they would remain friends, their relationship had run its course. Some in the church believed Tom had a real shot at a high academic office—perhaps even the presidency of Notre Dame. A doctorate from Harvard would help; a partner would not.

In spring 1979, Tom finished *The Monk and The Activist*, a project that evolved from a thesis to a 363-page treatise on Berrigan and Merton's reflexive qualities, and what they meant for the church. By the time he defended the work to his dissertation committee, he'd seen nearly a decade of pastoral service and spent more than half that time advocating for gay Catholics. In the dissertation, he offers a meditation on action regarding the "social order," work inspired by Berrigan's protest efforts that he was keenly familiar with:

> Today ... it is clear that Christian action demands participation in the reconstruction of the social order, in concrete social action for justice. The choice of "detachment" in the face of injustice and conflict, especially when silence and non-action might indicate compliance, "stands as far from the gospel as it does from the thought of men like [Popes] Leo XIII and Pius XII and John XXIII."

Tom's direct naming of Catholic inaction in the face of injustice—because of a misinterpretation of the Gospel, according to him—provides an insight to his faith and the evolving nature of his ministry at that time: "Resistance to the corrupt powers and structures of society is a basic form that Christian action must take in contemporary times." He further wrote of Berrigan's lament that monastic orders had failed to become "centers of resistance" like those in Buddhism.

For Tom, the struggle of the faith was the balance of love of God with love of neighbor, and how both were necessary to living a Christian life and fighting for civil rights. Berrigan and Merton presented, as Tom put it, complementary alternatives of Catholicism:

> they give us a model for resistance and active service (yang) that is determined and directed by their union with God (yin). And their contemplative spirit (yin) inevitably issues forth in active resistance to the forces and myth dreams that destroy and oppress (yang). Yin and yang; complementary alternatives. Each without the other is bankrupt and distorted. And in our case, each without the other fails to mirror Christ.

This suggests Tom made the idea central to his own theology, a yin and yang of a person's union with God and their service to the larger world, and that he believed it was necessary to adopt in order to follow Christ's teachings.

Chapter 8

Stonehill College

Tom was hired by Stonehill College a few months after he spoke at the New England Clergy Institute, which had been hosted on the college's Easton, Massachusetts campus. His first year as a full-time instructor was 1977, when the college published a multi-page media release on his work with Dignity and ministry to gay Catholics. If in more conservative and traditional circles he was derided for his work, here Tom was recognized for Dignity's efforts, and several initiatives—including a push for federal lawmakers to add sexual orientation to the 1964 Civil Rights Act's discrimination clause—to improve the lives of gay Catholics and those struggling to reconcile their faith and sexuality.

At Stonehill, Tom was known for teaching courses on human sexuality and the church and society. A popular and visible assistant professor whose opinions on homosexuality and gay life were different from the norm of a small Catholic college (his past work with Dignity was well known), Tom quickly became a local expert on the topic, and he participated in at least one public debate on the church's approach to human sexuality. While at Stonehill, he remained associated with Dignity, and continued to serve as chaplain to the Boston chapter and on the national organization.

Not long after graduating from Harvard Divinity School, Tom and Dignity were once again on the defensive with the larger church. In early July 1979, Cardinal Medeiros sent a letter—originally dated May 22—to priests under the domain of the Boston Archdiocese. The letter came after Paul Shanley had been reassigned to another parish in the area, leaving Boston without a priest ministering full-time to gay Catholics, as Medeiros had previously allowed. It is possible that his reassignment came after his attendance at the conference on sexuality that birthed NAMBLA, where he remarked on the value of sexual relationships between men and boys. If this was the true reason for his reassignment, it was not divulged to the public. But the cardinal's tone was drastically different from what the Dignity activists were used to.

The sixteen-page letter Medeiros sent that summer reiterated church teaching that homosexual acts "can in no case be approved." He excoriated those priests and theologians condoning homosexual acts—like Tom—as "personally enriching," and reaffirmed *Persona Humana*'s statement that homosexuality was "intrinsically disordered." He further declared he would not appoint a replacement for Shanley's gay ministry, and said priests should not encourage that parishioners join "gay groups"—like Dignity—out of precaution for their possible "embrace [of] a homosexual culture and even a homosexual way of life." While he tried to strike a sympathetic tone, suggesting that gay Catholics should be treated with understanding and "pastoral love," his stance was clear: The Boston Archdiocese would close ranks against groups like Dignity, and priests like Paul Shanley, as other dioceses had been doing for years.

Tom, now quoted as "Stonehill College professor" in addition to Dignity's national chaplain, said that he was "disappointed the cardinal does not fully understand or appreciate the work of Dignity and the need for specialized ministries to the gay community," while he appreciated the bit about pastoral love. He had worked with Medeiros in the past, and the letter must've produced terrible whiplash for its blunt definitiveness.

While Tom continued his work with Dignity after the Mederios letter, his focus turned toward the classroom and his involvement at Stonehill. For the tenth anniversary of Thomas Merton's death, in the dog days of dissertation writing, Tom published an op-ed on Merton for the college newspaper *The Summit.* It is clear from Tom's writing that Merton's work had a profound impact on him, as he spoke of the power of Merton's 1948 autobiography *The Seven Storey Mountain*—likely a book he had snuck in during his Novitiate. In contrast to Merton's early work, however, Tom noted that Merton had redefined the popular image of monks in his later years, "shatter[ing] many of the stereotypical images of the monk as a pious, world-denying ascetic, walking around on a cloud and hoping for death," since he eventually came to reject "a spirituality that seeks to escape this world." In light of successive challenges to Dignity's work and his own, Tom must've taken a page from Merton knowing that, even in a contemplative and inward looking period, one must not wall off the world in favor of solitude with God.

Tom believed Merton's most impactful contribution to the world came with his opposition to racism and discrimination of Black Americans in the 1960s. Writing about Merton's work in the arena of race politics, Tom recounted his service in DC and Baltimore, the experience of which can be felt from his description of the issues he and Merton encountered:

> It was this Trappist monk who spoke most perceptively of the frustration and violence that was building in the black community, of the destructiveness of the ghetto, and of white society's responsibility for much of the impending explosiveness because of its refusal to treat the black with justice and respect.

While his language on race in today's context is imperfect, speaking to the responsibility white Americans had for the conditions suffered by the Black community and communities within American cities shows that he was well aware of those conditions, and their roots. He closed his piece with a call to action for the readers at Stonehill to take wisdom from Merton's life and work to help influence their own. "Perhaps during this Tenth Anniversary celebration at Stonehill," he wrote,

> all of us might receive anew Merton's challenge to build a society of justice and peace, to ground that work in an intense relationship to God, and to travel with many brothers and sisters of all faiths in a common journey toward truth.

Tom's ecumenicalism, while not always front and center in his advocacy for gay Catholics, was nevertheless an important piece of his ministry. His first objective was never to convert, only to introduce those who came seeking to the things called God, Gospel, and Scripture.

Always a good teacher, Tom became a candidate for greater station at Stonehill while continuing to be a public face for the gay rights movement. In 1981, he appeared in a thirty-minute documentary produced by the Boston CBS affiliate, WNAC-TV. *All God's Children?* focused on the differing opinions of religious denominations toward gay people, and their own gay congregants. The program interviewed several individuals with varying degrees of separation on the topic—a psychologist, a Christian fundamentalist, a traditionalist Catholic priest, and Tom. The footage leading into the show's title card showed Tom, in his vestments, applying ashes to the foreheads of gay parishioners for Ash Wednesday. As he drew each cross, Tom told its recipient the customary greeting, "Turn away from sin and be faithful to the gospel." While the footage of his interview now appears lost, this imagery of Tom ministering to his people was part of a powerful and historic broadcast.

1981 also saw the publication of two essays by Tom for the sixth edition of *Theological Pastoral Resources: A Collection of Articles on Homosexuality from a Pastoral Perspective.* The first essay, titled "The Minister's Challenge to Guilt," offered perhaps Tom's greatest extrapolation of the anxieties and hardships gay Catholics endured within the church, and which most likely reflected his own experience. Tom started by quoting John Powers's *The Last Catholic in America*, where the author reflects on the wisdom of a nun from childhood:

> If you commit a mortal sin, you are spiritually dead in the eyes of God. And if you die with it on your soul before you get a chance to tell it in confession, you go straight to Hell. The only thing that can save you between the time you commit the mortal sin and the time you go to confession is saying a perfect act of contrition to God. But a perfect act of contrition is actually a perfect prayer of love to God. Very few people are holy enough to make a perfect act of contrition. And since those people love God so much, they never commit mortal sins anyway. Yes children, I'm afraid that perfect acts of contrition are very hard to come by.

He then expounds on why he chose that quote as an epigram for the essay:

> I thought that the above passage might be an appropriate reminder of the presence and power of guilt in the Catholic tradition. In Catholics over 30 the passage should spark immediate recognition and perhaps even a vivid recollection and recreation of the terror and fear that often surrounded our image of God and our understanding of sin. Our Catholic tradition was not alone in its fostering of guilt and fear as motivations for moral behavior, but perhaps it enjoyed more outstanding success, especially in the realm of human sexuality. Many of us grew up with the image of a God "out to get us," hiding behind a tree and calculating each indiscretion of deed or thought, focusing on our genitals as his greatest chance of "catching us." Many Catholics can [recall] (and perhaps even continue to experience) the cold sweats surrounding every errant thought, impure desire, lust-filled touch, or acts of intense lovemaking. All of these received the same mark of destruction in God's horrible record.

Tom added that, "for gay Catholics the terror was even more severe, for the 'occasions of sin' lurked all about, present in every friendship or glance." His relation of these daily anxieties is a window into the realities of gay life in the 1980s, desperately trying to live it but resourceful and aware of the risks, especially in the church. Tom believed that those involved in gay ministry could help ease the guilt among gay parishioners, people who had developed inner shame over their identities and behaviors, and build a "sense of mature, responsible, decision-making in [them]." Tom continued by citing a line from the Bible, John 10:28–29, where Jesus proclaimed, "There is NO snatching out of (God's) hand" of his people. Tom said that gay Catholics:

> do not have to *climb* into God's hands, carefully struggling past obstacles he/she has sadistically placed there. We do not have to hang on by the skin of our teeth, scrupulously repeating acts of contrition in the hopes that a "perfect one" will eventually be mouthed. No, this God, as imaged in Christ, has his/her fingers clasped firmly but gently around us, and no one or no thing can snatch us out. How forcefully the gay community in particular needs to hear that message in the face of a society and church that spend too much time trying to snatch away this hand of God.

Tom said that "Bad News," personified by war, nuclear armament, hunger, human rights, prisons, economic instability, and crime (for which Tom cited Boston's eleven gay murders that year) can cloud over the "Good News," but that nothing could snatch the faithful from God's hands. Not even gay Catholics' own internalized guilt and homophobia, which he believed took people out of their faith:

> No one (not ourselves) and no thing (not our guilt) can snatch us from God's hands. Not even the things we chase after, the distractions that we think will satisfy us and enrich us—not even our real sins—none of these can remove God's hand. I hope this does not sound too harsh, but not even our Church can separate us from God's love or unbend his/her fingers already molded firmly around us. Fortunately, Dignity is working hard to remind our Church of that reality.

Tom's writing clearly illustrates the moral and ethical decisions required of LGBTQ+ people of all faiths, including his own. Throughout his priestly life, he would've confessed many times, and passages like these makes you wonder what he felt particular guilt about. His distinction of "real sins" from the church-observed sin of homosexuality and usage of different gendered pronouns in reference to God are of particular note. If God could be a woman, what else could be misunderstood about the Gospel?

His second essay, "Tempering the Myth of Gay Ministry," sought to answer the question he received from a Midwest priest hastily assembling a local Dignity chapter's annual retreat. The priest said he wasn't sure he had the time or ability to "write all those 'gay talks'" and wanted advice on how to plan the event. "Tempering the Myth" is both a critique of the idea that gay ministry needs to be so specialized and unique that only a gay person could provide the service (Tom uses the example of joking about how psychiatrists, then, would need to be schizophrenic to help their patients), as well as the idea that all priests should be skilled in gay ministry. After all, recent history had shown that ordination as a priest was not an end-all, be-all insight to every parishioner's problems.

Then, having firmly established that notion, Tom responded to Cardinal Medeiros with two years' worth of angst in his rebuttal:

> In the summer of 1979 Cardinal Medeiros of Boston wrote a letter on the pastoral care of gay people. He disapproved of any "particular ministry" to gay people, claiming that they belonged in "the parishes" and that every priest was trained to deal with this "problem," especially in the confessional. While I saw the letter primarily as an unfortunate attempt to justify the removal of Boston's Fr. Paul Shanley from his specialized ministry to sexual minorities, it did seem to speak to me of an ideal. Wouldn't it be wonderful if lesbians and gay men were indeed welcomed in their parishes! Wouldn't it be wonderful if all parish ministers were indeed comfortable and competent in the pastoral care of gay people. Unfortunately, to my reading Cardinal Medeiros was articulating much more a *future* ideal than a present reality.

Tom took the Cardinal's words and clarified what they meant from his perspective, the same tack that previously got the Boston Archdiocese in hot water, and forced Medeiros's personal correction. Medeiros most likely did not believe gay Catholics had an ideal future in the church, but that they were better suited repenting for their sin and staying quiet. Tom, in contrast, used the essay to talk about the need for integrated pastoral training on gay ministry within seminaries, a focus that can be found in many of these institutions today. In both cases, Tom presents a progressive and accepting form of Catholicism built around the concept of a loving God, who made their creations exactly as they were. According to Tom, there was no confusion in divine planning: Gay Catholics were born that way.

A third essay from this period, undated but written after 1981, may have been delivered as a talk to the Paulist Center, a progressive Catholic congregation on the edge of Boston Common about two miles from St. Clement's. He gets to the root of the issues he spoke about, and reaches the same conclusion as "Tempering the Myth." Titled "Gay People Within the Church," the essay sees Tom looking back on a decade of new voices "speaking out with increasing regularity within American society and within our churches" about their homosexuality, and their advocacy for "increased understanding, affirmation, and sensitive pastoral care," a reflection of his work with Dignity and DignityUSA.

In that same decade, Tom writes, the social sciences tried to understand homosexuality, consistently declaring it an orientation that was a "discovered rather than a chosen reality," one that was "a deeply rooted primacy of response rather than simply an arbitrary behavior" and that meant as much about who someone "[falls] in love [with]" as it did their sexual attraction. He cited the infamous Dr. Alfred Kinsey and the Institute for Sex Research at Indiana University, both theorizing homosexuality could be found in up to ten percent of the world's population regardless of how the members of that subpopulation identified themselves.

Tom discussed several theories on where homosexuality comes from: first, recounting the failure of contemporary scientists to find a genetic origin; a second theory, prevailing through the 1970s, held the cause was a biological factor, like a hormonal imbalance in men, also without evidence; and a third theory, that it was some unknown factor or something relating to the child's upbringing, carried with it controversial suggestions and little to no supporting data. He wrote about how environmental theories suggested that the child's parents "did [something] wrong," when that was very unlikely the case. Calling the period until the 1970s the "sickness model," Tom notes that understanding homosexuality from a biological and psychological basis required confronting widely held beliefs and myths about gay people, which he laid out in detail:

> Few psychiatrists, even among those maintaining the sickness model, report any great success in "curing" gay people, in permanently changing the sexual orientation of constitutional homosexuals. Instead, significant numbers of apparently happy and healthy homosexuals have come forth, celebrating it as a reality to be used in the service of others, even proclaim-

> ing it as a God-given gift. The more public and self-affirming they have become, the more myths and stereotypes have been shattered.

See if you recognize any of the following myths and stereotypes Tom wrote about:

> Gay people cannot be "picked out" within our parishes (Gay males do not lisp, have limp wrists, and swish around the room; lesbians do not look like truck drivers and smoke cigars. These are horrible stereotypes). Gay people do not "prey on little children." (Statis[ti]cally, one should worry much more about heterosexual child abuse, though our stereotypes unfairly imply this is so typical of homosexuals). Gay people will not "attack us in the halls" and "do perverse things." (Few gay people seek relationships with people who cannot respond mutually; few are interested in "public" expression, and the so-called "perverse sexual actions" are all practiced by heterosexuals as well!) Gay people are not "recruiting." (The above data about causality does not at all suggest that one is brought into a sexual orientation by trying the behavior). And finally, gay people are not all promiscuous, running frantically from encounter to encounter. (Many gay people [look] for long-term, faithful relationships, though there is so little in society and church that supports such stability).

Tom then suggests that, despite its best efforts, the church may not be adequate or helpful in addressing the concerns of gay Catholics, indeed all gay people:

> Scripture and traditional Catholic theology have not always provided a helpful framework. Certain Old Testament biblical passages refer to homosexuality as [an] "abomination", while certain Pauline New Testament passages imply that homosexuals are excluded from the Kingdom. However, many contemporary biblical scholars find these apparent condemnations quite culture-bound, that is, linked inevitably to the particular concerns which prompted them, pagan fertility cults, emphasis on grogeny [*sic*][8], and abuse of young boys within Greek and Roman society. They suggest that the authors of scripture had no knowledge of constitutional homosexuality and could not have been addressing the phenomenon as we know it today.

8. Most likely "progeny."

This essay was most likely written the year Tom was made Acting Chair of Stonehill's Religious Studies Department, or shortly after. It contains clear lines around how the church should treat gay people that suggest even the Bible was erroneous in its understanding of their plight. These were not, and still are not, minor declarations. He continued by saying:

> Strangely enough, even the most traditional Catholic theology has never condemned homosexuality as an orientation. It is, supposedly, perfectly morally acceptable to be a homosexual, to find oneself in the condition of being attracted primarily to the same sex. The Church effectively recognized, even before it was commonly understood, that orientation is not a matter of choice and therefore cannot bear moral weight. Sin enters the picture, in this traditional theology, only when one acts homosexually; it is homosexual actions that are sinful. Therefore, according to Church teaching, all 20 million U.S. homosexuals must be celibate, non genitally active, and presumably they all receive the "grace from God" to live in such celibacy.

For Tom, and for many gay Catholics like him, such an approach led to lives filled with guilt and internalized shame, lives "of loneliness and isolation, for any friendships became 'near occasions of sin.'" I can imagine Tom wrote many of these lines from the heart, from having lived these experiences himself. And he said that contemporary theologians believed "all is not well" with the church's theology of homosexuality, holding that three distinct camps had developed. The leading belief was the "traditional position," where homosexuality is evil and lacks the procreation inherent in heterosexual couples, and as such is considered immoral. A second belief, one championed by Father Charles Curran and others in Tom's circles, proposed a "middle position," where homosexual actions are not automatically immoral, and there is an inherent desire for long-term monogamous relationships with others. A third belief, advocated by Father John McNeill, and perhaps one we can refer to as the "values position," said homosexual actions must be judged based on the embodiment of values heterosexual actions are held to. One criterion Tom suggested was the 1977 study of the Catholic Theological Society of America's Committee on Sexuality, which proposed seven different values: "Self-liberating, other-enriching, honest, faithful, socially responsible, life-serving, and joyous." By these metrics, the committee believed homosexuals should be judged, with little consideration of attraction or sexual preference.

Tom cited two other recent events in the church as proof that a more inclusive theology was possible: the NCCB pastoral letter *To Live in Christ Jesus*, which established gay Catholics' rights to respect, friendship, and justice, among other recognitions, and the 1976 Call to Action Conference that same year in Detroit, also hosted by the NCCB. The conference had been a controversial, at times rowdy event which brought together over 1,300 Catholic clergy and laity to discuss the church's positions. By its conclusion, many of the US Bishops believed the conference had been less than effective, giving way to populist declarations that appeared largely unactionable, including the ordination of women. Tom, however, cited a handful of the conference's resolutions that related to gays in the church—statements suggesting the church should "seek to serve [their] pastoral needs," "provide pastoral care to all sexual minorities," and "encourage and affirm the pastoral efforts of Dignity"—as signs of progress.

In closing, Tom said that gay people were always a part of the Paulist Center, and the church; that they came to church to experience the Gospel, to share in the riches of the faith, but they needed to hear back "ever more strongly a welcoming, understanding voice, a recognition of common humanity. And they need to find the unconditional acceptance that was characteristic of Christ's outreach to all people." The last line is perhaps the greatest summary of Tom's belief system, and the modus operandi of his activism: "Such love made flesh through the community casts out fear." If gays could be accepted, even loved by their church, the fears of their lives and those of their detractors could finally be vanquished.

These were the things Tom spoke about in his later years at Stonehill, at the end of his Dignity decade. He served in the Acting Chair role in the Religious Studies Department through the 1981/82 academic year. It was his first position in academic leadership, and where he learned his first real lessons in college administration. While he had a small team of faculty, and the department he managed was important if somewhat-overlooked, Tom was set for a career in faculty circles, teaching students and administering programs. In Easton, he felt at home for the first time since Notre Dame, and would later remark that he'd seen himself teaching forever, either at Stonehill or a place like it. But events already unfolding on the other side of the country would ensure his path was permanently redirected, his future history rewritten. Whether it was Divine Providence or a happy accident, one day in early 1982, Tom got a phone call: He would soon be visited by a Holy Cross superior, who would need a ride from Logan Airport. The night he was due in, Tom bundled up and drove to Boston, oblivious to one chapter ending as another one was being written for him.

Part Two: Challenger

1982–1986

I hope to be a rallying point around whom the already-present strengths of this University can receive direction. I hope as well to be a challenger, to move this University into an even more vibrant position within the world of scholarship, within this city, within the Church.

Tom Oddo,
Inaugural Address (1982)

Chapter 9

Portland in the 1980s

More than a decade before *Twin Peaks* introduced the Pacific Northwest to the larger American public consciousness, the region was a hodge-podge mix of new and old industries, old and new money, set against a pristine green backdrop of Douglas firs in the shadows of the Cascades. As the leading timber producer in the US, logging and paper companies had remained major employers throughout the state for many years. The Kaiser shipyards in North Portland, which hired thousands of workers to build Liberty ships and ready-made craft for World War II, produced an employee health benefit called Kaiser Permanente, a major health insurer. Oregon has functioned then and now as a major producer of hazelnuts and wine due to its optimal latitude and fair weather. It has also manufactured aircraft parts, electronics, and apparel—with Nike, Pendleton, and Jantzen swimwear each headquartered in Portland and the surrounding area.

For years, tech companies were clustered in Washington County's Silicon Forest, a short drive west from Portland. But job growth in the industry had slowed to 18.3 percent annually, one of the lowest among American cities. Highway projects envisioned by Robert Moses in the '40s sought to make rush hour drives shorter until protestors halted expansion of the Mount Hood Freeway in 1974. Highway building efforts resulted in the creation of an enclave within Portland, the City of Maywood Park—a neighborhood of homeowners who refused to sell their land for an expanded I-205, which had destroyed many neighbor's homes. For the first time in the city's history, urban growth was overruled by community activism.

But beyond the simple economics, the culture of Oregon began to change rapidly after the war. Terry Schrunk, Mayor since the Eisenhower presidency, left office in 1973 and died two years later. His successor, thirty-three-year-old City Commissioner Neil Goldschmidt, opened City Hall to women and BIPOC appointees for the first time, and established the MAX Light Rail system now synonymous with Portland. But the veneer of Goldschmidt's political success masked his surreptitious sexual assault and harrasment of a teenager over a three-year period during his term. He would later become President Jimmy Carter's secretary of transportation and a one-term governor of Oregon. The *Willamette Week* exposed his crimes in a 2004 story, forcing a public reckoning with the Goldschmidt years and a reassessment of his legacy that continues to the present.

Those years saw a wild mishmash of pop culture phenom, drug proliferation, and subversive entertainment in the Rose City: The Portland Trail Blazers rallied to their only NBA championship title in 1977; their inability to replicate the achievement led to a steep drop-off in fan engagement. Until 1977, pinball machines had been illegal in the city due to gambling concerns, while police and municipal corruption reached all-time highs. Governor Tom McCall, who had once championed public ownership of state beaches and the only publicly funded rock concert in US history, now banned outdoor display lighting to save energy, leading to periods of darkness throughout the state. Cocaine flowed as freely as prostitution and porn, while Portland would eventually boast the most strip clubs per capita in the nation, a record it still holds today. *Animal House* filmed at University of Oregon in Eugene that October, while a drag queen named Darcelle XV entertained her patrons with "X-rated female impersonator" drag shows at the Darcelle XV Showcase in Downtown Portland, now a historic venue.

For such a wild time, things were not well in the Pacific wonderland. Oregon was hit hard by the transition to the '80s, starting with the eruption of Mt. St. Helens, and fueled by the consolidation and later collapse of the timber industry. These events in combination over the first years of the new decade made the state's path a fraught one. New arrivals to Portland in particular began to drop year over year in 1979, with an average 2.2 percent or more population growth cratering to 1.26 percent in 1981 (meaning only 13,000 people moved to the Portland metro area that year, even as the city proper saw a net loss of residents). The influx that once necessitated Governor McCall's famous quip, "We hope you enjoy your visit, just don't move here," in a tourism ad only a decade prior had reached its limit.

Life on the Bluff, the high ridge dividing the city that's formally known as the Willamette Escarpment, had also been tumultuous. For many years, Father Paul Waldschmidt had been the steady, traditional hand guiding the University of Portland. As Waldschmidt left to assume the role of auxiliary bishop of Portland, the university picked from its faculty ranks Brother Raphael Wilson, CSC, an experimental biologist known across the country for his work with David Vetter, the immunocompromised child dubbed "The Bubble Boy," to serve as UP's sixteenth president. Wilson accepted the role despite suffering a heart attack in 1976, in the midst of his work with Vetter. He saw the the appointment as an opportunity to advocate for UP's faculty, a constituency group he believed had not been thoroughly represented in the Waldschmidt years.

In assuming the office, however, Wilson inherited problems outside of his control, then mishandled their optics. Increasing operational costs necessitated large increases in tuition each year, jumping by 12.5 percent in 1980 alone. That didn't stop him from approving a 10–10.5 percent increase in faculty salaries the same year—so closely timed *The Beacon* put both stories on the same front page. The economic malaise hitting the national economy hit Oregon too, causing worry among new graduates over job opportunities, and making prospective students think twice about taking out student loans.

Then came the issues related to Arthur Luther, an assistant professor of philosophy who was popular among UP students. When Luther was told his annual teaching contract would not be renewed at the end of spring 1981, he was effectively laid off. Before the tumultuous firing, he had been passed over for tenure and an advancement in academic rank, both requests he would deny to *The Beacon*, UP's student newspaper. Despite these discrepancies in stated facts, Luther's firing became a minor cause célèbre which, through no fault of his own (and due to institutional confidentiality in personnel matters), Wilson was unable to answer for.

By March, *The Beacon*'s Letters to the Editor pages were inundated with messages supporting Luther. So fervent was the backlash, Wilson wrote his own letter to students in response, running in *The Beacon* a few weeks later. In it, he again refused to explain the reasons for Luther's termination, only to confirm that Luther had been informed of the institution's reasoning, and had received numerous notices from him and Father Richard Berg, CSC, the dean of the College of Arts and Sciences.

Unsatisfied, a group of ten student protestors started a hunger strike, with the stated aims of reopening Luther's case for review by a new independent committee of administrators, faculty, and students—and subsequent action to make the committee permanent. If the demands weren't met, the strikers would call for Wilson's resignation. After 200 hours of striking, the UP Academic Senate announced they would form an ad-hoc committee to review Luther's case, and the students ended their fast. To their dismay, Luther was not rehired, and the episode cast a shadow over Wilson's presidency. That August, the Board of Regents received a report from their Presidential Review Committee, critical of Wilson's performance. In response to the report's concerns, Wilson sent a nearly eleven-page rebuttal letter. The regents were unmoved. During a special meeting called to consider his termination, Wilson resigned. With his term over on the Bluff, Wilson returned to teaching, and would later relocate to Pennsylvania, where he was ordained and served the Diocese of Scranton (as Father Joseph Wilson). It was also there where he sexually assaulted two boys, cases which were settled out of court. These cases were revealed in a 2018 grand jury report on sexual abuse by Pennsylvania priests. His presidency remains a controversial chapter in the university's history.

In that short tenure, despite the headwinds of the national and local economies, Wilson had increased enrollment and campus improvement projects. One such initiative was a plan to build the first real chapel on the Bluff. The project, led by UP's Father Richard Rutherford, CSC, and noted architect Pietro Belluschi, would see its marvelous crescendo some years later, ending in blessings by a friendly priest named Tom.

Chapter 10

New Man on Campus

The winter of 1982 saw some of the fiercest weather in decades around Boston. At Logan Airport, the cold had already made for a perilous travel season: In January, a World Airways DC-10 landed on ice and slid off the runway into the harbor, killing two passengers. Now, a few weeks later, a mammoth blizzard was building, posing danger to incoming air traffic. One flight from a far sunnier Florida carried Father Richard Warner, CSC, then-provincial superior of the Congregation of Holy Cross. He sat, anxiously looking over his notes and checking his watch, wondering whether the plane would run out of fuel before it landed. Passengers around him smoked as they saw the airport lights come into focus. When they landed, it was past one o'clock in the morning.

Father Warner was a transformer of priestly lives, strategically selecting good men for positions of leadership within the Congregation. He had been tasked by the University of Portland's Presidential Search Committee to draft a list of potential candidates for the role of president, recently vacated by the resignation of Brother Raphael Wilson. With Wilson's short presidency in shambles, the 2,800-student University was desperate for a new type of leadership—radically different from what Wilson, and even Father Paul Waldschmidt had offered in the years following World War II and the onset of the Cold War. They were desperate for change; the consideration of lay candidates was on the table for the first time in the university's history.

An April editorial in *The Beacon* titled "Priests Shouldn't Get Preference" underlined the real possibility of a layperson assuming the role. The thought was controversial with many in the congregation, where tradition dictated a priest was necessary to keep the university truly Catholic. But Warner was unfazed. Nothing, not a blizzard nor lack of obvious candidates, would stop him from completing his mission. Portland author

Christopher Boehme wrote of the common experience with Warner: "A young priest sets out with Father Warner unaware and comes back with a new job, a new life."

Waiting near the gate at Logan, Tom Oddo was unaware of his friend's purpose for visiting. The two had known each other for years through Congregation circles, but he had not been told why the Provincial Superior had left the Florida sun for Boston, where over a foot of snow would fall in the next day. As the airport shut down behind him, Warner's flight was one of the last to disembark. Stepping off the plane, the two hugged and took each other's arm. Their conversation would last several hours, and throughout Warner would ask Tom to apply for the UP presidency. With some convincing on Warner's part, Tom agreed. God's plan had taken a curious turn.

When the search committee met on March 15, a few weeks later, the members cut a pool of ten applicants to five. The finalists for the role were Fathers Richard Berg[9], David Schlaver[10], Charles Sherrer[11], James Watzke[12], and Tom Oddo, all Holy Cross priests. The announcement released to press outlets on April 9 mentioned a series of interviews scheduled through the end of the month. Tom was now thirty-seven, a young and intense figure. Boehme wrote of a search committee member who later recalled their impression of the man:

> Tom Oddo came in with those piercing dark eyes, that charisma … had something special that we all sensed, an agape love that one associates with people like Mother Theresa [*sic*] … the kind of love that loves unconditionally.

Tom's personality and zeal had shown through. Keeping up with his Notre Dame routine, he maintained a swimmer's build and trimmed brown hair which made him appear closer in age to the average UP student than to those on the committee. But beyond his personal charm, the committee appreciated Tom's philosphy of education. Whatever specific quality won them over, one by one the search committee members were convinced he was the pick.

Young, energetic, loving, he was still inexperienced in administration. Tom had only served as an *interim* department chair at Stonehill College

9. Dean of the College of Arts and Sciences, University of Portland—45 years old
10. Director of Campus Ministry, University of Notre Dame—39 years old
11. Former President, King's College (PA)—46 years old
12. Former Director of the Day Hospital Program (Chicago)—45 years old

for a year. He was never a vice president, or dean, or even director of a college office. But then again, Ted Hesburgh had been younger than Tom when he became president of Notre Dame. Since then, his term had made Notre Dame a national name in higher education, and his own name a regular contact for presidents to call on in times of spiritual duress. That same day, the committee nominated Tom for the job. One finalist later said the process was far less of an open question than it publicly appeared, revealing he agreed with others on the short list to appear as fill-in candidates. At no point was there a question: Tom Oddo would be the University of Portland's seventeenth president. The process was merely a formality laying the foundation for his term.

The announcement went to the press on May 20, and a formal announcement was held on campus at the Buckley Center the next day. Chairman of the Board of Regents Robert Franz introduced the university to its youngest president ever, a priest who *The Oregonian* noted taught three courses the previous semester at Stonehill: Western Religious Traditions, Church and Theology in Controversy (which dealt with topics like the ordination of women and the church's role in topics as varied as war and biomedical ethics), and "Religion and Sexuality." When asked about the latter course, which dealt with topics like homosexuality and abortion, Tom said that "It draws students by the hundreds. Anything with 'sex' in the title will." The article also included biographical information about his childhood in Queens, his pursuit of the priesthood, and his time at Notre Dame and Harvard—including a few lines on his dissertation about Daniel Berrigan and Thomas Merton. Noticeably absent was any mention of his work with DignityUSA, as a chaplain or as a former national officer of the organization.

The Oregonian's article and a flash published by the Catholic News Service both highlighted Tom's focus on improving connections between the university and the larger Portland metropolitan area. Genuine connection existed between UP and the Portland business world: The Bluff had hosted the Greater Portland Industrial Exposition in 1950, and marketing materials through the 1960s called UP "A Community Asset … A vital link in a new era of growth and prosperity for Portland and the Northwest" as graduates left the classroom for offices around the city. And yet, there was a disconnect between the university and the larger community. Tom saw in the disconnect an opportunity to reset relations disrupted by the disorder of the Wilson presidency, and said he planned to join several civic organizations as part of his effort.

Prior to his selection, Tom had visited the campus only once, for a weekend conference in 1973. When asked about how he viewed UP before assuming the presidency, he said that the campus was "flourishing," but still faced challenges posed by the local economy and cost of attendance. The environment he described was largely the result of the Reagan administration's hacksaw approach to financial aid—which cut $600 million from Pell Grants and loans for FY 1981 and requested an additional $332 million in cuts for FY 1982—coupled with the Wilson presidency's 18.2 percent tuition hike for fall 1981. To that end, Tom planned to be a president at the cutting edge of "advancement," a relatively-new approach to institutional fundraising that involved soliciting private donations from community members, businesses, and organizations. The model had not yet been tested at the Bluff, as UP relied largely on donations from a single angel-investor, Earle Chiles, Sr. and his family. As Tom planned the beginnings of his presidency, work with the Chiles family would be fundamental to complete major initiatives, including the completion of an athletic stadium named after Earle. But other donors would be necessary to grow, even maintain, what the university had built over seventy years. As enrollment held around 2,800, Tom would've been thinking about the economics of things as he sat down to write his first letter to students.

In the August 6, 1982, edition of *The Alpha*, an annual supplement to *The Beacon* published around the start of the academic year, Tom's letter ran on page two next to a photo of the new president from the Office of Public Relations. His opening offered a bit of frank honesty:

> It is difficult to say "Welcome to the University," when the one offering the welcome is not yet fully present himself. Like you, in September of 1982 I will officially come to the University for the first time, assuming the presidency during this summer. I hope that you are as excited as I am about this new beginning and about the community that we will become a part of in September.

Despite his unfamiliarity with the campus and newness to the university, Tom described UP as "an outstanding institution of higher education," citing graduates from thirty-four states and fifty-seven countries and UP's "wide variety" of programs that had gained a "reputation for excellence." He also described the Bluff as "a family, a community of people—administration, faculty, staff, and students—who enjoy together the working/learning/living project that we share," a "vibrant, growing community," and those employed by the university as "dedicated to [students'] enrichment" and "ready to serve in whatever way we can." Tom closed his letter by further describing UP as a "learning community, a family focused upon Judeo-Christian wisdom and values and enriched by other perspectives as well."

The last bit, referring to other perspectives, was a new tune for a president on the Bluff. Prior to Tom's hire, UP had frequently included the word Catholic in marketing itself as "The Catholic University of the Northwest," on the assumption that sticking to tradition would be more beneficial to the institution than opening the doors to ecumenicalism. And yet here was a new president, younger than most students' parents, talking about "other perspectives" in the same breath as Judeo-Christian wisdom and values.

A sense of change in the current was not lost on *The Beacon* editorial staff, who wrote "One gets the feeling that 'because it's always been done that way' will not be a stock-and-trade answer for Oddo," and that "[Oddo] knows that an 'ivory tower' approach will get him nowhere," concerning Tom's need for collaborative campus governance. He said so himself:

> I think the best advice I've received is to listen ... My major stance toward all segments of the University is to be one who wants to learn from them, one who listens to the concerns, the ideas, the directions that are proposed.

Without listening intently and learning intentionally from all campus constituencies, and without their direct engagement with him, he would get nowhere. *The Beacon* editorial closed by calling on students to give their input and ideas for how to make the university a better place. After all, "Oddo says he will listen to everyone, not just a select few. This means that changes previously thought unlikely to occur may soon become very possible." And what was the harm in trying?

Tom finished his teaching duties at Stonehill that summer, and moved westward to Portland. Several friends helped him move into a residential dorm apartment sometime in August, as was customary for UP's presidents. It didn't take long for the Bluff to get to know him. A series of extended interviews with *The Beacon* made clear his views on numerous topics.

He agreed with the regents that a Holy Cross priest was necessary for his role, since they were better able to "carry forth U of P's 'Catholic character,'" but acknowledged the contributions of laypeople to the university's Catholicity. He talked about the effects of co-ed housing at Stonehill, a major topic of discussion at UP, and believed they had caused no major problems. They were, to the contrary, "very natural" and did not promote promiscuity, and if a similar proposal were made at UP to establish such housing options, he said he "wouldn't have any inherent objections with it."

He cited multiple capital projects as top priorities, namely the fund-raising and building of the athletic facility that would become the Earle Chiles Center and the completion of the university chapel, whose design had recently been approved by committee. In a later piece, he mentioned a new tennis and racquetball facility, "The Racquet Center," as another priority project. Financial aid was another focus, specifically finding what he called "'creative' ways of helping students to afford college."

Father Charles Schreck, in a *Beacon* op-ed titled "School faces new directions," reflected on what Tom Oddo's infant presidency meant for the larger institution:

> We wonder about Tom Oddo and where his leadership will take us. We are curious about his dreams and directions, about what his unique contribution to the University will be.
>
> His first weeks at the University have given us the picture of an outgoing intelligent man interested in and concerned about all aspects of campus life. There are, however, many questions which lie ahead, questions only time will answer.

Questions about his leadership style, his competencies as an executive leader, and his ability to deliver on institutional priorities mixed with wonder about what kind of priest he was, and how he would minister to the university. Though wondering about Tom Oddo would only be so productive. Schreck added:

> But one of the biggest questions we face deals not with Tom Oddo, but with ourselves. I suppose it is our p[r]erogative to wonder about him, but I feel such speculation should also involve a close look at ourselves.
>
> Questions about our school's direction, [its] need to improve and grow, are questions we all must face. We need to ask ourselves if we are ready to work with our new president to make this the best school it can be.

If student opinion meant anything, a new direction was needed for the university. His selection prompted high hopes that such a course change could be delivered.

Chapter 11

Inauguration

On Friday, October 8, Tom and members of his family who had flown in for his inauguration attended a stand-up set by Milton Berle at Howard Hall, a feature of that week's Homecoming Weekend. Berle, a television icon who was known to multiple generations as "Mr. Television," had lived a sour final chapter in the years prior to his visit to the Bluff. At the end of his NBC contract in the 1960s, an unprecedented thirty-year deal, he had been subjected to hosting a bowling show, *Jackpot Bowling*. His singular stint hosting *Saturday Night Live* in 1979 was so bad, between his constant mugging to the camera and antics on- and off-stage, showrunner Lorne Michaels banned him from appearing on the show ever again. And in September 1982, a few weeks prior to his performance at UP, he made an ass of himself presenting an award at the Emmys. Reluctant to cede the microphone, then repeatedly interrupting the winners for Outstanding Writing, Joe Flaherty of *Second City Television* told him "Sorry Uncle Miltie … go to sleep." Many who attended his October 8 show would've seen the Emmys exchange boradcast live.

His performance at Howard Hall didn't do him favors. In a review published in the October 14 Homecoming/Inauguration issue of *The Beacon*, Editor Michael Raffanti lamented how a 1981 performance by Martin Mull was so crude, many had anticipated a better, cleaner show with Berle, "something of the family variety." It was neither better, nor cleaner. Berle began by jabbing at the state of Howard Hall, a combination of athletic facility and speaking venue, sarcastically calling it "classy." He then began a string of what Raffanti called, "vulgar remarks and crude anecdotes." What the review noted as his best material was his crowd work, which particularly centered on Tom's family, sitting in the front row. Said Berle to a woman in the group, "The last time I saw a mouth that big there was a hook in it." Whether these jokes played for laughs isn't noted, only that the show was two hours long. It included a highlight reel from Berle's time on *Texaco Star Theater* in the 1950s, described as an "exercise in ego satisfaction—and a prolonged one at that." Afterward, he took questions from the audience. The whole performance left Raffanti to close his piece on an observation Berle made on stage: "'The young spirit is great,' Berle said. But not tasteless."

The next day, over 300 UP alumni descended on the Red Lion Hotel at Jantzen Beach in North Portland for a reunion banquet. At the event, Tom gave the official Homecoming Message to alumni, his first as president. Of Berle he spoke little, only to say he "gave us a bit of a hard time. He had no idea what he was getting into, appearing in Howard Hall." He instead reflected on the "great history of the University as it unfolds before us" and what the university meant to him as he prepared for his big day:

> Oddo said that with all the Homecoming festivities and preparation for his inauguration, he has "learned something about protocol." He jokingly added that "only after (the inauguration will) students carry me around in a high chair."
>
> He complimented "the sense of family and community here," the "warmth and high esteem held" by alumni of U of P, the "faculty and staff committed to teaching," and the students concerned with the "pursuit of wisdom." These qualities, Oddo said, make the university "so great," and the feelings "carry on into the future" by its graduates.

He spoke on the importance of alumni contributions and emphasized giving back to the university. It would be the first of many donor asks he would make in his tenure, one that redefined the donor/university relationship.

Tom's inauguration was held on Sunday, October 10, 1982. Howard Hall once again became a speaking venue, with floral arrangements and an American flag filling the backdrop. UP's Concert Choir squished onto risers at the front. Multnomah County Commissioner Gladys McCoy, the first Black elected official in Oregon, was in attendance and said both the university and the city were lucky to have Tom. State Treasurer Clay Myers lauded Tom's "special kind of energy and vitality." Portland Mayor Frank Ivancie sent a letter of congratulation via his executive assistant. Dr. Robert Glennen, Jr. '55/'57, president of Western New Mexico University spoke on behalf of UP alumni, calling the ceremony Tom's "confirmation" (since he had already been "baptized" as president).

Then Father Ted Hesburgh rose to give the guest address, a homily of sorts on the role of university president. Hesburgh had famously resigned as chair of Richard Nixon's Commission on Civil Rights over disagreements on busing, desegregation, and the Voting Rights Act. So public a figure was Hesburgh, that he was considered as a running mate for George McGovern's 1972 campaign after Thomas Eagleton dropped out. Hesburgh declined the offer, and ten years later found himself on the Bluff as the elder statesman of Catholic higher education in America.

Hesburgh declared "One cannot be a good president all by himself." He said that university presidents needed to be forceful yet stay human, despite the powers entrusted to them. And he spoke on the constituencies Tom would serve: first the Trustees, the most important group, then the faculty, then students—who sometimes harbored views in contrast with the first two. All three would need a president with vision: "[He] may be the best administrator in the world," Hesburgh said, "but without a bright vision … nothing will matter and he will not be able to lead anyone."

Tom had spelled out his vision to the *Sunday Oregonian*, albeit broadly, in a feature that ran the day of his inauguration: "One of the roles of the university is to pursue wisdom. What happens to its students is that they receive an increased social consciousness … to do something for the betterment of the world." While he mentioned the need for better training in tune with business and industrial demands, and the need to improve the presence of UP in the city, Tom made no major declarations about his philosophy: "I came to Portland only with the vision of the Holy Cross Fathers—the pursuit of wisdom and a concern for social justice." The article reported on speculation that, with such a young appointment to the role, Tom was now on track to eventually succeed Hesburgh at Notre Dame. But Tom had no aspirations to the role, at least not at first.

As Hesburgh returned to his seat, the floor was now Tom's, first to receive the university chain and medallion from Board Chairman Robert Franz. He then assumed the podium, arranged his notes, and began his Inaugural Address. The top of his first page marginalia reads "(Opening comments of a very light nature)." From there, he explained how six months prior, he'd never envisioned being where he was:

> But those of us who are people of faith cannot help but feel there is a hand at work here, a gentle guiding hand that can't be fully understood and which points us to an uncertain future. But it's a hand and voice to which

> we can only respond like the prophets of old: "Here I am Lord, I come to do your will."

Keeping things light he remarked, "This is a wonderful group of people gathered in this less than wonderful building," to quiet laughs. But he went further to describe the assembly before him, and their collective mission:

> It is a marvelous community of University personnel from our University and others spread across the land. It is a community of students, regents, my family, civic leaders, alumni, contributors and friends, all of whom are saying yes not to just my being here but to the task we begin together. I thank you all for being here today to inaugurate this common pursuit and to step into the future boldly.

In spite of worrying words and darkening storm clouds in higher education, and those who'd ask why anyone in their right mind would want to be a university president, Tom was optimistic for the future and he made a point of saying so. He said he'd never accept such a responsibility without such a community who would "never let me do the task alone." Their community was one that, according to Tom, stood strong because of five distinct pillars holding it up.

First, the university held the "heritage of the Holy Cross Fathers and our long experience in higher education. That heritage has always enabled us to carry on the richness of our Judeo-Xian[13] tradition while creatively responding to contemporary challenges." Tom said that this tradition was what brought him to UP and motivated him to "nothing short of excellence."

Second, the rich community of employees found on the Bluff, faculty and staff who'd made the mission of the university into a personal devotion of sorts. Tom called it a passion: "The passion for good clear teaching, the passion for trimming shrubs or maintaining a building in just the right way, the passion for typing and counseling in ways that serve others most generously and sensitively."

Third, he talked about the students: "young, vibrant people, eager to be touched by the wisdom of the ages" that each held their own vision, their own passion. He said these students came to UP knowing its academic and professional reputation, but also because "it is a family in

13. Alternate spelling of "Christian" popular among Tom's generation of priests and parishioners.

which they can feel at home and be nurtured and move away from better prepared to do something about the world in which we live." To Tom, the students meant everything. "I'm confident in the success of this University because its students thirst for wisdom and a better world."

Fourth was the community of people Tom described as "friends" of the university: regents, alumni, supporters from Portland and beyond, who helped UP solve major urban problems. Tom said it was "because of the cooperation of so many, the faithful support of so many that the future can only be bright."

Last, but far from least, Tom cited the presence of God. Here, he publicly spoke of his own exegesis, his image of God, and what God's purpose was on the Bluff:

> I am confident because we have a God who is present with us guiding the course of our lives, guiding the life of this institution.
>
> Of course, I don't mean this in a simplistic sense—the hand of God reaching down to erect buildings, raise faculty and staff salaries, tap thousands of students on the head to send them our way.

Taking a pause, he made an aside: "We could certainly use all of those actions, but they're not characteristic of the God I know." As the crowd chuckled, he continued on with his premise:

> We prosper because we believe in a God who marches with us into the future, a God (in the words of this morning['s] Mass Gospel) "for whom all things are possible," a God who holds truth before us like a beacon and ever draws us toward it with a firm but gentle hand.
>
> We express today a faith in a God who is truth, truth here with us on our journey, truth to which this University tries to conform.
>
> With all of these to guide us, I have utmost confidence in our future.

He then pledged himself to several things: to "listen sensitively to every voice;" to "respond with honesty in comfortable times and in times of tension;" to find, through prayer and vigor, "the wisdom and compassion to do this job well." And he described what he hoped would be his part to play:

> I hope to be a rallying point around whom the already-present strengths of this University can receive direction. I hope as well to be a challenger, to move this University into an even more vibrant position within the world of scholarship, within this city, within the Church.

In closing, he shared his appreciation with the crowd, an uneven mix of older alumni in suits and their Sunday best with priests and parents and teenagers: "Thank you for inviting me into that very bright future that lies before us. We step into it together this day."

The crowd rose and applauded for the new president. Father Paul Waldschmidt, now auxiliary bishop of Portland, placed the Chain of Office over Tom's shoulders. As he fixed it across Tom's vestments, the UP Concert Choir began a rendition of the Alma Mater. The campus doors opened as they had in Rome seventeen years prior, fresh air flowing in. It was the last page of the university's darkest chapter finally being turned, and by a boyish Sicilian priest from Queens of the most unlikely persuasion.

Chapter 12

The First Years, 1982–1983

The initial wonder about Tom was quickly replaced by his growing visibility. Within days of his inauguration, he started a campaign to be omnipresent in campus life. In a schedule akin to a barnstorming politician, Tom held the first of dozens of town halls in UP's dormitories, starting with visits to Shipstad and Villa Maria Halls on October 18.

That evening's events provided many students with their first look at what their new president was all about. When someone raised the issue of co-ed dorms, one of the first questions asked, he responded with the thoughtful diplomacy that helped him secure the position: "To put it safely, I do not object to finding some ways of increasing a more 'natural' contact between men and women." *The Beacon* staff writer Pat Johnson explained what he meant, adding that Tom had presented "no philosophical problems on the issue, just practical ones," including potential backlash and hesitancy from parents, the need for regent approval, and more logistical matters. As Johnson noted in the article, "Oddo believes that co-ed living may help students see values that are part of U of P." It was the first indication that such a change could be possible with Tom at the helm.

Another question involved building plans during his tenure. He mentioned the projects on his radar: athletic facilities, starting with a new tennis and racquet center and a "Sports Convocation Center." Soon after, there was a question about why tuition was so high. For many, the experience of the 11 percent hike in 1981 had still elicited shell shock. For Tom, it was simple economics: UP survived off a budget where revenues were 90 percent tuition dollars. But Johnson pointed out that Tom "firmly stated, with much relief from students, that the tuition cannot be raised anymore."

Tom made clear that he was there to support students, first and foremost: "I will always be honest with you, listen to your concerns and do anything possible to help you." The photo accompanying the article showed Tom relaxed, sitting back with his leg up in an armchair, explaining his point. He would live up to his vow less than two weeks later, in the October 28 issue of *The Beacon.* On the op-ed page, he made a rare contribution in the form of a correction:

> Dear Editor:
>
> I wish to commend the editors and staff of *The Beacon* for the excellent quality of the publication and the great contribution it is making to campus life.
>
> May I make one slight correction in the article entitled "Oddo visits dorms" in the October 21st issue. I am quoted as saying that University tuition "cannot be raised anymore."
>
> While I might certainly hope that we find a magic formula to eliminate any future tuition increases and I would like to be able to make such a promise, what I actually said was that the administration realizes we cannot continue to raise tuition **at the same high rate**, that there will be a point at which highly qualified students will no longer be able to afford to come here.
>
> Sincerely,
> (Rev.) Thomas C. Oddo, CSC
> President

This engagement was new, and used when needed. While former presidents had responded to requests for comment and sat for interviews with *The Beacon*, this polite correction to the record feels unique from a university president. Tom would later co-sign an apology on behalf of a professor who disparaged an Associated Students of the University of Portland (ASUP) candidate's character and campaign to his students, another instance where he used his position to reassert the university's standing and communicate directly to the campus at large, a departure in style from the Wilson years.

Early in his presidency, Tom's governance style was largely personal and involved, despite the wisdom of at least one elder in the field. On Inauguration Sunday, *The Beacon* ran a special edition two-page insert on the ceremony, which included an interview with Father Ted Hesburgh after the event. Following his address, he expanded on his thoughts and answered questions posed by the Editorial Board. While he commented on what was needed to make a presidency successful, and by extension a university, his own reflection on being selected to lead Notre Dame offered an arguably more useful piece of wisdom for Tom: "I personally thought it was a dumb thing to select me at age 35. I had a zillion things to learn ... there were enough people around to keep me out of trouble, though."

Tom gradually learned to delegate, to surround himself with people capable of managing the minutiae of campus operations. The first year, however, according to Father Joe Corpora, CSC, he would be frustrated by little things like an unattended coffee cup left on a hallway windowsill. Such concerns would not matter to him by the end of his tenure, but those details were top-of-mind at the beginning. Joe, a resident director at the time Tom assumed the presidency, took a liking to him quickly. They connected over swimming, both making regular use of Howard Hall for laps in the pool. Soon, they started coordinating swim schedules, a practice that would become ritualistic for both of them. And before long, Father Joe had his own set of keys.

Before long, Tom was a fixture of the Bluff and the larger city. He participated in Portland State University's November 11 Convocation event "Solutions to the Nuclear Arms Race," offering his thoughts on peace and nuclear war. Six days later, back at UP, he was the inaugural guest of Christie Hall's annual speaker series. The next week, he cooked a meal for four female students who bid for one hour of "his services" at the university's Thanksgiving auction. The photo in *The Beacon* shows the students seated and laughing while Tom handles a frying pan in the background. He's wearing a chef's hat embroidered with "Kiss The Cook" on the brim. The image of students swooning over their president would become a cliché in short order. It was not uncommon for students to develop, for lack of better phrasing, strong feelings for him. It didn't help that he was also a regular sunbather.

In an early example of the "Hot Priest" archetype that has become popular in modern film and television series, Tom was featured in 1983's "The Bacon," a satirical edition of *The Beacon* produced annually by the paper. The story was "Oddo becomes AC," a report on how Tom had been appointed area coordinator for the women's residence halls "effective immediately." The column noted that while Tom's new apartment was done up, he'd be on the seventh floor of Mehling Hall. It also noted resident reactions:

> Some of the reactions from hall rsidents [*sic*] are: "I think Fr. Oddo would be a nice addition to this residence hall," said Kathleen Laslowski. "He would be a great father-figure to have around," stated Theresa Tichy. "Fr. Oddo could certainly generate more enthusiasm for floor activities!" commented Lori Bisio. Jean-Marie Vaculin said, "I'm definitely moving to seventh floor, **immediately!**" A resident who wishes to remain anonymous said she was excited about having Fr. Oddo around!!

Call it sex appeal, or call it appeal in general; Tom would ingratiate himself with students. His kind and gentle personality drew people to him and made him a caring surrogate father to an old cat named Henrietta, who'd become his close companion. And he showed an appreciation for both culture and the zeitgeist in his role. In fall 1982, he had awarded one of his first University Medals to band leader Lawrence Welk, whose show many students (and surely Tom) had grown up watching. At the time, Welk's health prevented him from traveling, and Tom would eventually fly down to present him the award at his office in Santa Monica. Then in February, two mentions in *The Beacon* showed a conversely future-thinking president.

A story ran on February 10 about a report that showed American colleges and universities weren't adequately preparing students to use technology of the future, primarily computers. Tom gave a comment on the Department of Education/National Science Foundation report at the center of the story. While UP had a "tolerable" nine-hour core of math/science combined with the undergraduate liberal arts curriculum, a computer literacy course could better prepare students for real world experiences and market needs than additional math/science hours. On February 24, a second story, titled simply "Students need computers," reviewed efforts nationwide to increase computer access and literacy on college campuses. It also included comments from Tom, and his thoughts on what UP should be doing for its students:

> The University of Portland may soon follow the lead of these universities, according to Rev. Thomas C. Oddo, CSC, U of P president. Oddo feels that the computer will be an essential tool in the future education of U of P students.

> "Just as you carried your typewriter off to school, expecting to write your English papers and type them, so will the computer be a component of everyone's approach to studies, and an approach to University administration and faculty development," Oddo said.
>
> "Twenty years ago, the slide rule was an important educational tool; I think the computer is going to become that [important educational tool]," said Oddo.

More than just important, Tom believed the computer would soon become ubiquitous in its regular use: "I think all of us here are going to have to be so computerized that we are able to have information at our fingertips." While that didn't mean UP would buy computers for everyone, Tom conceded the idea would have to be considered within the next decade. His attention to future job needs accompanied a deeper concern for the future of life itself.

CHAPTER 13

Talking Peace and Ethics

Growing up in Queens, and throughout his days at school, Tom lived in a world on edge from the threat of nuclear war. His father had served with millions of other Americans in the Second World War, and for decades after the question of whether a third would start in their lifetime was a frequent topic of conversation. While in New York City and Boston, Tom would've felt the anxiety of living in a potential target area, passing fallout shelters on his way to school, or to St. Clement's on Boylston Street. The threat of major conflict pushed Tom to speak out about peace, and his philosophy on the subject became clear when he used the presidency as a platform.

One year after his inauguration, in November 1983, Tom addressed a Thanksgiving event held by "Generations for Peace," a non-profit once active in Portland through St. James Lutheran Church. Portlanders were no strangers to the anxieties of nuclear war, and in some ways more acquainted than most city dwellers: Besides possessing targets on Soviet hit lists like the Swan Island shipyards, a CBS documentary that dramatized an American city under nuclear attack was filmed in Portland. *A Day Called X* had given 1957 television viewers a real-time simulation of something they would need to prepare for in their own city, featuring locals as actors and city officials portraying themselves. Mayor Terry Schrunk was featured heavily. It's likely many attendees to the "Generations for Peace" event would've seen *A Day Called X*, either when it premiered or in rerun airings.

The event was a community breakfast held at a local synagogue, the Wednesday before the Thanksgiving holiday, less than a week after the airing of another TV movie, *The Day After*, on ABC. Still considered one of the scariest movies ever made, it depicted global nuclear war and its destructive aftermath across the world. More than one hundred million viewers watched its initial broadcast. If those at the Thanksgiving breakfast hadn't seen *A Day Called X* when it aired, they almost certainly caught *The Day After.*

Tom's remarks began by referencing the latter film, and the fear it had instilled in the audience:

> This is, indeed, a time for Thanksgiving. Perhaps for some of us, it's especially appropriate after Sunday's viewing of *The Day After.* Maybe we're especially ready to give thanks that it is still The Day Before—that there are so many voices calling for peace and horrified at the prospect of total destruction. We give thanks today because there are more and more people ready to say "no" to the scenario that was laid out before us, ready to strive for other directions.

He talked about how there were discussions to be had about depictions of religion, or lack thereof, in *The Day After.* Some clergy, Tom said, had disapproved of the absence of prayer among those caught in the film's calamity (most instead were depicted in a "numb despair"), and how the one scene of "explicit" faith came from a tent revivalist–type character who implied the destruction was the coming of Armageddon. Tom did not share the same feeling. Instead, he assured the crowd, there was "another religious perspective" with "a much more solid foundation[:]" the convergence of peoples and faiths on the topic of peace.

For Tom, peace was a subject anyone—be they Christian, Jewish, Muslim, atheist, or any faith whatsoever—could agree to, that anyone of any age or profession could agree to. It was a remarkably unifying subject in an increasingly polarizing world. He cited Isaiah's comment about "Swords into plowshares," the "Wisdom and Compassion for Peace" of Buddhism, Jesus's beatitudes declaring, "Blessed are the Peacemakers," and Islam's Mohammed teaching that "God's Name is Peace" as examples of the concept's universality among the world's faiths.

Tom also talked about how peace had, somewhat subversively, transcended social structures in its attraction of advocates. As a cause, it was no longer attached to any one segment or group:

> No longer can we say that the peace movement belongs to the disenfranchised, the hippies and the radicals. Today, we find the rich and the established, the simple mother or father, people in the mainstream of our

> society. The Challenge for Peace seems to be touching a wide spectrum of concerned individuals.

Tom cited a recent publication by his infrequent adversary, the National Conference of Catholic Bishops. A pastoral letter issued in May, "The Challenge of Peace: God's Promise and Our Response" had explicitly condemned nuclear war and advocated for a just peace, with human rights and dignity at its core. The letter also called for increased diplomacy, the use of nuclear deterrence in the absence of peace, a freeze on nuclear arsenal build-up, and a comprehensive nuclear test ban. On this issue, Tom was "particularly proud" of the NCCB's work, which he called "marvelous." With this action, supported by a broad stroke of ecumenical organizations and experts, Tom revisited *The Day After* and the impacts it had on its audience:

> The film, last weekend, sparked us to a sense of crisis, but, I hope it did not leave us with despair. For it is so necessary that we recognize, as well, the progress we have made.
>
> The Scriptures, themselves, move from the image of the warrior God to the image of peace and tranquility present in Isaiah, the lion lying down with the lamb, the swords being turned into plowshares, the new covenant of love written on people's hearts.

From Tom's perspective, more than just people, theology itself had evolved to meet the moment:

> We have moved from a theology of "an eye for an eye" into a "Repay no one evil for evil, but live peaceably with all."
>
> From our rather simple Just War Theory, we've moved to a great appreciation of the tenuousness of such a position in the face of nuclear weaponry.
>
> From our crusades and jihads, at least we've moved to a new recognition of brotherhood and sisterhood.
>
> From a less than forceful outcry from [the] pope and religious leaders during the Holocaust, now we hear so many voices of all our denominations saying "War, NO, Never Again."

The latter comment would've caught peoples' attention: A priest criticizing the response of the Vatican and Pope Pius XII to the Holocaust, an event still fresh in people's minds. Some attending the breakfast may have survived the camps themselves. He spoke to the dark spots of the world, those that would someday occupy the pages following the Holocaust, "we still have the pains and scandals of our Lebanons and our Northern Irelands, and our Central Americas." But, Tom asserted, age-old religious traditions held out "a tremendous challenge for peace," and those traditions were "inviting us to become ever more dramatic activists ... for the renewing of our earth in peace and harmony."

Tom closed his remarks by citing Jewish theology and its "recognition that there cannot be true and lasting peace unless there is justice." By this metric, Tom explained, there was much to do in order to make the world just:

> It's clear therefore, that the religious challenge to all of us this morning is to rebuild a society and a nation (and indeed a world) where justice flourishes, where growth and development are offered to the many, rather than simply to the privileged few, where resources are generously shared, rather than selfishly guarded. Like that covenant community of old, we must [recognize] our relationship to <u>all</u> others, even the strangers and the aliens. We must give thanks for the common vision that is emerging.

He concluded by reciting a poem by Jane Blewett titled "What Will It Take to Prevent Nuclear War?" It spoke of the people needed to end the threat of nuclear annihilation, the parents, and poets, the soulful and young, men and women of all stripes. But Blewett's list had started with:

> *prophet-people who dare to lay bare the fallicies [*sic*]
> that choke and blind us
> even if we cannot hear their words nor dream their dreams;

Tom's advocacy inspired and contributed to a rash of activism around the issue. The last week of March 1984 was designated "Peace Awareness Week" on the Bluff. Each day, the UP chapter of Pax Christi USA held a prayer service, and a keynote speech by Dr. Gordon Zahn of the Center on Conscience and War at University of Massachusetts rounded out the week.

Tom expounded on topics beyond peace and conflict, and their religious implications. In February 1984, he spoke to a group of international students about the importance of a university education. He gave the assembled group three reasons why: First, a university education provided the chance to "develop knowledge of the great ideas, figures and movements who have brought the world where it is today." Second, the university helped students "learn a profession" and "begin a career." Third, Tom described the process of transformation a student experienced once they had completed their studies: "Something happens," he said, "you become an educated person who can think clearly—think well, communicate well, care well, about all other people." He ended his talk by saying he hoped the students found UP to be "a family with outstretched arms," an image well in line with Tom's philosophies on peace and love.

In April 1983, Tom and Reverend Lincoln Reed of First Congregational Church participated in the opening ceremonies of Lifeyard, "an outdoor art exhibit of banners and sculptures portraying a concern for life in the nuclear age" next to the Oregon Historical Society in Portland. The show featured dozens of works by local artists and school children. It was the first of multiple events Tom would be involved with that concerned the topics of peace and nuclear warfare, one of several issues he would become identified with either explicitly or by association over his presidency. In May, Tom was a featured speaker in a local conference, "The New Idea is Peace," held at St. Ignatius School in Portland. His talk was titled "Peace Education: Our Common Responsibility."

The following April, the Portland Rotary Club invited Tom to join a panel on ethics as a local official and academic leader. Moderated by Bill Johnson, Training Director of the Federal Reserve, Tom joined Louis B. Perry, the Chairman of Standard Insurance, and other notables. Despite his position as a university president, Tom was included on the panel as a "theologian," to speak on a religious approach to ethics. As a result, his thoughts are unique among his fellow panelists.

He began by speaking about the Judeo-Christian tradition, how it paralleled other systems of faith in assessing human ethics, and how it proposes "the infinite worth of every human being." Tom called ethical behavior "all that which enhances human dignity and human potentiality, all that which respects human uniqueness and beauty and destiny." He said that society's ethical codes, the Golden Rule and the Ten Commandments, were not just pulled from the ether, that they were not meaningless, nor just "commandments etched on a stone within a Cecil B. DeMille movie." They were, in fact, "reflections of what is hidden within the human spirit." Tom finished by, again, taking stock of what work needed to be done, on a societal level:

> Of late we have come to realize that religion cannot simply concern itself with prayer and piety, with all the so-called formal religious behavior. It must have a direct impact on human behavior and the way we relate to one another. This was the cry of the prophets of old and it has taken us a long time to catch on.
>
> We need to promote behavior that enhances life—to develop a *consistent* ethic of life, individually, societally.
>
> May we truly live toward one another as we would have others live toward us.

In his remarks on peace and ethics, one can't help but hear echoes of the Dignity years. The next year, during the historic Reykjavik meeting between President Reagan and Mikhail Gorbachev in November 1985, the university community was encouraged to light a candle and turn off their lights to show support for world peace. And throughout the '80s, students regularly saw adverts for the Peace Corps and other organizations in *The Beacon*. These were distinct examples of Tom bringing Christ's teachings to his work, as he used the presidential pulpit to call for the end of global conflict and to promote kinder relationships between people.

Chapter 14

Chiles Center

Throughout those first years, Tom hinted at his thoughts on how the university could operate, and how it could function as part of a larger urban organism. At the time of his appointment, Tom had been quoted by papers nationwide saying he wished to improve the university's connection to the city and larger metro area. One idea was the availability of campus facilities for community use, and the design of new facilities with community use in mind. Where prior efforts by the university saw students graduate and filter out into the city's workforce, now the focus would be on welcoming in the university's neighbors.

In October 1982, a few weeks after Tom's inauguration, the Board of Regents announced the creation of Challenge I, a $46.5 million capital campaign fund to finance faculty salaries and new construction. One of the latter projects was a "sports and convocation building," an ensphere concept dome designed by Wendell Rossman, most recently associated with building another ensphere arena nearby: the Tacoma Dome. An initial $7.7 million of the campaign fund would be dedicated to finishing the new arena on the Bluff, to be built on the campus's northwest corner. Conceptual drawings of the center's dome and the interlaced wood-spar interior ran alongside a photo of Tom with UP's head basketball coach Jack Avina and Athletics Director Joe Etzel. All three were smiling big.

Reaction to the announcement was not all positive. The November 4 *Beacon* ran the story "Oddo explains capital fund drive" at the top of its news page, in which Tom clarified what exactly was being asked of potential donors, and what everyone could realistically expect from Challenge I. Waiting any longer to announce the campaign wouldn't have made a difference in assuaging shock, he deduced, since plans for the stadium had been shelved for several years already. The story published a more detailed breakdown of the fund's allocations.

Step one, the convocation center, budgeted at $6 million ($2 million of which had already been raised, mostly by the regents). Step two, the completion of a tennis racquet center, budgeted at $1.3 million. Step three, the re-siting of the athletic track, involving its slight relocation to allow for an "adequate soccer field," and conversion to meters, budgeted at $250,000. The rest of the fund would go toward a combination of other improvements: $16 million to raise faculty salaries and fund sabbaticals, $8 million in additional student aid, and $7.2 million in new capital building projects. $700,000 would go to the fine arts, and $250,000 to remodel St. Mary's. Another $1 million was set aside for property acquisition in the neighboring Portsmouth neighborhood. Tom hoped to dispel any notion that the campaign was frivolous, or prioritized athletics over other departments, by detailing each goal of the campaign.

While informative to the campus population, campus neighbors began to squirm at the idea of the coming construction hell they'd have to endure. Some wanted to know "just what is in it for *us*?" if their quiet, wooded street was suddenly crowded out by cones and construction equipment, jackhammers running, and mammoth trucks blocking up traffic. In January, UP and the North Portland Citizens Committee held a community meeting to discuss Challenge I and its potential impact on the neighborhood. Tom led the presentation, outlining the steps as he did in *The Beacon*: Step one was the sports convocation center, and while it was meant as a new home for the UP Pilots basketball team, Tom "stressed … that it would also be a center for other campus events such as concerts, speakers, workshops, and even a place to hold U of P's graduation ceremony." Step two, the racquet center, built over already existing courts, would add spaces for handball, squash, indoor soccer, and a new pool. Step three, the reconstruction of the campus's athletic track and soccer field, was sure to include bleachers for spectators.

Tom offered himself and a panel of UP officials for questions and feedback. Wendell Rossman was also on the panel. While the obvious concerns of noise, traffic, and parking space were raised, what may have surprised local homeowners was the eagerness of Tom and his cabinet to answer those concerns. As *The Beacon* reported, "What started with mixed feelings basically turned to support for the University and appreciation of U of P's effort to reach out to the community." Staff writer Pat Johnson noted it was the first meeting of its kind in a decade, and that attendees firmly recommended creating a committee between UP and area residents.

By May, Tom had eased the neighbors' fears, and UP was ready to break ground on the "University Center."

The Board met on May 18, and afterward converged on the corner of Willamette and Portsmouth. There Tom, alongside Portland Mayor Frank Ivancie, Multnomah County Executive Dennis Buchanan, Board Chairman Robert Franz, Wendell Rossman, and Earle A. Chiles, Jr. shoveled a line of dirt that would one day make up the venue's footprint. It would be, as Tom described, "another entree into people's view of the University," and "a great contribution to Portland itself." The facilities proposed were themselves the greatest investment seen in Northwest Portland in decades, if not its entire history.

In his remarks that day, Tom said the venue, now officially referred to as the "Chiles Center," would not only match the quality of UP's education but would be a project befitting the memory of its namesake and benefactor, Earle Chiles, Sr. The stepson of grocery mogul Fred G. Meyer and a longtime company president of Fred Meyer, Inc, Chiles passed away in December 1982 and left a sizable endowment bridging the gap in funding for the project. Tom said that Chiles had "provided a call to all of us to be generous servants of our fellow human beings," and that "we hope that it will be a welcoming place serving the University, our North Portland neighbors, and the entire city."

Work began overnight. Throughout that summer, the corner of Willamette and Portsmouth was a construction zone. Day by day, the dome grew from a blueprint to a skeleton waiting for skin to be laid over its bones. In *The Beacon*'s first edition of the 1983/84 year, Tom spoke on the status of the project now encircling the campus. "The roof should be finished somewhere around October or November [1983]. Possibly it would be done for graduation, but we don't know for sure yet," speaking to a question on the minds of the Senior Class. Elsewhere in *The Beacon*, UP's site representative Marvin Swartz was less optimistic about a graduation opening, but reported things were "a little ahead of schedule" and that work with Viks Construction Company, UP's hired contractor, had been "right on target." He gave an estimated opening of July 6, 1984.

Soon, though, the realities of the project came into focus as the last bits of roof beams were slotted together. In late September, *The Beacon* reported Challenge I was "short $2.5 million—$800,000 on the dome alone." Because of stipulations by the Chiles endowment, the campaign had to solicit donations from a wide swath of the community, not just a few wealthy individuals. As such, Tom had overseen the collection of $5.7 million, raised from "40 major donors," while a larger campaign to the general public (including UP alumni) was also prepared. Challenge I, once a booster campaign for campus improvements, had evolved into UP's first real capital campaign. With a special film created about the project and a slate of fundraising dinners scheduled, Tom championed the project with the goal of reaching full funding by February. Falling in line with his prediction, the roof went onto the Chiles Center at the end of October 1983. Sixty-five feet at its apex, it was an impressive structure, though its real striking point, George Pasero wrote in *The Oregonian*, was "looking up at the very attractive wood of the ceiling." Huge wooden beams criss-crossed the inside of the arena's roof, high above the planned center court.

The April 26, 1984, edition of *The Beacon* gave readers a sneak-peek: A black and white photo of the Chiles Center interior shows the roof draping over a half-complete venue, with workstations and scaffolding and piles of lumber still wrapped together on the floor. The photo was taken from the high-rise seats now built into the structure, designed to seat 5,000. And already, the Chiles Center's calendar was being booked out: Contracts were already signed to host the state high school boys' wrestling tournament, and the state high school girls' volleyball and basketball tournaments in 1985, with talk of adding the boys' basketball tournament as well. UP was also already negotiating with external vendors to host their own conferences. The Order of the Eastern Star bid for a June 1985 event of up to 2,500 people; the Pacific Northwest Presbyterian Marriage Encounter Reunion, a bid for 1,500–2,000 attendees, was also planned for summer 1985; the Chiles Center had appeal even for events several years out from its scheduled opening, as the American Society for Engineering Education bid for the space to host their 1988 conference. With these, and every future Commencement between its opening and the year 2000 booked, the Chiles Center grew in stature just as quickly as it was built.

UP was not without standards for what the Chiles Center could be used for, however. Larry Scruggs, UP's director of auxiliary services, noted that the center would not play host to concerts featuring "punk rock, or acid rock, or heavy metal" music, nor would it plan to rent out space to the small but growing professional wrestling scene in Portland, though even those minor standards on exhibitor or performer content did not dissuade promoters from calling. Joe Etzel predicted revenues would increase significantly enough from venue rental to keep tuition rates level—something UP had not done successfully for many years. He called Chiles "a window to the University" which would attract not only future events, but future applicants and students on the Bluff. By then, Chiles was scheduled to open on August 3, slightly later than expected but still three weeks ahead of schedule.

Soon after came the announcement that the coveted OMSI Auction, to benefit the Oregon Museum of Science and Industry—then located at Washington Park—would be hosted at the Chiles Center later that year. The announcement was carried by a who's-who section in *The Oregonian*, which noted that "The Rev. Thomas C. Oddo, who looks more like a movie star than a university president, was on hand to express delight at having one of the major events on Portland's social and fund-raising calendar come to his campus."

The delight would continue as one of Tom's prospective community partners responded to his entreaties in kind. On October 2, a building materials company, Louisiana-Pacific Corporation, announced they would build and donate the 24,000 square foot tennis and racquet facility originally included in the Challenge I master plan. The construction would cost $550,000, with a projected opening date in March 1985. Athletics Director Joe Etzel called it "a tremendous asset" to campus recreation, and said it was "another step in the fulfillment of Challenge I." Tom himself called it "a pretty significant gift. A very nice gift."

As news of the L-P donation circulated, construction crews finished out the last of their work to finally open the Chiles Center for Parent's Weekend—October 20 and 21, 1984. A ribbon-cutting ceremony and other festivities would officially welcome the community inside. *The Beacon*'s News Editor Brenda Braxton—who would become a local broadcasting icon at KGW Portland after her time on the Bluff—interviewed several people involved with the project for their take on it. Tom called the Chiles Center "first class all the way," and echoed the refrain that it would serve as a window for the community to the university. While drawing in new people, like prospective students, was a good thing for the university, Tom theorized the greater gain was from the arena "serving the community and giving them an alternative place to meet."

At the ribbon-cutting and subsequent dedication, attended by over 1,700 people, Portland Archbishop Cornelius Powers added another, deeper moniker to the building: "Hereby, this is now a church as well as a pavilion." To cap off the festivities, a display on the new scoreboard read THE LAUNCHING OF THE EARLE A. CHILES CENTER as the theme from *2001: A Space Odyssey*, Strauss's "Also Sprach Zarathurstra," boomed from the loudspeakers. It underscored how the Chiles Center represented not only a modern sports venue, but an example of what the future of Christian education could bring. More than anything, the saucer-roofed arena was *something new*, something futuristic that would forever alter the landscape of the Bluff and the trajectory of the university.

Chapter 15

The Gipper Visits the Bluff

In his address at the Chiles Center dedication, Tom commented on the larger state of affairs in education, namely the peculiarity of a celebratory moment such as theirs:

> In these difficult times for much of higher education, what we're doing today makes a dramatic statement about our vision and [courage]. The many friends who have supported this building are expressing their confidence in the greatness of this University. They know we are moving ahead and want to be a part of it.

Two days prior and two thousand miles away in Washington, DC, White House Deputy Press Secretary Larry Speakes announced that the new arena was getting a top-billed first event: President Reagan would stop at the Chiles Center for a re-election rally and speech, the only stop he'd make in Portland that year. Tom issued his own release on the news, mentioning the vote of the deans to cancel morning classes prior to the event to allow as many as possible to attend. The venue was quickly cleaned and reset from Parents Weekend to accommodate the president's entourage, as Reagan wrapped up a whirlwind debate performance in Kansas City. The Secret Service surveyed every inch of the new facility.

The Chiles Center was a brand-new venue, with a single entrance and exit along Portsmouth, and facilities that proved extremely favorable to the Secret Service. In retrospect, the campus's perch high above the streets of Portland, nestled in the Overlook neighborhood was, aesthetically, the perfect place for a Reagan rally. 1983 data from the Portland Office of Fiscal Administration suggested the "West/NW" quadrant of the city, with Overlook at its center, was 9 percent whiter and 45 percent more college educated than the city's averages. Median home value was a whopping 94 percent higher, and its subpopulation of people aged sixty-plus was 45 percent higher. A predominantly white outcropping of college-educated homeowners, Overlook was a doppelganger for Reagan's mythical "shining city on a hill," a metaphor he'd reference throughout his administration.

Ronald Reagan was a name Tom would've recognized from movie marquees in Queens, or from his time presenting the show *General Electric Theater* when Tom was at Notre Dame. He would've remembered Reagan's impassioned plea for Barry Goldwater, which aired during Tom's final summer in South Bend, decrying the spread of global communism and underlining Goldwater's America First approach—before such phraseology was resurrected by modern politicians for the same ends. It is unclear how Tom voted throughout his life, or whether he did at all. Solely by his religious ethics and approach to Scripture, it is unlikely he saw a kindred spirit in the California governor, and later the thirty-fifth president.

As governor, Reagan had used his power to slash the budget of the University of California by 10 percent and led an effort to fire Clark Kerr, the university chancellor who refused to put down student protests at UC–Berkeley in 1966. As president of the United States fifteen years later, Reagan took a similar approach to federal higher education programs, seeking to cut all parts of the government—especially those under the jurisdiction of the Department of Education, an agency created during Jimmy Carter's singular term.

By 1984, Reagan had used the power of the presidency to cut the funding of the department, and hobble federal financial aid programs. By some accounts, federal financial aid suffered the worst of any program cut by Reagan while president, a tenure marked by hacking away at the governments' outlays year after year, budget after budget. When he appeared at Chiles, Reagan was responsible for over 25 percent in direct cuts to financial aid, and 50 percent to the department budget, flipping a historic balance that once had the federal and state governments covering the majority of public college funding. Now, it was supposed by Reagan's White House, if students *really* wanted to go to college, they'd work for it. Reactions to the Reagan educational agenda were varied, especially on the Bluff. For Tom's part, while observant of the Vatican edict on political activity, he would frequently acknowledge the challenges and hardship students faced in affording college, in no small part due to Reagan's policies.

A few days before the president's event, Father Joe Corpora met with Tom to discuss his attendance. Meetings were an informal affair that could develop spontaneously at UP, and Tom sometimes stopped by Joe's office to say hello without a pre-set agenda. This time, Joe sought him out. He walked into Tom's office in West Hall and let his friend know that he planned to protest during Reagan's appearance. He wouldn't be chanting, but he would be holding a sign throughout the speech. Tom understood and thanked him for the heads-up. The two had become close over long talks and shared Sunday afternoon swimming hours in Howard Hall. And Tom wasn't completely unsurprised by Joe's opposition to Reagan. He probably expected some form of demonstration and vocalized disapproval, regardless of its source.

When the president came to town, a minor shuffle of high school bands nearly rewrote the whole rally plan: The Woodrow Wilson High School[14] marching band had originally agreed to play during the event, but Portland Public Schools Superintendent Matthew W. Prophet intervened, citing a state law restricting the usage of public resources in favor of a political candidate. In light of Wilson High's inability to participate, the University of Portland sent an invitation to Parkrose High School, a school in an adjacent district, who happily accepted. One of Parkrose's band directors claimed, from the information they received, "we are playing for the opening of the [university] dome, and it just so happens that Ronald Reagan is going to participate."

After Air Force One touched down at PDX International Airport, Reagan's motorcade pulled into downtown and drove to the Westin Benson Hotel on Broadway. Along the far side of the street, over 1,000 people gathered—some supporters, but mostly onlookers—to try and see Reagan as he stepped out of his limo. With memories of his near-fatal 1981 shooting still fresh, Portland Police brought out horse units and barricaded the street with motorcycle officers. Helicopters provided overhead coverage of the crowd and the motorcade route. Any glimpse Portlanders got of him was momentary, as he walked in his own crowd of Secret Service agents.

The next morning, the motorcade drove up the Bluff to Chiles Center. On the stage with Reagan would be Oregon Governor Vic Atiyeh, Senator Bob Packwood, and Representative Denny Smith—all Republicans—Virginia Chiles, the widow of Earle Chiles, Sr., ASUP President Kelly Krautscheid, and Tom, who took a spot at the far end of the stage. As Reagan paraded in, the crowd shot to their feet, many waving signs

14. Now Ida B. Wells High School

that the campaign distributed. Joe Corpora was there too, with his own handwritten sign: *The rich are getting richer, the poor are getting poorer!* A nun who stood near him read the message and said, with a hint of disgust, "Oh Father, you really shouldn't have that sign." Corpora, incapable of mincing words, gave a trite response: "Fuck you, Sister."

Reagan came to the stage, smiling and waving, as the Parkrose High School band played "Hail to the Chief." A camera operator caught slivers of him through the river of signs as he found a seat three to the left of Tom's. A blue banner with a pair of matching roses hung from the ceiling that read *The University of Portland Welcomes President Ronald Reagan.* For a moment, the stage headliners sat and mingled. Then, an announcer's voice came through the center's speakers, once again welcoming the president, honorable guests, and the public to the University of Portland. The announcer then proceeded to individually introduce the officials onstage, leading to Governor Atiyeh, who gave his own brief remarks. He then introduced President Reagan, as "the man who has walked with us, and restored our faith in ourselves and our nation." Tom rose with the crowd to applaud him as he rose triumphantly to the podium. After a minute's ovation, the crowd descended into a chant of "Four more years! Four more years!" Reagan retorted "Thank you! I hadn't thought about it, but you talked me into it!" Even Tom laughed.

As he thanked the crowd again for a warm welcome, Reagan heard his first heckler of the night off to his left. What the heckler said is not clear on the recording, but it's possible to make out one shout: "Warmonger!" Reagan heard the man berating him and told the crowd, "You know what? I may just let Mondale raise his taxes!" gesturing to the heckler as the crowd cheered. Multiple hecklers continued shouting through his remarks, as he said how nice it was to be in Oregon, and at the "home of the mighty Pilots," which brought more cheers. Reagan then said, "This unique, new center is a tribute to the spirit of voluntarism exemplified by the Chiles Foundation." And he thanked the crowd for sending such fine Republicans to Washington, saying more were needed.

He joked about how he felt at home in Oregon, especially since a state official had jokingly proposed renaming the state "Oreagan." He recalled the story of the city's founding, where two settlers chose the name over a coin toss. "I'm involved ... in a kind of contest now," he said, that would not be chosen by tossing a coin, but by the "wisdom of good people like yourselves." After that point, the hecklers became louder and clearer.

As Reagan spoke on how four years prior, the American people made a great turn from the past, someone in the crowd shouted, "And turned towards war!" Reagan said the federal government had, prior to his term, created all forms of chaos. Someone else yelled, "What about the deficit?" As he talked about tax cuts and government spending, a heckler yelled, "Liar! Liar!" Reagan, paying no mind, talked about increasing defense spending, and how inflation had been "the quiet thief" before the shock treatment of Reagan and Paul Volcker's Fed. He then asked the crowd:

> But what already has come of our efforts? A great renewal. America is back, a giant reemergent on the scene—powerful in its renewed spirits, powerful in its economy, powerful in the world economy, and powerful in its ability to defend itself and secure the peace.

As the crowd applauded, the camera panned back out. While Mrs. Chiles and others clapped, Tom did not. Reagan then said to go back to the old ways was to invite back "the days of torpor, timidity, and taxes." After a moment's hesitation, Tom clapped politely.

Reagan then moved into a section of his speech devoted to trashing former Vice President Walter Mondale, his Democratic opponent for president. He nabbed him for ignoring the Misery Index, a calculation Reagan said the Democrats invented for the 1976 campaign, which he claimed had improved significantly from Carter's term. He poked Mondale over oil prices and how his administration had seen them move downward. By then, the hecklers had intensified when Reagan ragged on Mondale's proposed tax increases, so much so that the president remarked, after a pause in his speech, "you know, I know I'm no concert baritone, so I know those can't be an echo of my voice." Seeing that he had hecklers on both sides of the arena floor, he joked that this was a "perfect example of where we solid citizens are—caught between the right and the left," to more cheers from his supporters.

He declared that while Mondale's campaign wanted to make every day Tax Day, his campaign wanted every day to be the Fourth of July. He made a meal out of Mondale's apparent lack of tact regarding foreign policy, offering "but then there's so much that baffles him." He talked about the "[liberating of] Grenada from Communist thugs," and how Mondale complained it was against international law. A heckler shouted, "It's called terrorism!" By now, more than a dozen hecklers were consistently shouting through Reagan's speech, but the president continued. As he spoke on the Sandinistas in Nicaragua, someone in the crowd blew a whistle. He spoke of the Sandinistas' cruelty toward church leaders, their slandering of the Pope, and their anti-Semitism. Reagan asked why his opponent would say the Sandinistas were ushering in "democratic progress," and why Mondale wouldn't repudiate Reverend Jesse Jackson for saying, "Long live President Fidel Castro" while in Havana. Each question prompted a harsher rebuke from the Reagan crowd, each line firing them up.

He spoke on the need for a line-item veto, something he had while governor of California, and scoffed at how Mondale didn't believe in it. He chided the former vice president for flip-flopping on tax free "enterprise zones," and for opposing the creation of the Space Shuttle program, citing the recent achievements of Kathryn Sullivan, the first woman astronaut to walk in space, and the belief that cures to diabetes and heart disease would be developed in sub-zero orbit. He hit the crowd with a few pop culture zingers, saying if Mondale's campaign were a TV show, it'd be *Let's Make a Deal*, and if it was a Broadway show, it'd be *Promises, Promises*—the Burt Bacharach and Neil Simon–helmed musical about a junior insurance executive who opens his apartment up to sexual trysts to get ahead in his job.

He said that, by that point, some in the crowd would agree he'd gone on too long. The hecklers yelled in disjointed unison. So, he began to wrap it up, saying that Americans had been right to make the turn toward conservatism in 1980, and that the country had changed: Instead of saying "SOS," America was now saying "USA," sparking off a minor chant of "USA! USA!" He expressed his appreciation for the enthusiasm and support of the young people assembled, calling their generation "something special." Even as hecklers called him "Murderer!" he ripped, "You know, I got interrupted on the debate when I was trying to talk about this same subject. I'm going to finish it this time." As he finished on a note of turning over a more prosperous country to the youth, and the crowd again chanted "Four more years! Four more years!" Reagan thanked them and said, "I'll tell you a secret. If the capital was on the West Coast, I'd go for 40!"

"America's best days are yet to come," he finished, saying "I know it galls my opponents, but you ain't seen nothin' yet. Thank you very much for your support. Thank you all, and God bless all of you." ASUP President Kelly Krautscheid then rose and took the podium, saying that while she didn't know how to follow "an act like that, it's tough," she wished to present, alongside Wally Pilot (UP's mascot), a UP jacket to President Reagan. He held it up to the crowd: a purple track jacket with white letters and numbers, which said REAGAN and 84 on the back. "You've really touched a nerve," the president said, "my high school colors were purple and white!" And then the balloons fell, a pile of red, white, and blue helium balloons held by a net above the crowd.

As the Parkrose band played "Stars and Stripes Forever," Reagan shook hands with his stage neighbors. While making introductions with some of those in the back, Mrs. Chiles mentioned he should meet Tom, and he made his way over. They shook hands and met for a moment, which the cameras caught. What they said to each other isn't known, but it appears Tom said something which Reagan appeared to brush off, gesturing to the crowd and possibly saying the words "once or twice." Tom most likely apologized for the hecklers, to which the president seemed unfazed. In many respects he was. As he left the Chiles Center, Ronald Reagan had good reason to be optimistic: National polls showed his lead on Mondale gaining, and Oregon had been reliably Republican since it went for Nixon in 1968.

Portland, however, was a scene of major discontent toward Reagan and Reaganism, hinting at the liberal and progressive counterculture that would evolve into more violent and explicit acts of political dissent over the next decade, an evolution which inspired George H. W. Bush's staffers to nickname the city "Little Beirut" when Bush was president in the early nineties. A week after Reagan's visit in 1984, a consultant contracted by the city's Bureau of Facilities Management wrote a cruel joke about the president's supporters in draft plans for emergency evacuations of public buildings. He had written that, in the event of a national emergency (such as the outbreak of nuclear war), officials should "Go up to the 15th floor [of the Civic Building] to watch the blast. If you voted for Reagan, you're going to get what you deserved, and you'll burn in Hell for dragging the rest of us along with you!" While he insisted it was a joke, *The Oregonian* said the bigger joke was the city deducting $6.92 from his consulting contract, reflecting the time it took a secretary to type up and print out the joke recommendation.

Tom, while limited in his abilities to control the dissent settling among the Chiles Center crowd, did little to quell the hecklers. Most of his reactions are not documented in film from the event, sitting outside the camera's view except for wide shots of the stage. From his political involvement and academic output in the 1970s, we can assume he likely did not approve of President Reagan and may have even voted against him that year. But we can only guess.

Many at UP felt the spectacle had been at their expense. *The Beacon*'s article on student reaction to the rally focused largely on the criticism that the event was strictly political and appeared to be an institutional endorsement of the president:

> According to one student who preferred to remain unidentified, "We were used by the Reagan–Bush campaign committee, for what was to look like a total endorsement for the president by a reputable, upper-middle class Catholic University. He needed to show the country he was scoring points with the younger generation."
>
> Dr. Tom Lasswell, director of theatre, agreed saying, "Students were used. The cheerleaders, the band, and Wally Pilot were combined with tuition money and class time to promote a partisan event. All of this implied an endorsement."

Kelly Krautscheid, the ASUP president, agreed to feeling used. But she felt the event provided positive exposure for the university to the public, and that it had not hurt the institution's reputation—although some would believe UP now endorsed Ronald Reagan.

When asked for his viewpoint, Tom was less certain the event had been a successful optic for the Republicans: "If they wanted to use us to create a sense of unanimity it didn't work." He further stated, "It is hard to believe that that kind of rally would play a significant role in anyone's judgement of the issues." Even so, he believed that some of the crowd's outbursts "bordered on disrespect and some were disrespectful." Even Father Corpora was surprised at the contentiousness of the crowd, telling *The Beacon*, "I don't know where the enthusiasm came from. I don't think those were U of P students."

In the grand scheme of things, Tom was right: the Chiles Center visit was not imperative to Reagan keeping Oregon red. The state voted for the president 55.9 percent over Vice President Mondale's 43.7 percent, a lead of nearly 150,000 votes. It was a national blowout. Reagan beat Mondale in forty-nine states, leading to a 525–13 finish in the Electoral College. But on the Bluff, he was not met with uniform support or admiration, despite the thankfulness for his welcome and the joyfulness his new Pilots jacket brought.

The visit remains a historic curiosity, a moment trapped in photographic amber, shown in black and white photos and color film now held by the Ronald Reagan Presidential Library. Even now, some dissent over the event still lingers. In a nod to the old adage usually attributed to Winston Churchill that says, "History is written by the victors," transcripts of the speech held by the National Archives do not include a majority of the comments heard from Reagan's hecklers that day. Many simply read "[inaudible]."

Chapter 16

Apathy

While the 1984/85 school year opened with the great success of the Chiles Center reveal, followed quickly by the raucous Reagan show in the new arena, a sense of apathy had been developing across the Bluff since early 1984, when Tom led an effort to change the operating rules of the Board of Regents. What started as an effort to make university governance more efficient became one of Tom's first gambles as president, and one that resulted in a mixed reception on campus.

The regents empaneled an ad-hoc committee, of which Tom was a member, to study the board's composition and offer recommendations on structural changes. The committee announced in February 1984 that it was considering the removal of "in-house" board members to limit conflicts of interest in the regents' decision making. In practice, it would remove voting privileges from anyone on the board who was not a regent—effectively disenfranchising faculty, staff, and students, whose student regent position would be eliminated under the proposal. While some may have taken issue with the idea of removing voting rights from non-regents, the larger issue revolved around board decisions regarding employment or termination, which previously involved the direct votes of administrators, professors, *and* student leaders. Tom described it as employees voting to fire their bosses, and believed a change was necessary to avoid future conflict between constituent groups. The move did not inspire confidence among student leaders.

To assuage concerns, Tom and Dean of Students Guy Sievert floated the idea of resurrecting the Committee on Student Affairs, a long-dormant group that would focus solely on student issues and report back to the regents its findings. The ad-hoc committee's formal recommendations came in April, largely following expectations that had been set that spring:

the Board of Regents would remove all non-regent members except Tom, then serving as board vice president, and it would encourage all interested non-regents to join one or more subcommittees. A further recommendation suggested that the regents adopt a more intensive orientation process for members, to better acquaint them with the board's expectations and obligations. Tom called this self-study "a very positive step, almost like a self examination." In time, it would serve as a model for even greater self-examinations on the Bluff. But for students, it was a setback in representation and real power in university governance.

Then came the clash over Good Friday. An April 1984 editorial board op-ed in *The Beacon*, published on Maundy Thursday (three days before Easter), urged Tom to cancel Friday classes in observance of the Holy Week. Alongside the op-ed ran a two-panel cartoon: the first panel had Tom welcoming students to campus, saying UP was "a school deeply rooted in its Catholic tradition!" The second panel showed a teacher wishing students good luck on a one-hundred question test and a good Easter; the chalkboard in the background reads April 20, Good Friday. Despite the dual plea and appeal to the university's Catholicity by *The Beacon* staff, nothing came of it. The next year, a renewed, if abbreviated effort was launched. The ICC, UP's club council, circulated a petition to cancel classes after member clubs voted 18–1 to support the proposal. And again, nothing came of it.

Calling the refusal to cancel classes "business as usual," *The Beacon*'s staff urged the administration to respond, citing the lack of traction with the holiday as indicative of a pattern:

> It has been our hope that the administration would take notice of these issues and if at all possible, respond at least one way or another. Apparently the administration believes that no response or maintaining the status quo is equivalent to an adequate response.

During this time, Tom put his name to the first of two political campaigns, despite the Vatican's rule. In November 1984, Tom was mentioned in an op-ed supporting Measure 28, a $5.1 million levy that would increase jail space, correctional resources, and specialized services. Among the expected asks for more prosecutors and speedier trial proceedings, the measure also planned the opening of a mental health center, a women's rehabilitation center, an alcohol treatment facility, a community service program for sentenced offenders, and juvenile services like a youth sobering program. The measure, a property tax on homes in Multnomah County, became Question 28 on the ballot. Despite the backing of local notables, the plan was defeated in a tax-averse election climate 98,982 to 115,373.

The annual Toga Dance that year, co-sponsored by campus fraternities, turned into a grift for members of Sigma Tau Omega, who were later found to have misappropriated $1,800 in admission fees from the event, leading to Sigma's repeated suspension as a campus organization. Soon after the dance, a Christmas-time edition of *The Beacon* reported on student employees hired at the center to be ticket sellers suddenly finding themselves laid off as the Athletics Department moved to hire professional ticket sellers for events. Then came a lawsuit, filed by the university, against Wendell Rossman and his firm for design flaws in the final construction of the Chiles Center. According to the lawsuit, filed for $750,000 over breach of contract and negligence, Rossman and his team had deviated from the university's building plans from the beginning, and had created significant issues with the structure of the new arena as a result. Doors swung the wrong way, sightlines were messy, over one hundred seats that were originally planned could not be installed, and hot water stagnated in the pipes, among other problems.

The next month, *The Beacon* ran a staff op-ed titled "Promises, Promises," which described the mood developing on-campus that year: "Students at the University of Portland lately have become uniquely acquainted with broken promises." Two groups in particular had received bad news: The ASUP, with President Kelly Krautscheid's push, had announced their intent to move offices from the Student Communications Building to Howard Hall, the athletic facility which was slated for renovations with Challenge I fundraising, to be more accessible to students. This push was halted when it was determined such a move would overcrowd the building as renovations began; as for moving to St. Mary's, the basement chapel, Krautscheid said, had almost no foot traffic to speak of, largely defeating the purpose. The op-ed suggested that while nothing was gained or lost from the aborted move, the greenlighting of such a major campus relocation earlier in the school year by UP administration to only be rescinded weeks later was "Not a real popular decision."

The op-ed also covered the staff and DJs of KDUP, a beleaguered start-up FM radio station on the Bluff originally scheduled to go on-air that month. Because of ongoing conversations with campus officials and station leadership over the right kind of cable to lay—one which needed to accommodate phone service and computer access—the station was not able to keep with its planned January 1, 1985, timeline. In the interim, UP had also nixed funding for the station's carrier current transmission system. With the plan to outmode this tech still moving ahead, Tom said it would be like "throwing money away" to keep funding it. Still, there was a feeling that the institution had started to veer off track.

"Riding Shotgun" was a regular column by student David Rex Schmitke featured in *The Beacon*'s Commentary section. His January 17 column, which ran in the same edition of the paper as "Promises, Promises," was titled "'Self-seriousology,' lack of fun invades campus." Schmitke described a chronic happening among UP students where, seemingly hungover from the earlier years of partying and having fun, they snap into gear and become uber-focused on their careers. Schmitke called this future-obsessed anxiety "self-seriousology." He recommended readers curious about the phenomenon perform a test while walking around the Bluff:

> First, when walking to class next Monday, secretly glance at the person coming towards you. Look at their face, and try to remember the expression.
>
> Secondly, next time you're in the Pilot House, eavesdrop on your neighbors' conversation ...
>
> Now, add "A" and "B" together and ask yourself: "Are these people having fun?"

Indeed, whatever honeymoon Tom had received for the first years of his presidency appeared to be winding down quickly. As Ronald Reagan came to town, the National Conference of Catholic Bishops (NCCB) had issued a letter detailing the need for social justice in the modern economy. The letter draft accompanied public forums on its contents, one of which was held on the Bluff. It was a message that both the AFL-CIO and the Western Council of Lumber Production and Industrial Workers (LPIW) decided should be front-and-center for Catholic institutions working with external vendors, like the University of Portland. The LPIW was the professional union representing over 1,700 Louisiana-Pacific workers that had been on strike since June 1983 for unfair labor practices.

The union's case had merit: The National Labor Relations Board (NLRB) had originally ruled in the union's favor in spring 1984. Then came the resignation of Don A. Zimmerman, the board's only Independent, leading to a two-to-one Republican majority. The commissioners reversed course on the case and ruled in Louisiana-Pacific's favor instead.

The addition of a third Republican, Wilford W. Johansen, to the NLRB would ensure the case's death. Regardless, the LPIW encouraged the university to disavow Louisiana-Pacific and reject the donated tennis center. Tom viewed this change of fortune as the last word on the subject, believing the NLRB's final ruling was objective, and offered to answer any questions on Louisiana-Pacific's labor practices.

He was not without some reservation about the allegations raised by the LPIW. The university had conducted its own review but had not found anything to substantiate the union's claims. Regardless, Tom said, "even if we have greater questions, we stand a better chance of having an influence by not washing our hands of the situation. It is our job to examine and assist," hinting at the university's role in holding its constituent partners accountable. It is unclear what, if any, work the university did in response to the LPIW's case, as construction on the Louisiana-Pacific Center moved forward.

In February, a prank in the residence halls went too far: a "raid" of the all-female Mehling Hall by two male resident assistants in Villa Maria Hall, long an abode of male athletes on the Bluff. Five other students participated. The group had entered Mehling at 3 a.m. on Saturday, February 9, with shaving cream and toilet paper—although other items somehow found their way into the raid, including a bit of dead squid bought from a seafood market. The situation devolved quickly and the group of students split up, resulting in the squid first being dumped in a trash can, then having it and its pooled water spread across three floors of the building. The entire hall stunk of rotting fish.

The consequences for the seven were swift: All were placed on disciplinary probation. They were forced to apologize to the residents of Mehling, pay for the cleaning of the hall's carpets, and banned from Mehling for the rest of the semester—the right of intervisitation between male and female students being a privileged one in the days when UP's residence halls were gendered. It was also determined that the two resident assistants at the center of the prank would not be able to do their jobs while on disciplinary probation, and both were fired as a result. Some students felt the hammer fell too harshly. Following front page coverage of the incident in *The Beacon*, an edition which included a Staff op-ed that called the dismissal of the RAs "hasty and overly harsh," students opposed to the decision staged a sit-in protest, to no avail. The decision was final.

Then, a campus-wide investigation for asbestos was announced in late February, following an incident where facilities workers had cracked open asbestos insulation while repairing a boiler leak in Howard Hall. The state fined UP as a result, and the EPA sent a team of experts to train staff on the Bluff in asbestos handling and removal. The larger review of campus buildings for asbestos was something the aging campus desperately needed.

A confidential report created by George Ebey Associates in 1962 entitled "Future Development: University of Portland," now found in the Oregon Historical Society archives, included a survey of campus facilities. Several buildings which were still actively used during Tom's presidency by students, faculty, and staff—including Howard Hall, the Pilot House, and West Hall—had been deemed "inadequate" two decades prior. That unknown asbestos was still present in the older buildings created a greater cause for alarm. Institutional decay, a problem Tom had met in his work navigating Church directives on homosexuality while national secretary of DignityUSA, was becoming visible and manifesting in a series of ways.

In another of his "Riding Shotgun" columns, David Rex Schmitke wrote about a pervasive apathy among students as ASUP elections loomed:

> The subject is similar to the weak attempts of Pilots fans to do "the wave" during a hoop game, and is the one thing you won't find at a Bruce Springste[e]n concert. The subject is apathy.
>
> Apathy is a scapegoat. Whenever people don't like the attitudes of the masses, it's always attributed to apathy, and in particular cases they may be right. In this case it appears to be a lack of involvement through stagnation. We don't give a damn, because for the past two years we've never given a damn and changed nothing.

To Schmitke, no promises any ASUP candidate could make were worth their salt, since officers changed but school administrators largely remained the same. Among students, there was a real feeling of disconnect between what they wanted and what the university delivered.

In March 1985, the state legislature brought a revenue plan to the floor that would've hobbled the university. The plan would introduce a 5 percent tax on purchases, including those by churches, private schools, universities, and social service agencies. Only textbooks were exempt in the legislation passed by the Oregon House of Representatives. Tom joined other non-profit and charity leaders at the capitol in Salem to call for exemptions to the proposed sales tax. He told state lawmakers that UP alone faced about $65,000 in new tax obligations, in addition to whatever costs suppliers would pass on. In his testimony, he stood his ground in defense of private colleges:

> It seems to me most incongruent and unfair under the proposed legislation that monies received from the private college would, in effect, be turned over to the public college, thus subsidizing them an additional time at our expense.

The plan was ultimately defeated, but it would not be the last time Tom would resort to politicking to protect his institution's well-being.

If the university wasn't caught up in taking itself too seriously, as David Rex Schmitke wrote, it was caught in a bind with student engagement. It may have contributed to Tom's decision-making in a few areas: One was a proposal from Father Joe Corpora to open a new office on the Bluff focused on community engagement in the larger Portland metro area, specifically volunteer and service work. After much discussion across campus, and Father Joe's persistent advocacy for the idea, Tom was the only person who believed the office had long-term sustainability and usefulness. He authorized a $5,000 budget for materials and a used station wagon for transportation as Joe wrote his own job description: director of the Office of Volunteer Services. The new office opened in spring 1985 and soon was nationally recognized for a program which asked students to take a meal of soup, bread, and water in exchange for donations to local food banks, with other initiatives in the works.

The success of the Office of Volunteer Services was a particularly bright spot in an otherwise somber, if lackluster year. In June 1985, Tom's father, Dominick, passed away. A normally relaxed and celebratory post-Commencement mood was waylaid by the elder Oddo's death, as Tom flew out to Florida to be with his mother, Catherine, to pray the Rosary like they had when he was a boy, saying the *Apostle's Creed*, the *Our Father*, the multiple *Hail Marys*, the *Glory Be*, while working through each of their prayer beads. The tradition is used to encounter the spirit of Mary and explore the mysteries of Jesus Christ, a profound experience for Catholic adherents that can provide comfort in times of loss and mourning. That same year, long-time chemistry professor Father Joseph W. McCoy, CSC, suffered a heart attack and died as he was driving out of the university parking lot. *The Beacon* ran a story on McCoy's untimely and somewhat-shocking death, quoting students who responded to the ailing professor as his car came to a stop. It was also the year when Tom's cat Henrietta passed away. She had been a loving friend to the new president, an old rescue living in his campus apartment. Now, his presidency was no longer new, and it was time to say goodbye. Through the tears, he no doubt prayed the rosary for all of them.

The apathy continued through the 1985/86 academic year. In September, a thief dressed as a maintenance worker cased UP's administrative offices, making off with cash and two wallets stolen from Guy Sievert and from Arthur Schulte's administrative assistant Rose Marie Corah, whose kind demeanor led her to assume the impostor was genuine. Corah's wallet and ID were later found in a dumpster in Eugene, over 100 miles south. That same week, *The Beacon* reported that the "UP for Africa" benefit concert in the Chiles Center, expected to attract over 3,000 attendees, only sold 225 tickets and barely raised $700 for charity, a major disappointment. This was followed by an announcement from the ASUP Major Events Committee that they had failed to book any major acts for the year. Requests for John Cafferty and the Beaver Brown Band, Dr. Ruth Westheimer, and other possibilities either went unanswered or could not be worked out.

Two additional developments that year, brought on by palpable campus stagnation, involved other areas of fatigue: UP basketball's lagging fortunes and the lack of campus worship space. The first required a major leadership change to revive the university's athletics program, the second a capital building solution long in the planning. Results would vary.

Chapter 17

The Coaches

Jack Avina was the longtime head coach of the Pilots men's basketball team. He came to UP in 1970 after making a name for himself in high school and college basketball in California. As head coach at San Mateo Junior College, over an eight-year stretch he became a popular figure, running up a 140–80 record of wins and losses. When the college began limiting its athletic recruiting outreach, Avina decided to move on. The coaching job at UP had recently opened with the death of Pilots head coach Earnie Smith, who died of a heart attack after a single season. A succession of one-year coaches had preceded Smith including Joe Etzel, who briefly took on the role as interim before being named UP's Athletics Director. The Pilots needed someone to reinvigorate a relatively lackluster men's athletics program, starting with basketball. Avina was so interested in the role, he signed on and planned to move a thousand miles north, even while taking a pay cut from his San Mateo job.

Avina was initially given many tools to resurrect UP's sport fortunes: a guarantee of "15 to 18 scholarships on which to rebuild the retreating … basketball program," financial resources to assist with recruiting top high school athletes, an assistant of Avina's choosing, and leadership of a summer basketball camp on the Bluff. Once relocated, Avina set to work, and quickly started producing results. In his first decade at UP, Avina built a deep bench of talent which would come to include future NBA players Darwin Cook of the Detroit Pistons, Rick Raivio who originally signed with the Philadelphia 76ers, then moved to the LA Lakers, and Jose Slaughter of the Indiana Pacers. He also led the Pilots to multiple upset victories against Oregon State and other formidable NCAA opponents in Portland's Memorial Coliseum, prior to the completion of the

Chiles Center. But by the mid-1980s, it was clear that, like Tom's presidency, Avina's coaching tenure had begun to stagnate.

In 1985, that year of emergent apathy, Avina's men's team went 0–5 in the first two weeks of the West Coast Athletic Conference, effectively ending their chances of any season pennant or advancement by early February. The losses hit Avina so hard, he told his wife that, while he wasn't worried about losing his job, he was—for the first time in his life—worried about failure. Never before had the Pilots started a season so poorly. In contrast, the Lady Pilots under coach David Olmsted (whose record was a remarkable 117–39 over five years) ran up successive wins year after year, sending them to three NAIA basketball championships between 1983–1985. In the 1984 contest, they lost the NAIA championship to the UNC Asheville Bulldogs by two points, 70–72, in overtime. Yet Avina's team languished, unable to find its groove after fifteen years of growth and forward momentum.

The Bluff's avid sports fans, including Tom, couldn't make sense of it. Some wondered aloud about problems with Avina's strategy, but Tom deferred, as he often did, to his subject-matter experts. His trust in Avina, despite ominous signs, was clear when he told *The Oregonian* that February, "There are expectations between the coach and the university's [athletics] office. To run a good program, to fulfill the NCAA's regulations … Winning seasons are certainly part of it, but that's not all of it." Privately, he prepared for the worst.

Sports culture was present at UP before Tom arrived, but more than any prior president he made his own attendance at games and matches a priority. He became a ubiquitous presence, even at the most sparsely attended events. Tom's passion for UP's teams traveled beyond the Bluff too, attending away games and recruiting Father Joe Corpora to give him the latest score updates by phone while on business trips. In one emotional moment, Tom wept at the news of UP's loss to the Indiana University Hoosiers' soccer team. He even helped write a new victory march for the university's teams which continues to be played today:

> The University of Portland goes forth with courage and pride.
> The University of Portland, will shout out its message far and wide.
> PURPLE PRIDE! The University of Portland, rides on with triumph over all.
> Our Pilots stand tall, can't fall, will march on to victory.
> Raise your voices high Pilots battle cry … V-I-C-T-O-R-Y
> The University of Portland goes forth with courage and pride.

> The University of Portland, will shout out its message far and wide.
> PURPLE PRIDE! The University of Portland, rides on with triumph over all.
> Our Pilots stand tall, can't fall, will march on to victory.

As university president, he had reason to consider changes when it meant the success of the larger sports franchise. UP's women's athletics programs continued to dominate national competitions—including the Lady Pilots cross country team winning the 1985 NAIA championship, the first national title won by a UP team—but the overall men's athletics program on the Bluff continued to lag. Cross country coach Mike Johnson remarked on his women's team's national triumph that year, "Not bad for a bunch of runners without a track," referring to the Challenge I objective to rebuild and reposition UP's track, which had been increasingly delayed as workers finished the Louisiana-Pacific Tennis Center. The center had run $130,000 over projections but opened on-schedule that fall.

In January, the upcoming NCAA convention of colleges and universities had Avina thinking about Proposition 48, a move by the conference in prior years to create uniform academic standards for student participation in Division I sports. Originally, the criteria called for a 2.0 GPA or higher in an eleven-course curriculum track (not including PE courses) plus either an SAT score of 700+ or an ACT score of 15+, which many institutions agreed to. It was when Historically Black Colleges and Universities (HBCUs) in the NCAA fold agreed to protest the rule, calling it racist, that it was reconsidered at the 1986 convention. Avina found his greatest success in courting BIPOC players, some of whom did not have stellar academic records but became essential players regardless. The realities he saw in recruiting and retaining players convinced him that Prop 48 needed a rewrite. Tom agreed with Avina, and was so persuaded by his coach that he requested to speak at the conference in support of the move. Despite their best efforts, Prop 48 went unchanged; so were the Pilots' fortunes in 1986/87.

Around the same time, UP decided to move the Lady Pilots, and other women's teams, into the NCAA—in order to keep its status with the organization. This meant all head coaches would become full-time, in addition to other institutional policies for full-timers: They would be expected to assume a dual role on the Bluff (like teaching) and hold a master's degree. Olmsted, despite his coaching record, did not have teaching experience, never attended graduate school, and felt passionately against enrolling for the sake of the requirement. Avina, meanwhile, was grandfathered in, having assumed his position before UP adopted the new rules for coaches. So, on March 1, days before the Lady Pilots would defend their district champion title, it was announced that Olmsted had been let go. Rather than continue with coaching he told *The Oregonian* he'd return to his previous line of work, real estate.

While Avina signed a two-year renewal contract in 1986, he again found himself in a rut as the Pilots dropped farther and farther down the list of the WCAC. For a second year, the team was out of the running for the league championship by February. The Pilots ended their season with a breakeven 14–14 record. Even as the fledgling Athletics Marketing office dropped $20,000 on city-wide advertisements highlighting the men's basketball season, Avina could sense things weren't improving. After some reflection and prayer, he requested a meeting with Tom and Joe Etzel on March 10. That afternoon, Tom accepted his resignation.

Avina ended his seventeen years coaching the Pilots with a 222–243 record. It was noted in both *The Beacon* and *The Oregonian*—each devoting multiple column inches to the story—that Avina was not asked to resign, and was not "under fire" for his team's losing streak. Instead, Joe Etzel told reporters, it was because he had fallen out of love with the job. In the three years since the Chiles Center's opening, he felt increased pressure to deliver wins, which largely failed to materialize, and stepping away was a chance to make a change. "I've been here a long time," he told *The Oregonian* reporter Ken Wheeler, "I think it's time that someone new coming in can do a better job. After you have been in one job for such a length of time, the time comes when you lose your effectiveness, when you are not as productive." In the span of ten days, UP had lost both of its basketball coaches.

Tom, despite this sudden turnover of events (and coaches), restrained himself. Rather than try to claw Olmsted back, after spending months to find a suitable dual role for him, he graciously allowed his exit. And rather than stand in Avina's way and keep him to his contract terms, he bid him a fond farewell and thanked him for his service:

> I am tremendously grateful to Jack Avina for his 17 years of service at the University of Portland. Under Jack's leadership, our men's basketball program has made significant progress. I have always appreciated his integrity and his deep care for our athletes. I wish him well as he pursues other career opportunities.

Tom was hasty in replacing Avina, telling *The Beacon* he would not let the Pilots effectively forfeit the season while searching for a coach. And, despite a purported national search, Tom wasted no time reaching into local circles of talent for Avina's successor. He began making calls to the city's most successful sports franchise, the Portland Trail Blazers. On May 31, 1987, it was announced that former Blazer Larry Steele, who had played on the 1977 championship team, signed a five-year coaching contract for the Pilots. His acceptance came after a former teammate, then-Blazers Assistant Coach Rick Adelman, turned UP's offer down.

The move to hire Steele, a big get in athletic coaching, did not translate to a better record: Steele's inaugural and sophomore seasons were worse than any season for UP men's basketball since Avina's inaugural year in 1970. But the Pilots pressed on and would eventually build on small successes through the end of the decade to better position themselves for the '90s—when elusive success finally came.

Dave Olmsted decided against leaving college athletics altogether. Soon after his dismissal from UP, he was hired by Pacific University's athletics program, becoming their women's basketball coach. The university still belonged to the NAIA, Olmsted's original conference, allowing him to take the role without the additional expectations of NCAA coaches. During his time at Pacific, he would rack up a 195–150 record, and from 1989–1992 the Pacific Boxers would win four consecutive Northwest Conference championships under his leadership. In the 1989/90 season, they would go 27–3, still a record for the program. Ultimately, Olmsted became the winningest coach in Pacific's history and was inducted into that university's Athletic Hall of Fame in 2007.

The end of Avina's time was a pivotal moment for UP athletics, a historic chapter ending at the height of an institutional malaise which finally began to show signs of clearing. He would go overseas and coach professionally in Brazil and Türkiye before retiring. A father of six and grandfather of thirteen, he passed away in 2018, and was admitted to the UP Athletic Hall of Fame in 2022. Today, Avina is still the winningest coach in the history of the Bluff. His and Olmsted's removal as head coaches remain rough spots in the memory of Tom's presidency, a difficult period when the campus stood on the brink of major reinvention.

Chapter 18

Chapel of Christ the Teacher

The years following the Reagan visit were marked by campus-wide challenges beyond the shake-up in athletics. A growing problem was the deterioration of campus buildings, like the Pilot House—an aging arcade and food stop that served as a de facto student union—and UP's residential halls, both in need of replacement structures. *The Beacon*'s February 6, 1986, edition, the first edition to report on the Challenger space shuttle disaster, also reported on a minor ceiling cave-in at Christie Hall, where a student escaped serious harm as a slab four square feet in size fell to the floor. Yearslong internal water damage was the most likely culprit, another instance of campus infrastructure showing its age.

Around this time, the campus would roll out its first policy on littering after an explosion in trash accumulation outside Villa Maria and other residence halls. Students found in violation could now be fined for their discarded pizza boxes and bottles. As facilities staff cleaned up the mess, they also furiously patched buildings around campus however they could.

St. Mary's Chapel, the sole on-campus church space, was one of those looking worse for the wear. It was also becoming a ghost town: The ASUP turned down office space in the building, citing the lack of student traffic. For all the importance St. Mary's held on the Bluff, it still felt like a converted space rather than its own sanctuary, having previously served as the campus dining hall. In the entirety of UP's history, even while operating as Columbia University, the campus had never built a standalone chapel. Father James Fogarty, CSC, an economics professor who lived in Christie Hall, wanted to change that. He had a theory that a small seed fund could grow into an account big enough to finance the building of a chapel on the Bluff. Fogarty started the fund in the 1950s, but would die in 1965 before his dream materialized.

Through effective stewardship and investment in the years after his death, Fogarty's fund eventually grew to $820,000. In 1986, the fund was given to the university in his memory, announced as the "University Chapel Fund." Tom and other university leaders found donors to bridge the remaining $180,000 needed in funding. The total budget, a flat $1,000,000, was a fixed number without flexibility, managed by a committee tasked with organizing the chapel's construction. At the head of the committee, Tom appointed Father Richard Rutherford, CSC, a theology professor with extensive background in the minutiae of Christology[15]. If anyone on the Bluff knew how to build a chapel worthy of the fund, Father Richard did.

Also named was the project's builder and co-leader: renowned architect Pietro Belluschi. Former dean of the MIT School of Architecture and Planning, Belluschi had previously made his name in designing dozens of churches, multiple symphony halls, and office buildings: most recently the US Bancorp Tower (also known as the Big Pink, still the second tallest building in the city and the largest office building in Oregon). Belluschi made Portland his adopted home with a massive mansion he designed himself in the West Hills and saw his newest project on the Bluff as the chance of a lifetime: Where he had previously been held back by the expectations of conservative congregations, the chance to build an *academic* chapel opened new doors in Belluschi's mind.

The resulting design of the chapel was radical, modern, and utilitarian. Instead of traditional pews set in rows facing an altar, UP's chapel would be a largely open space with moveable chairs. Instead of setting the clergy at the front of the space, their position was moved to the center of the room, similar to a 360-degree circular concert stage but on a much smaller scale. The space itself, though, would be large enough to hold up to 500 people, with balcony seats on three sides of the second floor. Three offices would give ministry staff professional spaces, and separate contemplation and confessional rooms were also sketched in. At the entrance of the chapel would be a massive stone baptismal font in the shape of a cross.

Tom hailed the design as the "the most up-to-date liturgically," and said the built chapel would "create a warm community space where people can come together in their worship. The focus of this church is on the community gathered around the table," exemplifying his idea of a campus community in brick form. He said the future chapel would be "a beautiful symbol of our [C]atholic identity" once it was completed. Tom, Belluschi,

15. The study of Jesus Christ.

Father Rutherford, Father Thomas Hosinski, CSC—trustee of the University Chapel fund—and members of the Board of Regents spoke at a groundbreaking ceremony on September 22. Archbishop Cornelius Power blessed the site as spadefuls of dirt were turned over next to St. Mary's. While those on campus celebrated the inception of the project, several items were still required before building could begin, like obtaining a land use permit from the City of Portland, which would require the involvement of homeowners surrounding the campus.

As construction crews assessed the chapel site. and the university administration submitted their land use requests, Tom held a "birthday party" to celebrate the Chiles Center's first year in operation. Not everyone on the Bluff was in a celebratory mood: A disgruntled resident on Willamette Boulevard circulated a petition complaining about the increase in traffic, and subsequent lack of parking resulting from Chiles Center events. Echoing the concerns of residents voiced at the listening session UP held two years before, twenty-five residents signed on. They delivered the petition at a hearing to issue a conditional permit for the project. In response, Tom reminded the neighbors that a newsletter was regularly distributed to residents for community input on building projects. He also said that campus security was doing what they could to get students to park on-campus, rather than on neighborhood streets—a difficult proposition after a rash of car break-ins that year had led to over $2,500 in property loss from cars parked at UP. Despite the minor protest, a permit was granted and the project moved forward. The hearings officer suggested, if nothing else, that notes could be left on the windshields of unwelcome cars.

By December, whether assuaged or merely uninterested in escalating their complaints, no appeals had been made by local residents to the conditional use permit, allowing UP to pursue a formal building permit. Pietro Belluschi filed the paperwork, which Tom expected would take around two weeks to process—with approval just before Christmas—and construction to begin as soon as possible (depending on the winter weather). While the snow would be largely delayed, a major windstorm swept the West Coast over January 16–17, 1986. The product of a cyclone that came ashore on North Vancouver Island, BC, and stretched as far south as Northern California, the storm brought rainfall, lightning, and sustained winds of nearly 30 mph in Portland, with gusts up to 48 mph on the night of the sixteenth. Snowfall would come later, throughout the month of February.

Set back by weather, but determined to start, construction crews erected a security fence to keep intruders out as they poured the chapel's foundation. By Easter weekend, students filing into St. Mary's for services would've seen the beginnings of a wood skeleton develop on the dirt site next door, growing day by day as crews built upward. A short walk away, a second crew was gutting the Pilot House, finally cleared for renovations after years of student complaints. As the chapel grew, so would the Pilot House: Tom, Guy Sievert—now vice president of Student Services—and Christie Hall Director Jim Barbieri shared a plan to double the space inside, while potentially adopting a debit system for food service, a first for UP.

St. Mary's, meanwhile, would become the new home for multiple student outlets, including *The Beacon* and *The Log*, UP's yearbook, as the rotting hut that housed student communications for decades approached its final days. The same month, a new card-access system was installed in campus residence halls, including Christie, to the tune of $14,000. The next month, Tom and UP administrators considered the purchase of a new campus phone system, estimated to cost up to $500,000. The end result was the selection of a cheaper system, the NEC-2400 from US West Information Systems, to replace most of UP's aging Centrex system. To save money, a handful of old Centrex lines were preserved, limiting total costs to around $185,000 (with estimated future savings between $6,000–$7,000 per month). The NEC-2400 installation work was completed in August, ahead of the fall semester. All told, 1986 became the second largest building year of Tom's presidency, after the Chiles Center blockbuster year of 1984.

Students who left campus for the summer would return weeks later to find the new chapel almost complete. On the exterior, bricklayers set their bricks in a unique pattern: Laying one directly over the other, instead of a traditional off-center arrangement, they appeared to be stacked in great piles over a row of sideways bricks, which created an indented band running around the structure. Nearby, the Pilot House was still draped in tarps as workers finished the interior. Both projects were scheduled for an August 15 completion date, timed with the start of the academic year. While UP planned a formal dedication and blessing of the chapel on September 14, the unforgiving weather earlier in the year pushed the event back to October 5.

The Pilot House received a humbler opening: Its dedication, outside in the late summer sun, ended with Tom cutting a ribbon with ceremonial enlarged scissors. In St. Mary's, crews put the final touches on the last space renovated there, an additional student lounge. With Campus Ministry completely vacated from the building, *The Beacon*, *The Log*, the UP Residential Hall Association, and Father Joe Corpora's Office of Volunteer Services, moved into their new home.

The Beacon dedicated a portion of its October 2, 1986, edition to the realization of the chapel fund's goals. The story, by copy editor Nikki DeBuse, cited how the project took thirty years to develop from Father James Fogarty's initial donation. It had seen the deaths of both Fogarty and Father James G. Anderson, the first trustee of the fund, and a complete redesign of the structure before completion. The first proposed design, a four-towered hexagonal building to be set in front of rather than next to St. Mary's, showed the evolution in thought which had carried the project forward. Between Fogarty's chapel fund, and additional donations sought by UP to complete the building, the chapel would cost just short of the expected $1 million total.

Despite its somewhat plain appearance on the outside, the chapel's adornments were spectacular in their detail: massive black walnut doors, collectively weighing six tons, hand carved with a multitude of Christian symbols including the fish and the Chi-Rho (☧), each designed by local sculptor LeRoy Setziol; a century-old marble crucifix, donated by a university patron, placed in the confessional room; a stained-glass mosaic of a dove in flight on the wall opposite a private sanctuary space; the baptismal font, standing in the entryway under the chapel's skylight, its tall candle welcoming parishioners and newcomers alike.

Belluschi said of his work, "A church is a spiritual shelter. You need to be extra careful designing the meeting place of people coming to worship. It takes more of yourself." *The Oregonian*, in its feature about the chapel's opening, noted the mixture of Scandinavian and Japanese architectural touches in the structure. It also highlighted Belluschi's personal distaste for gutters, a feature he kept out of the final design. The rain, instead, would roll down the roof eaves, onto rounded stones within the chapel's landscaping. The image still evokes the line from Amos: "Let justice roll on like a river, righteousness like a never-failing stream."

The opening ceremony and dedication were held the morning of October 5. Tom joined, in white robes and vestments, Father Chris Johnson, director of campus ministry, Col. Jack Roscoe, a local deacon and retired US Air Force commander, and Father Paul Waldschmidt, former UP president who now served as auxiliary bishop of the Portland Diocese. The dedication of the space was one of several dedications planned that day, as Father Rutherford explained to *The Beacon*, "The first time each part of the mass is (performed) it becomes dedicated." Following the blessing of the chapel and words from the officials assembled, Father Johnson opened the doors and the campus community proceeded inside for the Dedication Mass. A brunch was held in the Commons, followed by guided tours of the space and a concert by the UP concert choir and chamber orchestra. The day concluded with the chapel's first Community Mass, an event which has now been held thousands of times inside.

The name *Chapel of Christ the Teacher* was selected out of a flurry of suggestions from the campus community. As Father Rutherford remembers it, the name spoke to the mission of the university. "There is almost a theology of education implied in the title," he told me in 2023, "It is the risen Christ continuing to teach." It spoke to Tom's mission, and the mission of the Holy Cross brothers to educate students in their service to God, in a way befitting of the university's Catholicity. Flying overhead, one could see the Bluff's landscape changing rapidly as UP added more buildings and finished renovations on others. The once little college on the escarpment, with paths that traversed open fields and treelines, was quickly becoming a world-class university under Tom's watchful guidance.

School photos of young Tom Oddo, 1957 and ca. 1961. Source: University of Portland Archive.

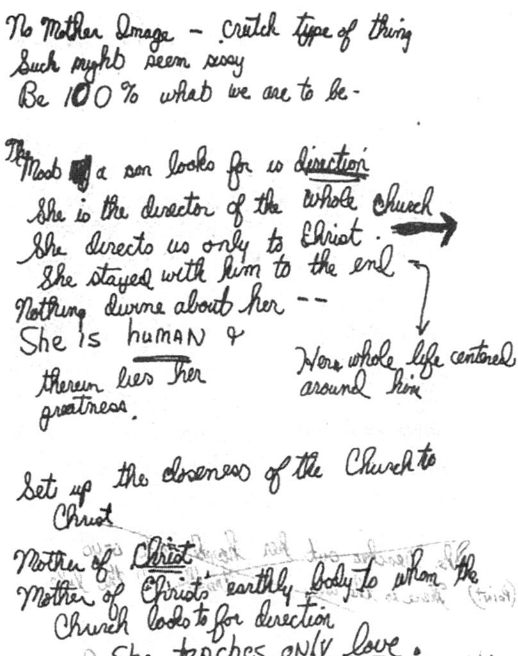

No Mother Image - crutch type of thing
Such might seem sissy
Be 100% what we are to be-

The Most a son looks for is direction
She is the director of the whole Church
She directs us only to Christ.
She stayed with him to the end
Nothing divine about her --
She is human &
therein lies her greatness.

Her whole life centered around him

Set up the closeness of the Church to Christ

Mother of Christ
Mother of Christ's earthly body to whom the Church looks to for direction
She teaches only love.

Tom's notes about Mary for a speech he likely gave at the last visit of his Notre Dame class to Sacred Heart Church, 1965. Source: University of Portland Archive.

Tom, now a young priest active in DignityUSA, on a visit to San Diego, ca. 1976. Source: Pat McArron.

Addressing the camera at a Dignity event, explaining the mission of the organization, 1977. Source: "Being Gay and Catholic with Dignity," 1977 film.

With Paul Diederich (right), DignityUSA's first president, ca. late 1970s. Source: Pat McArron.

A clip from Tom's appearance on WNAC-TV's program "All God's Children?" showing him ashing the foreheads of Dignity members, 1981. Source: Alex Frisbie (director).

Tom receives the presidential Chain of Office at his inauguration ceremony, 1982. Source: University of Portland Archive.

Addressing student questions at a town hall in Villa Maria shortly after his inauguration, 1982. Source: University of Portland Archive.

Cooking Thanksgiving dinner after University of Portland students bid for the experience, 1982. Source: University of Portland Archive.

Sitting on the campus lawn with students, 1983. Source: University of Portland Archive.

Looking over papers in the presidential office, 1983. Source: University of Portland Archive.

Tom's building efforts were not without criticism, as this cartoon (with the finished Chiles Center in the background) suggests following the announcement of tuition hikes for the 1984–1985 school year, 1984. Source: University of Portland Archive. Cartoon by "M'Lou."

A second cartoon critical of Tom's non-response to student demands for a Good Friday vacation, by *The Beacon's* editor-in-chief, 1984. Source: University of Portland Archive. Cartoon by Paul Pimental.

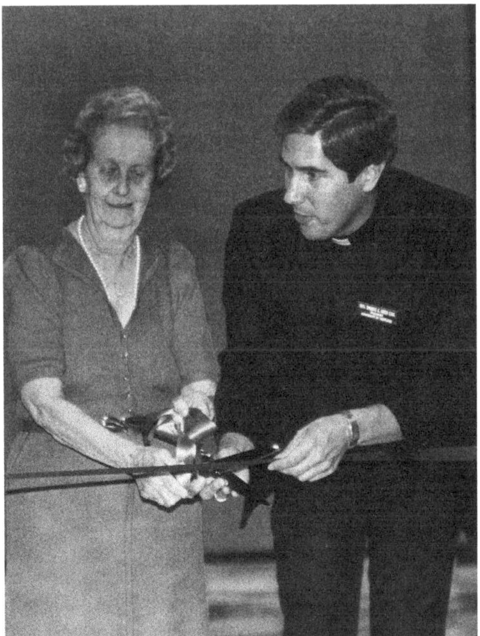

Opening the Chiles Center with Virginia H. Chiles, his biggest building achievement, 1984. Source: University of Portland Archive.

Shooting hoops with Executive Vice President Arthur Schulte, Jr. (middle) and Athletics Director Joe Etzel (right), 1984. Source: University of Portland Archive.

Shaking hands with President Reagan at a controversial re-election event, the first major booking in the Chiles Center, 1984. Source: University of Portland Archive.

Leading opening ceremonies for Chapel of Christ the Teacher with Director of Campus Ministry Father Christopher Johnson, CSC (left); Deacon Jack Roscoe (second from right); and Portland Archbishop Father Paul Waldschmidt, CSC (right), 1987. Source: University of Portland Archive.

Pictured with his cabinet (from left to right): Father George C. Bernard, CSC, Academic Vice President; Dr. Harold Westby, Vice President for University Relations; Tom; Arthur Schulte, Jr., Executive Vice President; Dr. Guy Sievert, Vice President for Student Services, 1986. Source: University of Portland Archive.

Walking with Sen. Bob Packwood (left) during the lawmaker's visit to the university's AFROTC unit following its closure notice, 1988. Source: University of Portland Archive.

The pressures of the presidency began to show in Tom's hair by the last year of his service, 1989. Source: University of Portland Archive.

Playing donkey polo for AIDS youth charity House of Light, 1989. Source: University of Portland Archive.

Over 900 students met the hearse carrying Tom's body back to campus the day after his death, 1989. Source: University of Portland Archive.

Tom looks through the telescope of the campus observatory (1952–2009) with Dr. Merle Starr, who became the building's namesake, 1985. Source: University of Portland Archive.

Part Three: Camelot

1986–1989

Ask every person if he's heard the story
And tell it strong and clear if he has not
That once there was a fleeting wisp of glory
Called Camelot

Alan Jay Lerner,
Camelot (1960)

Chapter 19

Campus Life

A few weeks after the chapel's opening and the start of regular services, another comedian took his set to the Bluff. In its first celebrity get of the year, the Major Entertainment Committee invited Robin Williams to UP. Between the success of his third comedy album *A Night at the Met*, and journeying to Bangkok to film *Good Morning, Vietnam*, Williams went on a national stand-up tour of college campuses, and the committee wanted to book a big act after repeated missteps in 1984 and 1985. Williams was *major* entertainment, the first performer hired in two years, and one that required external sponsorship to pull off. With a mere $8,500 budget for a $40,000 event, the committee had to partner with a local entertainment group to cover the gap in funding. This would involve some trade-offs: The event was opened to the public and students were placed toward the back of the arena. But the booking paid dividends.

Williams brought the house down. The October 19 performance was the last of a fifty-city tour, and the Chiles Center was sold out. After an opening act involving a local juggling and comic duo, Williams came to the arena floor and shot into his material: He joked about how to pronounce "Willamette," and called the Chiles Center "the Sistine Chapel built by Black and Decker." He improvised bits off of suggestions from the audience, and kept them howling for two hours. When he finished his set and took his bows, he was sure to remind everyone in attendance to "thank the school" for his performance. It had been an overwhelming success, with over $10,000 in profit from ticket sales coming back to the ASUP and effusive praise in *The Beacon* in the days after. So successful was the event that ASUP would eventually adopt a buffer account to accommodate future excess revenue from major acts.

Campus life at the university even in the apathetic years remained somewhat lively and active, though there were still lingering issues generating interest in student leadership. At least one ASUP presidential election went uncontested, and other major outlets only received single applicants for vacant officer roles, like *The Beacon*'s editor-in-chief search in 1986. Despite this, a combination of student groups and administrative efforts kept many popular events going. From Orientation Week onward, the UP student's calendar would be peppered with campus happenings, like Casino Night, also known as Monte Carlo Night, a personal favorite of Tom's; the Lip Synch concert, sponsored by radio station KDUP, whose 1985 iteration led to over $500 in damages to rented music equipment; and the annual Toga Dance.

A self-explanatory romp borrowing from *Animal House*, the Toga Dance was co-sponsored by a pair of UP's fraternities, Sigma Tau Omega and Upsilon Omega Pi. Issues with alcohol abuse and misappropriation of admission fees would lead to Sigma's eventual suspension and caterers' refusal to supply booze to the event, eventually moved off-campus to the Memorial Coliseum. Alternative events to Toga developed, including a non-alcoholic "Untoga" dance, and its polar opposite: An event called "Coma" which drew over 300 students, some of whom attempted to literally drink themselves into a coma. The university tipped off the Oregon Liquor Control Commission (OLCC), whose officers charged multiple students and pulled the plug on the event. Throughout the '80s, the Bluff saw a pronounced culture of alcohol use and abuse, exemplified by the piles of empty bottles outside dorms and ads for Lowenbrau running in the latter pages of *The Beacon.*

Major entertainment events like the Robin Williams concert would fluctuate throughout Tom's presidency, with a gap in bookings between fall 1984 and spring 1986. Good reviews would come from performances by Michael Winslow in 1985, Freddie Jackson and John Denver in 1987, while jeers came for The Outfield, also in 1987. Fresh off their song "Your Love" reaching #6 on the Billboard charts, their concert lost so much money for ASUP Major Entertainment that *The Beacon* openly questioned the committee's future viability and whether to invite "major talent" to the Bluff at all. Campus Programming Board Director Brigid Driscoll, who tallied the losses from The Outfield concert at $17,017, admitted "I learned just how short-lived fame can be." When major entertainment wasn't available, other entertainers were: Professional clown and mime Rick Davis came to the Bluff for a weeklong artist residency and live show in the Mago Hunt Center in 1985. The Campus Programming Board also hosted several movie nights, including a double-header of *Top Gun* and *Sleeping Beauty* in 1987.

Tom's presidency welcomed a bevy of famous figures and notable speakers visiting the Bluff. Frequent non-performance appearances were made by James DePriest, the conductor of the Oregon Symphony, who Tom became friends with. DePriest would, in time, be granted an honorary Doctorate of Fine Arts and a humanitarian award in his name by the university. Another frequent sight on the Bluff was Father William Levada, archbishop of Portland. On-campus talks were given by ABC-TV news correspondent Bettina Gregory in 1984; language writer Willard Espy, Irish journalist Eamonn MacThomais, and Guardian Angels national director Lisa Sliwa in 1986; subliminal messaging expert Dr. Wilson Bryan Key and aviators Dick Rutan and Jeana Yeager, fresh off the nearly 25,000 mile flight of the Rutan Voyager in 1987; Congressman Les AuCoin, *Rolling Stone* international affairs editor P.J. O'Rourke, and science fiction author Ursula K. LeGuin in 1988. Notable guests also addressed the university's annual Commencement ceremony, including DePriest (1984), Archbishop of Manila Father Jaime Sin (1987), and Oregon Senator Mark Hatfield (1988).

Celebrations of diversity also started during Tom's presidency.[16] The week of February 20–24, 1984 was designated Black History Week at UP, with the theme of "Today's Students, Tomorrow's Leaders." Events and displays created by the Third World Coalition club sought to "expose the University and others to their proud Black culture," like a UP for Africa benefit concert later that year (which played to underwhelming attendance). In other efforts, the university sought to connect BIPOC students to communities within a still largely segregated Portland: UP's Minority Assistance Program ran a student support initiative, Family Away from Home, starting in the mid-'80s, and created other events with the university's Office of Counseling and Consulting.

But racism on the Bluff was not unheard of. The City of Portland has a regrettably racist history, an urban environment replete with Klan members and sympathizers in leadership positions, redlining in property deeds and zoning, disproportionate levels of police brutality, and perhaps the most thorough metropolitan segregation of neighborhoods in the western United States. For many decades, life in Portland was particularly difficult

16. One important student group, a gay–straight alliance, wouldn't exist at the university until the 1990s. This was not without efforts by student leaders to establish one; efforts blocked by administration multiple times over doctrinal differences. It is unclear whether Tom ever dealt directly with the organization of such a group during his tenure.

for BIPOC residents. Ample evidence and experience show it still is, often in the most unexpected places.

At UP's 1987 Lip Synch concert, for instance, a group in blackface and afro wigs called Hair We Are won second place, seemingly without consequence or reprimand by the institution. The group sang John Denver's "Thank God I'm a Country Boy," with one member using a tennis racket as a violin. The event was an unfortunate scar which Tom either did not address, or was not made aware of. Considering the prevalence of blackface even in the present day, it is possible the gravity of this episode did not register among the participants, university leadership, or Tom himself. These are regrettable truths we have to consider when no written opposition is documented.

A budding spirit for physical activity was egged on by the university, while the campus lagged in actual engagement for it. An outdoor exercise course built prior to Tom's presidency, by the mid-'80s, sat unfinished and largely unused. Major demand for physically active programming existed, not for outdoor courses and personal fitness but for practically applicable classes, like self-defense tutorials for women, and non-professional athletics, like campus intramural sports. While a physical challenge sponsored by ASUP would inspire everyone to go the distance with their chosen activity, the star finisher was Tom, who in one year swam over 1,000 miles in the Howard Hall pool. He had joked before his inauguration that students should expect to meet their president in his bathing suit, and it had already happened multiple times. In countless places, Tom provided an unending source of energy to a campus that, at times, struggled to keep pace.

Tom's particular commitment to technology came into focus in 1986/87. Institutional negotiations by the University Computing and Telecommunications Committee with Apple and IBM led to a student discount on individual computers. Then, in February 1987, UP's Buckley Center micro-computer lab opened. The lab powered eighteen IBM personal computers, ten Apple Macintoshes, nine Apple IIG devices and a single Apple IIGS, then the latest model from the growing tech company. Twelve additional VT220 terminals were connected directly to the university mainframe. Use of the lab was free to students, providing many with their first experience using a personal computer.

A spiritual underpinning of campus life sprouted directly from the newly opened Chapel of Christ the Teacher, which saw four baptisms and six weddings by April 1987. On Easter that year, five more baptisms were made in the chapel's font, three of which were adults. Meanwhile, a chapter of Alcoholics Anonymous began holding meetings in Columbia Hall. The meeting relocated to the Bluff after being evicted by Portland's Holy Cross School, their former host, in favor of a bingo night. A similar group, Students on Alcohol Problems (SOAP) also formed and met in the University Health Center, located in Christie Hall. Such groups were welcome news in the wake of the university's Coma event, and the increasing incidence of student alcohol abuse. Other institutional drives came from a desire to refresh the campus, with the first Campus Beautification Day organized by the UP Alumni Association that March. And throughout Tom's presidency, the Hawaiian Club sponsored an annual luau alongside an International Week of events organized by the International Student Association.

In his efforts to expand the reputation of the university, Tom joined the Louisiana-Pacific Board of Directors in August 1987. L-P Board Chairman Harry Merlo said that the new director was selected for "his administrative talents, his probing intellect, and, above all, his concern for people." His magnetism was on display as he traveled to Guam in March 1988 to help grow the UP Alumni Association. While there, he formally established the Guam Chapter, which had raised $10,000 in the two months leading up to the visit, and was welcomed by a recent university graduate, Governor Joseph Ada, '87. In Guam, Tom visited high school students and spoke about campus life and the experience of UP's education: He extolled the sixteen-to-one student to teacher ratio, promising students they would not be mere statistics, calling it a "comfortable environment" for newcomers to the mainland and a "good place to take that leap from the island life." The university's relationship with its Guamanian alumni would lead to the creation of a recurring grant for UP-bound students in 1989, a further strengthening of bonds to the Bluff. The success of the Guam outreach was typical for the later years of Tom's service, with UP's influence growing and alumni finding their way back to the university.

Despite a busy schedule that involved greater and greater amounts of travel, Tom found time to serve in the confessional booth. In 2023, Father Richard Rutherford, CSC, gave me a tour of Chapel of Christ the Teacher. When he showed me the chapel's confessional, a small room located off of the worship space, its simplicity belied its seriousness. Here, Tom and other priests listened to many hours of students' confessions each semester. Such a task remains rare for university presidents and would've only endeared him more to students who sought relief in confession—including LGBTQ+ Catholics.

These were happy moments on the Bluff as Tom matured into the presidency, moments students would look back on with reverence, the days when UP felt like Camelot, the mythical universe of the Kennedys. The university's evolution kept Tom's name in discussion for higher roles within Holy Cross circles. He was a young leader on the rise, and undoubtedly one to watch.

Chapter 20

Dark Horse

When Tom was an undergraduate in South Bend, the University of Notre Dame had been led for nearly a decade by Father Theodore "Ted" Hesburgh, CSC, chosen for the role at just thirty-five years old. Prior to his appointment, he had been an instructor and head of the Department of Theology, then executive vice president, a position setting him on a glidepath to the top job. When he became president of Notre Dame, Father Ted inherited a faculty of nearly 400 instructors and a $9.7 million annual budget. In the years immediately following WWII, the school needed a booster, a champion to set it apart from other public and private "Ivies." Already a known entity in college football, it was a school not yet known for its academic excellence.

Almost immediately, Hesburgh hit the ground running. A distinguished professor program, started in his first year, would eventually churn out over one hundred professors. Throughout his tenure, no fewer than forty building projects were completed—largely with capital fundraising—on the South Bend campus, transforming it into an academic city-state and forever coupling it to the city in the national consciousness. Average faculty salaries jumped tenfold from his first year to his last, the university budget ballooned to over $175 million annually, and the university endowment to over $300 million. When Tom came to Notre Dame, Father Ted was already a legend in Catholic higher education, his life and reputation already transcending to myth.

Like Tom, Hesburgh could not be confined to campus either. A tireless, restless advocate for God in a modernizing world, he was active in larger discussions on Catholicism in America. One such avenue was the Land O'Lakes Statement, finalized in Land O'Lakes, Wisconsin, in 1967. Tom was already two years out of his undergraduate program, but remained plugged into the Holy Cross world. It is likely he read and followed news of the statement with interest. Formed in the aftermath of Vatican II, and drafted in the same liberalizing spirit, the statement asserted a new and revolutionary streak among Catholic colleges and universities in the US: "To perform its teaching and research functions effectively the Catholic university must have a true autonomy and academic freedom in the face of authority of whatever kind, lay or clerical, external to the academic community itself." Strong words on campus independence which mirrored UP's move to an independent Board of Regents. UP president Father Howard Kenna would advise Hesburgh on how to replicate such reforms in South Bend. By the 1970s, both campuses had cut all formal ownership ties to the church, operating instead at a distance from Rome's intervention.

Whether it was his independent streak, internal theology, or outward appearance as one of a growing number of "public intellectuals," the Nixon Administration formally requested Hesburgh's assistance on matters of civil rights, making him chair of the US Commission on Civil Rights in 1969. He had previously served on the commission at the request of President Dwight Eisenhower, and continued as a member through the Kennedy and Johnson Administrations. While on the commission he was reportedly offered the job of NASA director by President Johnson, an offer he declined. Early on as commission chair, Hesburgh advised the president and Vice President Spiro Agnew on the mechanics of suppressing college protests against the Vietnam War, a conflict which he abhorred but nevertheless found himself on the institutional end of. Hesburgh himself had distributed a letter to students about Notre Dame's policy of breaking up student protest groups, which only ignited further student unrest toward the war.

He also stood for the equal rights of all races, while not always championing such policies at Notre Dame. His time as commission chair would come to an end over disagreements with Nixon on desegregated busing and slowing the integration of America's most racist schools. His dismissal from the Nixon Administration was so prominent, he was quietly considered as a replacement candidate on the McGovern '72 Democratic presidential ticket after Senator Thomas Eagleton dropped out. Despite his contradictions, Hesburgh would become the most visible, and perhaps most "well-known" Catholic in the US while he served as Notre Dame's head. By 1986, he had become one of the longest-serving college presidents in American history. It's plausible Tom joined a chorus of Holy Cross leaders wondering whether Father Ted, the same man who'd shook his hand over twenty years before, could keep going much longer.

Rumors of his eventual retirement floated around South Bend, although none ever seemed credible. The man was an institution within the university he led, and the prospect of finding a worthy successor added more and more weight to the Notre Dame Board of Directors with each passing year. An attempt at retirement in the 1981/82 academic year led to a five year contract *extension* for Hesburgh after the board was "[unable to] find a suitable replacement." When news of Hesburgh's renewed push for retirement became public, the Associated Press headline on June 13, 1986, read "Notre Dame President Trying Again to Retire." A search committee assembled to conduct a national search for his replacement, the first new president in thirty-five years. Tom's name made the rounds.

Early candidates for the position, called the "New Guard" by the Notre Dame *Scholastic* magazine, included Tom's friend from seminary Father Edward "Monk" Malloy, then serving as the university's associate provost. Joining him in the frontrunner category were: Father William Beauchamp, CSC, Hesburgh's Executive Assistant Father David Tyson, CSC, then Notre Dame's vice president of Student Affairs; Father Ernest Bartell, CSC, former president of Stonehill College, who had served while Tom was teaching theology there; and Father Michael McCafferty, CSC, a notable professor in Notre Dame's law school. A lack of experience in academic administration appeared to set Beauchamp and Tyson back, while concerns about McCafferty's recent battle with cancer made his candidacy appear unlikely. This left Fathers Malloy and Bartell for an early short list.

Also profiled in the *Scholastic* were a group of dark-horse candidates, less likely picks that were still in discussion for the role. Their names were frequently mentioned in conversation whenever people described their vision of Father Hesburgh's successor:

> Foremost among these is Father Thomas Oddo. Oddo is currently president of University of Portland, a Holy Cross school in Oregon. He got that job in 1982 amid heavy speculation that it was a grooming position for the future presidency of Notre Dame.

The article mentioned Tom's two degrees from Notre Dame and cited his year of teaching at South Bend in discussing his familiarity with the campus. This, however, appeared to be less than desirable experience for doubtful "campus observers," the article noted. Other such dark horses included the chair of Notre Dame's Theology Department Father David Burrell, CSC, and Father Oliver Williams, CSC, the co-director of Notre

Dame's Center for the Study of Ethics and Religious Values in Business. Though each brought their own serious credentials to the conversation, one name continually stood out. A November 2 *Chicago Tribune* story reported that Father Monk Malloy was the prospective choice to succeed Hesburgh the following year.

The report was quickly criticized by many on the South Bend campus. Assistant Vice President of University Relations Richard Conklin called it a "speculative piece," saying, "The people who know don't talk, and the people who talk don't know." Editor of *Notre Dame Magazine* Walton Collins also expressed surprise at the news. Even Monk weighed in, telling the student newspaper *The Observer* that "It seems foolish for them to venture such a strong assertion when (the trustees) haven't voted on it." Nevertheless, Monk conceded, "no one can stop them from publishing anything they want." In the *Tribune* story, unnamed insiders described the Notre Dame board coalescing around Malloy as the best candidate, in a gradual process that eventually led to their internal decision.

In truth, the process was far more choreographed than the public knew. According to Monk himself, he had been the desired candidate from the early stages. Tom was contacted and agreed to appear as a short-list name, as did the others profiled by *Scholastic*. In a parallel to Tom's hiring four years prior, the question of Father Hesburgh's successor had been long settled when the board announced their decision to the public on November 14. At the same meeting, per Monk's request, the board also named Father Bill Beauchamp as Notre Dame's next executive vice president. Monk's inauguration in fall 1987 would follow Hesburgh's last engagement as president, that year's commencement. At that ceremony, Hesburgh awarded honorary degrees to former First Lady Rosalynn Carter, Coretta Scott King, David Rockefeller, and Father Richard Warner—the man who convinced Tom to apply for the UP presidency—among others. Harvard President Derek Bok served as the keynote speaker, and also received an honorary degree. Hesburgh got no fewer than four standing ovations and chants of "We want Ted!" Even at the end, his popularity soared high.

Four months later, Monk was joined by his family at his own Inauguration, as was Tom in 1982. Beyond the waves of uncles, aunts, and cousins, many Holy Cross peers attended the event. Tom gave the homily at the Inauguration Mass, such was his talent. In his remarks that September morning, Tom invoked Mary—a figure he'd become so familiar with in his studies and prayers—and her answering of God's call. He also spoke on the nature of the university presidency, and echoed the words of Father

Hesburgh at his own inauguration, reflecting on how foolish one must seem to take on such a job:

> Numerous commentators have written in recent years that one would have to be crazy or masochistic to accept a presidency in higher education today. They say, with considerable cynicism, that the task is an impossible one. Why would one do this or say "yes" to the demands?
>
> Those of us with a passion for ministry and enlivened with a Christian faith say instead that you need to know that strength comes from outside oneself, that we have a God who inspires and empowers and who gives strength even in the face of the tremendous challenge. This is a God who comes to live within us, a "shadow streaming into our being" again and again. And this God gives us a community of brothers and sisters so that we do not stand alone in our task.

For Tom, the university president should be a "lover and promoter of wisdom," that age-old value which he called the "lifeblood of university life." Wisdom, after all, was the only way Monk "could understand university memoranda and committee reports!"[17] And Monk too, had the "let it be" spirit—as Tom called it—brought by the Annunciation of Mary, the willingness to go with God no matter the rough patches and struggles. He concluded by speaking about what this wisdom and spirit meant for the university, and for Monk's presidency. Tom then led an extended prayer for his friend:

> Paul's prayer for the people of Ephesus is certainly our prayer for Monk this morning as he both inspires us and assumes these weighty responsibilities. "May God give you power through his spirit for your hidden self to grow strong."
>
> You have the deep roots. You are indeed planted in love because you are grafted on to the Lord.
>
> You know God's love; you've sought his strength from youth; you bask in God's wisdom.

17. I thought that was funny.

> You become this day one more in [a series of] pointers to the wonders of God; a sage who celebrates wisdom; a Mary who says yes to an unknown; a Paul who knew strength comes from walking with God; a Jesus who showed us how to live with God; scores of the Notre Dame family living and dead who learned and taught wisdom and service here.
>
> May your leadership, Monk, and your ministry bear great fruit as you help the Notre Dame community to continue its faithful service to Church and society.

Father Monk Malloy would go on to serve many years as president of Notre Dame. Monk's executive vice president, Father Beauchamp, would build his own presidential career on the Bluff (2003–2012), as would Father David Tyson (1990–2003), another name on the 1987 short list. But these dreams would've been far from their minds as Monk ascended to the presidency. By that point, Tom was looking more and more like a long-term resident of the Bluff, and in more than one campus battle he further endeared himself to its students, using the same wisdom and spirit he attributed to his friend.

Chapter 21

A Value-Centered Education

Tom's opinion on Catholic education, and education in general, relied on a mix of ethics and values that invited the challenges of the world to the classroom, and by extension the church. It also involved universities like UP taking an active role in worldly affairs. An August 1985 talk he gave, titled "A Perspective on Catholic Higher Education," expressed how Catholic universities were looking at their larger roles in society, and their impact on the world outside the church. He spoke about the widespread shift among Catholic universities to adopt lay Boards of Trustees, as UP had seen in 1967, describing it as an institutional shift where universities became "'public trusts' with responsibilities not only to the Church, but to society at large."

This transition, however, did not mean the destruction of a university's Catholic identity as some had feared. Quite the contrary: Tom spoke to the qualities of the interfaith culture at UP, where fifty percent of students were Catholics, while the other fifty were an amalgam of "Christian and non-Christian traditions," the latter referring to the Buddhists and Muslims among UP's 350 international students. He said that, in light of this shared reality within Catholic universities:

> We must function with an ecumenical spirit, celebrating and witnessing our Catholic heritage, but unwilling to indoctrinate and appreciating alternative viewpoints. Like the Vatican II Decree on Ecumenism, we must celebrate our perspective, while realizing that we do not have a monopoly on truth, and instead must seek it together. Our spirit is one of welcoming, rather than driving wedges. We focus on the variety of perspectives that must be embraced by Catholicism.

Tom then asked, "How is a Catholic character maintained today at Catholic universities? How can we best enhance our sharing in the mission of the Church?" He had several ideas. First, universities had to continue offering the "finest intellectual development possible" to students. This involved the fostering of Catholic scholarship, the employment of Catholic and non-Catholic faculty, the encouragement to engage in real world discussions about the church, and the understanding that non-Catholics within these universities would agree to abide by common values if not the institution's religious theology.

Second, the total development of students, a "fostering of their intellectual, spiritual, social, cultural growth." Here, Tom spoke about how he believed a university education should apply to a student's life:

> We try to awaken in our students an appreciation of the values that have shaped Western civilization, and a desire to live in accord with them. We believe that education must be more than simply a passing on of abstract knowledge; it must make a difference in the way our students live.

And here, he reflected on how 150 UP students were now participating in a monthly fast day (referencing the work of Father Joe Corpora's Office of Volunteer Services), the savings of which were being used to feed the homeless in the Burnside neighborhood.

Third, a commitment to the liberal arts. Tom said that, while so many college students focus on career success, the inclusion of disciplines like theology, literature, and fine arts in their curriculum would give them "a perspective beyond their chosen career." He argued that, with this balance, "any excess materialism and narrow career-based thinking might then be tempered by a broader appreciation of the central questions that echo within the human spirit."

Fourth, Tom believed in the requirement of theology and philosophy courses for all students. These would not seek to indoctrinate students into Catholicism, but would "expose the students to the key questions about life and meaning" which would optimally produce the same questions in their minds. Similar to how a liberal arts curriculum would better prepare a graduate for their career, these would better prepare them for the complexities of life.

Fifth, an active campus ministry program. This would involve regular service to students, including celebration of the Eucharist, counseling, and other pastoral care. Followed closely, was his sixth requirement, the continuation of priests in areas of prominence throughout Catholic universities. They would provide a strong embrace of Catholic tradition, with the expectation that those employed by the university would work cooperatively with the laity in their roles.

Finally, it required placing universities "at the service of the church." Tom believed Catholic universities were instruments in fostering the church's larger mission, citing UP's homegrown efforts to train religious educators and to assist church theologians in perfecting pastoral care. He then harkened back to his talks on peace with his final thought on the point: "The University consciously and zealously affirms a common mission with the Church in breaking the fetters of ignorance and injustice and fostering a kingdom of peace and harmony, the very Kingdom of God." Tom concluded by saying UP's success lay in being "both excellent and Catholic."

Tom had good reason to believe in the place of educational institutions building moral literacy among their students. In a talk earlier that year titled "Service with (Com)passion," Tom had referenced UP students' sincere, consistent devotion to volunteer service projects in their community, and the impacts of their coordinated action:

> University of Portland students have been working with the elderly and the handicapped in special outreach programs; they have served as Big Brothers and Big Sisters to needy youth. Hundreds have fasted one evening a month to raise funds for the hungry in Portland and Africa. Scores of them have prepared and served meals in various soup kitchens of downtown Portland ... Some students are so deeply touched by these activities that their post graduation lives and careers are redirected, at least for a time, into activities like the Holy Cross Associates or Peace Corps.

Here again he spoke of the need for university organizations like the Office of Volunteer Services, and the role they played in offering enriching, real-world experiences. In his telling, those experiences were more important than nearly anything else in a student's time on the Bluff. Tom closed the talk with a decidedly firm statement on the obligation of modern colleges to their students:

> It is not enough that the University offer the finest of academic programs. It is not enough that we provide students with resources for a successful career. (I trust we will always do these extremely well.)

> I hope we can also consistently awaken in them a sense of responsibility for the world beyond themselves and a generous readiness to serve with passionate care.

In September 1986, Tom returned to his interest in ethics by moderating a multiple-day event at UP, "The Consistent Ethic of Life Conference." The conference was co-sponsored by the Oregon Catholic Conference and included talks by several notable guests: Reverend J. Bryan Hehir, secretary of the US Catholic Conference Department of Social Development and World Peace, spoke on foreign policy topics; Senator Mark Hatfield gave a pre-recorded speech titled "A US Senator's Views on Consistent Ethic"; Father Joseph Bernardin, archbishop of Chicago, spoke on a "consistent ethic of life" while Dr. Sidney Callahan from Mercy College in New York tackled the issue of abortion. Multiple UP faculty also offered rebuttals to the latter two speakers, in an effort to capture (as the Oregon Catholic Conference's executive director put it) "why the Catholic church speaks as it does on certain issues."

That December, Tom spoke to the Annual Meeting of the Northwest Association of Schools and Colleges (now the Northwest Commission on Colleges and Universities, a regional higher education accreditor that certifies UP's programs). His speech came at the end of the conference, though he felt "challenged to help [the event] end on a positive note." 1986's meeting had focused on the "harsh realities and new opportunities" in American education. In the wake of repeated cuts to financial aid and public school systems, educators had cause for concern looking to the future. Sunny as ever, Tom had an "excitement" for what was happening in education. But he did not initially elaborate his point. He summarized a *Doonesbury* cartoon instead.

At his inauguration, a friend of Tom's gifted him a set of the comic strip which focused heavily on the fictional Walden College, and its begrudging leader President King. The purpose of the gift was, Tom said, "so that I'd never get too comfortable in my position." One scene Tom described from the series had President King at his desk, grumbling over proposed cuts as his CFO, named Simpson, gives his recommendations:

> "And finally, I'd recommend firing the two new English Department appointees." But King laments: "Oh Simpson, what are we doing here? Aren't we cutting out our soul?" Then, in the next frame, he continues: "In my day, education was a many-splendored thing. The best minds of a generation led us through this garden of human knowledge and bequeathed

> us the divine gifts of reason, logic and judgment." Scene 3: "But today, Simpson, today we live in an era of limits. What kind of education can we afford to give these kids? What are we settling for?" And Simpson responds in the final frame: "Literacy sir. Sign here."

You can tell from a written speech where the speaker expects an audience's reaction. Tom knew his punch lines, corny as they could be. And for the jokes he told—including one about how the title of his presentation, "Value-Centered Education and Freedom of Inquiry: Some Perspectives on the Delicate Balance" came after he was given ten minutes to think of one by a meeting organizer four months prior—Tom touched on deeper, more existential issues than fiscal cuts and degrading educational quality. He spoke about the opportunity for modern education to pass down cultural values, while still respecting freedom of religion, and diversity of thought. Where some areas of his speech suggest laughs or pained expressions of simpatico over cigarettes and coffee, others paint a picture of an audience leaned in, considering the young priest's words. Tom then elucidated his thoughts on value-centered education, freedom of inquiry, and academia's responsibility toward both:

> It is a responsibility on the one hand to let our institutions pass on the values and grapple with the moral dilemmas that echo within the human spirit and the world in which we live; to expose our young people to the questions and the responses and the ways of life that educated people have wrestled with in the past, and wish to see lived out in future generations; and to not be afraid as institutions to "stand for something," to want to pass something on.
>
> And yet it is also our responsibility to let all ideas be thought, to [ensure] that every question is considered and every perspective respected. We must recognize that fear and censorship have no place within our institutions, that truth certainly has enough power to prevail, however winding and shaky the path it takes to recognition and affirmation.

The push-pull of the university "passing something on" while offering an open forum for ideas (even controversial ones) is a challenge many colleges and universities face. Tom's reason for working in higher education at all was to teach, to pass something on to his students, as he would do with classes throughout the 1980s usually titled Theological Problems in Human Sexuality. He also welcomed debate on class topics, in an effort to engage with students who wouldn't have considered taking it for their own program, and spoke to sexuality in a way more open and nuanced than students would've expected at a Catholic university. The course was popular, so popular it became known as "Sex with the President" among UP students. No one can argue Tom's connection with them: Beyond his magnetism, many who took the course found it to be one of the most engaging during their time on the Bluff.

Tom's defense of a similar, value-based education to the Northwest Association meeting was a reflection of this teaching record. For Tom, the idea of institutions standing for something, just as people do, was the cornerstone of developing a more moralistic academia. At the same time, the pull toward liberal inquiry, toward an open and accessible dialogue among all people, was equally as important to the modern university. In his view, the differences between the two mattered far more than the similarities one could find: "To speak of a balance," he told his audience, "is to affirm that both not only can go hand in hand, but that they are necessary correctives to one another." But, this did not necessarily mean that every idea was worthy of such inquiry. Just as a college administrator struggles with the balance between allowing free speech and giving certain ideas (e.g., fascism) a platform today, Tom assured his fellow educators that there could be a "right" and "wrong" in a world of liberal inquiry:

> In affirming that values belong in education, I wish to eschew any method which uses indoctrination rather than gentle leading and open inquiry. And I also wish to assert that "freedom of inquiry" or "academic freedom" does not imply that nothing can be "stood for," that every idea or behavior is of equal worth or moral value, that "freedom" means teaching nothing that really matters in life.

Tom approached the question, whether to lean into teaching of values or freedom of inquiry in education, with his position in mind. "As president of a Catholic university," he said, "I have great concern about the recent interventions of Church authorities in the lives of some Catholic institutions and Catholic scholars," a dig at Rome and the NCCB's meddling. But instead of harping on these complaints, Tom reasserted his responsibility, itself a delicate balance: "I work to teach church authorities that we can afford to lose neither 'Catholic' nor 'University' in our mission, that we do not have to be afraid of alternative, even dissenting, viewpoints." He emphasized to his audience, and wider critics, that "values can be carried forth, even in the midst of dissent." Such a declaration from a

UP president was strong, and may have turned heads among Catholic traditionalists, Vatican II opponents, even emeritus presidents.

Tom, his theoretical foundation established, turned his ire toward the trend of educational censorship as conference attendees shifted in their seats. He spoke about a study completed by the American Association of University Professors (AAUP) sent to its membership in December 1985. In it, the AAUP outlined how censorship was quickly accelerating, like a cancer, through the nation's schools. He didn't mince words about where this trend was stemming from:

> Again, as one who professionally and personally represents religious perspectives, I am embarrassed and offended by these usually religious-based efforts at censorship. The same people who should be supporting efforts to bring an excitement about values into our schools, instead turn their energy to eliminating *Catcher in the Rye* because Holden [Caulfield] uses four letter expletives.

On the topic of book bans, the AAUP report warned that removing books from school libraries over ideological differences or perceived obscenity, "increases in some measure the probability that the student will see suppression as an acceptable way of responding to controversial ideas," and Tom called such actions a "countersign" and "counterproductive."

He also criticized the decision of a lower Tennessee court in the case *Mozert v. Hawkins County Public Schools* (*Mozert v. Hawkins*). The case involved parents suing their children's school district over requiring the kids to read books with values they disagreed with. A lower court had ruled in favor of the parents prior to Tom's remarks. He said of the court's verdict that "these ideas are deeply hostile to (and fly in the face of) our American concept of education." The case would eventually be decided in the Sixth Circuit Court of Appeals, which ruled, partly, in favor of Hawkins County Public Schools in August 1987. The Sixth Circuit, however, found the schools had violated students' First Amendment rights by suggesting there was "no one way" to worship God. Nevertheless, it determined parental opposition could not be a hindrance to supplying ideologically diverse books in school libraries, a position Tom would laud in the pursuit of the liberal analysis of ideas. To him, such bans produced nothing but ignorance.

Tom then segued into his thoughts on secretary of education William Bennett, a conservative Republican he said was "generally not one to quote," to a collective chuckle. Bennett, Tom said, believed some campuses had no freedom because "many professors go into the classroom with a 'liberal bias,'" drawing a contrast to the idealized picture of free speech in the college setting. But on the topic of value-based education, Tom found himself largely in agreement with Bennett, who would later become Reagan's director of Drug Control Policy and a major supporter of Donald Trump. Tom said this was "a somewhat frightening realization" for him, explaining Bennett's approach on the topic:

> In the face of the controversy over whether we can and should teach what are vaguely called "values" in public schools, Bennett prefers to eliminate that word and refer instead to "the effort to help form the young and to aid them in achieving moral literacy." But, he says, most definitely, schools can and must help form character; schools and teachers must teach morals; and that they can do so without falling into a narrow religious perspective or promoting a particular religious doctrine.

He then quoted verbatim a lengthy line from Bennett, speaking to sources from which American schools could derive lessons on values such as honesty, courage, kindness, and compassion. These included several Bible stories, like David and Goliath and the Parable of the Good Samaritan. Bennett had also emphasized how other disciplines were taught despite being complex and controversial, or prone to heated discussion, so there must be room for values-based education. Bennett had a formula to make students "morally literate" in schools and colleges.

First, he suggested that major curricular restructuring was not always necessary; instead, schools should focus on reworking their core curricula, the general education received in the first years of an academic program. Second, he asserted the need to continually "recruit caring and competent teachers who want to deal with these questions." Third, it was crucial to extend student involvement in service projects, such as the ones championed by the Carnegie Foundation, to, as Bennett had suggested, "shape a citizenry that can promote the public good." Fourth, it meant "setting our own institutional houses in order. By that, I mean we must watch how we deal with our own people: staff, faculty, colleagues. Do we create a respectful, honest, caring community? How do we deal with dissent and controversy … ?" Finally, it meant "clarifying the way, the method, we will use to transmit values." An overly dogmatic approach would directly undermine the truth and values Tom spoke of. "Our methods," he continued, "must include persuasion, respect for freedom (and again, I emphasize that that word must not imply valuelessness) and the truth lovingly and excitedly chosen."

Writing for *American Catholic Studies* in spring 2005, Father James T. Connelly, CSC (who would later write the definitive history of the Congregation of Holy Cross), explored UP's long-running identity crisis with its Catholic tradition in his essay "The University of Portland: A Catholic University?" In the essay, Connelly bases his approach on the 1990 declaration *Ex corde ecclesiae* by Pope John Paul II, a document which outlines the "norms" for Catholic institutions. Based on these ideas, and a study citing a trend toward secularization in Catholic colleges, Connelly examined the case history of UP from its early beginnings. He writes about a mid-'50s financial crunch on the Bluff, and the subsequent ascensions of Father Howard Kenna, CSC, and later Father Paul Waldschmidt, CSC, to the UP presidency. Under Waldschmidt, Connelly notes the creation of a lay Board of Directors, effectively resting control of the university from the Congregation of Holy Cross, and a proposal in the early 1970s to transform UP into an "ecumenical university," with numerous denominations represented in their own autonomous colleges similar to a model used in Canada.

These events, according to Connelly, led to the dropping of the word "Catholic" from various places, from bulletins posted across campus to marketing materials circulated throughout the state. A major reaction came from Waldschmidt's two presidential successors, Brother Wilson and Tom. Under Wilson, it was the assertion that faculty needed to understand the "expectations" placed on the university by the church, reminding them that Catholic teachings prevailed on "doctrinal matters." Under Tom, it was the completion of the Chapel of Christ the Teacher, despite Waldschmidt's prior opposition to building an on-campus chapel while he was president. Connelly described UP as a campus that was "drifting toward abandoning its Catholic identity in the 1960s and 1970s but reversed course in the 1980s and 1990s, thus indicating that a trend toward secularization need not be irreversible."

Without Tom's efforts, it is possible the university would've continued on a crash course toward complete separation from its Catholicity. On the contrary, Catholicity was something Tom embraced, even while embracing the world of secular ideas. He simply did not believe the two were mutually exclusive. Both were central to the campus environment he was trying to develop: a spirit of youth empowerment reminiscent of the Kennedy era seldom seen now.

Chapter 22

AIDS

Autoimmune Deficiency Syndrome (AIDS) first appeared in print in May 1981. Originally known as Gay-Related Immunodeficiency Disease (GRIDS), the disease spread around the world in the late '70s and early '80s, decimating communities with an untreatable new illness that disproportionately impacted gay men. In hundreds of cities across the US, hospitals and medical centers were engulfed by the virus, with many unwilling to provide care to LGBTQ+ people out of fear it could be transmitted through skin contact or aerosol droplets. Meanwhile, the topic was regularly the subject of jokes in the White House. President Reagan himself would not speak on the epidemic until 1986. By then, 6,000 Americans had died from AIDS.

Portland saw its first AIDS-related death in 1982, while the case numbers reported to the CDC from the city doubled every year through 1986. Year by year, the numbers crept upward. AIDS first appeared in *The Beacon* in early 1986, when a poll of readers asked for their opinion on the question, "Has the widespread fear of AIDS made you more conscious of blood donations and related health concerns?" Responses published varied from students to faculty: A senior business student replied she was more conscious because "you don't know where the blood comes from and the tests aren't a hundred percent." A freshman society and justice major replied that "I don't think about it. If I had an operation I'd just give my own blood then take it back later on since we can do that now." An associate professor in biology offered that "It's made me use a certain amount of restraint in terms of who I kiss." Another respondent, a senior electrical engineering student, countered by saying transmission through close contact had been debunked, and there was "[no] risk involved." But the range of responses alarmed campus staff.

A month later, *The Beacon* reported on a forthcoming forum dedicated to AIDS at Buckley Center. The forum, open to the public, had been in the planning stages since fall 1985. Tom would serve as moderator but the coordination of the event extended far beyond his office. A panel of experts contributed their expertise: Dr. Mark Loveless of the Cascade AIDS Project would speak on the facts of the virus; Reverend Terry Lally, director of the Office of Counseling and Consulting, would discuss psychological treatment for those with AIDS and their loved ones; Father Chris Johnson would offer a pastoral perspective on the virus, while Louise Allen, director of the Health Center, would offer her center's perspective; associate dean of students Kathi Marriott-Brave would consider AIDS from the perspective of the residence halls and residential students; and Jim Christopher, an AIDS-diagnosed patient would speak first-hand about living with the virus.

Altogether, the forum aimed to educate the community on the realities of AIDS, but also provide a space to voice concerns and answer questions. Father Johnson addressed the need for such a space, saying disinformation and fear about AIDS had gotten out of hand:

> There's an irrationality and a near hysteria about this thing that has got to be counteracted .... Intelligent people are not using their heads ... I'm thinking that preventive medicine is better than reactive medicine in this case.

The forum was held on February 25. Fewer than fifty people attended, making for a sparse crowd in Buckley Center, an auditorium built for six times that number. Nevertheless, the presentation was enthusiastic and largely positive. Tom began with prepared remarks, saying:

> It's our thought here at the university that the best way of easing fear is to replace it with knowledge and understanding. And we hope that because of knowledge and understanding, there can be an increased sensitivity to those people within our society who have AIDS.

Jim Christopher, a man living with AIDS from outside the UP community, spoke on his experiences with the disease, and on relevant services available to the public. Christopher and the forum's panel also talked about the stigma associated with AIDS, and how public misperception compared with the reality of life with the disease.

The forum was a direct assault on misinformation, and perhaps unexpected from a Catholic university. Gallup polls on AIDS at that time showed 60 percent of Americans believed HIV+ people should be required to carry a card identifying their status, while one third of respondents said businesses should be able to fire HIV+ workers. Between 1987–1988, 44 percent of respondents believed that "AIDS might be God's punishment for immoral sexual behavior." While most polled believed compassion was the right course to take with AIDS patients, there was a glaring lack of compassion in public responses to the virus. At UP, the forum was the first in a series of institutional steps designed to prevent the spread of the disease.

In fall 1986, UP formed an ad hoc committee on AIDS. Members included individuals involved in the forum earlier that year, like Father Johnson and Louise Allen. The group immediately set to work on a proposal for institution-wide education on AIDS. Thanks to the committee's efforts, resident assistants would attend the first in-service training on AIDS in residential life, as the university continued building a strategy of informed prevention and services. It would be a multi-year effort, and under Tom's leadership UP would stay the course.

By 1987, 143 people in Portland had died from the disease. AIDS would resurface in *The Beacon* in February. An op-ed by UP student Bill Cavanagh called the proposal for TV networks to air condom advertisements "important," explaining such ads would be a "responsible and fair" way to educate people on AIDS prevention, where conservative groups and talking heads saw the ads as a promotion of unsafe practices. Mere weeks before, an op-ed by Father Joe Corpora spoke to the virtues of celibacy, speaking on his life experience and explaining how celibacy and marriage shared "two sides of the same coin." That these op-eds ran so closely together shows some variation in campus opinion on the topic of sex.

In March, *The Beacon* ran a feature on UP's prevention effort titled, "AIDS prevention begins on college level." The piece reported on progress by the ad hoc committee, who had just approved their proposal for prevention education. Pending approval by the larger University Health and Safety Committee, Tom would have final approval over the plan's details. The article included information on how the virus was spread, debunking lies and myths about transmission that spread over water coolers and smoke breaks. It also included a quote from committee member Louise Allen on the proposal's intentions, a balance of public health and pastoral concerns: "The committee is going through the formal steps to see if we can distribute total information which includes safe sex practices without condoning premarital sex."

Allen stressed in the article that AIDS is an infectious disease that should be treated like any other illness, and should not be a reason to preclude someone from "living in the residence hall, eating at the Commons and continuing with normal campus activities." Guy Sievert, the dean of students, was also quoted on how the university opted to treat each person's health issues individually, on a case-by-case basis, rather than developing a singular policy on AIDS treatment. The message was clear: AIDS would be treated like anything else, and would not be singled out except for public information and education campaigns.

One such campaign was the publication, at Tom's commissioning, of a university brochure on AIDS covering multiple subjects, including questions on the morality of drug use and premarital sex as it related to AIDS, and a section of facts about the disease. *Portland Magazine*, UP's alumni publication, reported they would also "discuss 'safe sex' practices and the use of condoms," information that had become somewhat taboo in public discourse; so taboo that several Catholic institutions, including Tom's former employer, Stonehill College, had hesitated in disseminating similar literature to their campuses, primarily out of fear that such literature could be interpreted as an endorsement of unacceptable lifestyles and behaviors. Such a project needed institutional pressure from the highest levels. When UP published their AIDS literature, Tom made sure it was sent to every person in the campus community that fall. He called the brochure "an educational tool" that could help students "be informed regardless of their own personal behavior." For Tom, it was a question of preparedness: "They need to be aware of their neighbor and American society."

The brochure itself was not a progressive document. Developed by Louise Allen and Father Chris Johnson, it did not promote "promiscuity," while simultaneously recognizing that students would—despite their best efforts—have premarital sex. As such, Johnson said, "we would be remiss if we didn't provide information about AIDS that could prevent [students] from dying." Reception to its publication was very positive. *The Beacon*'s staff October 8 op-ed said:

> [Tom's] decision to allow the University Health Center to disperse a brochure on safe sex practices is of no small consequence. The decision is not only historic but thrusts the University into a position of leadership in tackling the problems of STDs headlong and educating students. The

> publication of a brochure on safe sex by a Catholic university is not a common [occurrence].

A key point the op-ed made was that anyone concerned over possible conflict between church doctrine and the university's approach to AIDS and sexual behavior should see the decision to publish the brochure as "really in line with Oddo's philosophy of enhancing student[s'] educational opportunities." Tom's philosophy was certainly at the root of the brochure, and by extension the AIDS ad-hoc committee and UP's overall response to the crisis. In every way he could, he fought against both a viral disease and the disease of misinformation, an effort no doubt fueled by his own horror at the crisis, and many heartbreaking phone calls.

Chapter 23

Co-Ed Housing

For most of its history, UP was an all-male college. At its founding in 1901, when it was still known as Columbia University, the Congregation of Holy Cross wanted to build an academy that could train a new generation of priests for the burgeoning Catholic population of Oregon, and the greater Pacific Northwest. For the next seven decades, there was little variation or desire for reform in this regard. But in 1971, a decision was made during the Waldschmidt presidency to finally admit women, and the first female Pilots moved to the Bluff that fall.

That same year, student protests and sit-ins attempted to convince the fledgling Board of Regents that co-ed dorms could work, alongside an intervisitation policy allowing male and female students to mingle in their respective dorms. While a policy was enforced at the time, the university put the idea of co-ed housing "under study." UP's Executive Council would later veto the proposal in the 1972/73 academic year. While students would continue to push for a change and push back against the university administration, their efforts were largely unsuccessful.

A decade later, UP was consistently enrolling large numbers of women, while keeping gender-segregated housing. The policy of intervisitation had largely governed relations between male and female students—rules that were constantly challenged by UP's dorm residents. Student dissent towards their living arrangements featured regularly on *The Beacon's* op-ed page through the early '80s, and into the beginning of Tom's presidency. Asked for his opinion on the issue in 1982, he talked about how co-ed housing at Stonehill College, implemented while he was a faculty member, had not contributed to any major issues and did not (as some contrarians warned) lead to a promotion of promiscuity among students.

Within the same few pages, alternative concerns were being floated: Guy Sievert, as Vice President of Student Affairs, originally supported co-ed housing on the Bluff, but by early 1984 had experienced a change of heart: "I used to think co-ed dorms would work here after some pushing and pulling and groundwork," he told *The Beacon.* "Now, I'm convinced a co-ed hall won't work here. If we tried to go co-ed now it would do more harm than good." Sievert believed that co-ed dorms would, ultimately, become unnecessary if UP got "the kind of mix we are looking for." Still, co-ed dorms were an official recommendation of Dr. Thomas Schoenk, UP's former Dean of Students, tasked with investigating multiple issues for the university's Committee on Student Affairs. The recommendation came after the university made the decision to swap residents in Kenna and Villa Maria Halls, giving female students more residential space and subsequently making Villa Maria a haven for male athletes.

This space swap was a temporary solution to a growing challenge. To some students, though, the issue needn't have been one. At UP's study abroad program in Salzburg, Austria, a popular destination for the Bluff's upperclassmen, men and women lived beside one another in co-ed facilities. This arrangement had never been challenged, since no problems ever came from it. Why, then, couldn't the main campus in Portland do the same? A group of students asking this question formed a lobby group, Change for Progress, to try and move the needle on co-ed housing. Their first op-ed in February 1984 didn't hold back, comparing UP's gender segregation to the military and to Puritanical families seeking to control their children. It also struck out at what they called the "ultraconservative administration," and said that Guy Sievert had "compromised" his position to satisfy that administration. While it conceded that Tom had vocally supported the idea of co-ed dorms, the op-ed asked why the recommendations to the Committee on Student Affairs had been put on ice, and dropped all pretenses about the criticism of co-ed living by saying the quiet parts out loud:

> Let us face the facts. There are no more pregnancies or wild orgies in co-ed living arrangements than in single sex dormitories. Men do not run around with their tongues hanging out looking for a free peep show. Women on the other hand can talk and relate with men without the fear of an R.A. [resident assistant] knocking on the door. In reality, the only thing that develops is a more healthy attitude between the sexes.

This effort, the newest iteration of a nearly-twenty-year fight, was unsuccessful at securing co-ed dorms in 1985 or 1986. For the time being, the swap of Kenna and Villa Maria Halls accommodated the spurt in female students as overall residential occupancy still lagged under 70 percent.

By fall 1986, his fourth year at UP, Tom resolved to finally implement some form of co-ed housing arrangement. Although the final decision was truly his, he did not want to make such a monumental change to residential life without extensive community buy-in. That year, he established a subcommittee of the larger Committee on Student Affairs to study the issue and offer a proposal with next steps. That group's process would take many months, involving discussions around the mission of the university, the logistics of such a change, and the potential implications if the change was made. Nevertheless, time was of the essence, and students were becoming restless: A survey conducted by the UP Residence Hall Association in February 1987 found that, from approximately 300 student respondents, 87 percent supported establishing co-ed housing. Further support was shown ahead of a March 31 meeting of the Committee on Student Affairs, when a rally in favor of co-ed housing was held. The ASUP even printed t-shirts.

The report by the subcommittee was delivered that afternoon. Despite a recommendation in favor of designating co-ed dorms in a five-to-three vote, doubt still remained. Further ridicule toward the university's conservative housing policies came in *The Beacon*'s April 1, 1987, parody edition, *The Bacon*. Tom had been featured in *The Bacon* previously, and in the 1987 edition he was featured twice on the front page: The first, a press photo of Tom crudely cut and pasted next to a larger picture of an iguana. The caption called him "Fr. Froddo Oddo," and explained that the giant iguana was a fuel efficient "econo-lizard" developed by the university to save Americans millions a year in fuel and driving costs. Beside this odd little section, another story reported that Tom, here referred to as Rev. Ohno, had ended the intervisitation policy:

> In a surprise move on Monday, Rev. Thomas C. Ohno, C.A.T.[18], announced to a stunned ASUP Senate that the University plans to curtail all intervisitation rights on campus next year.

18. A play on CSC, and a nod at Tom's reputation with students.

> According to Ohno, the change will mean that men and women will be kept completely separate in terms of living arrangements on campus. "We'll have the little boys' dorms over here," said Ohno, gesturing, "and the little girls' dorms over here, and never the twain shall meet."
>
> Asked to clarify what he meant, Ohno, clarified. "It is the University's position that intervisitation is the moral equivalent of accepting the serpent's apple," commented Ohno, "[i]t's like the Vatican operating a Motel 6."

Beyond the glib humor of student satirists, there were deeper cuts toward the administration, the university writ-large, and the larger church in the piece, with Tom at the center:

> Ohno was pressed further on the issue of [students'] rights. "Now don't go around thinking for a moment," responded Ohno. "That just because you live here on the University campus you have rights. That'd be chaos and contrary to our mission."
>
> Very few of the senators, however, agreed with Ohno's view, passing a unanimous resolution that called for the administration "to think about this thing really, really carefully as we'll all be p.o.'d in an extremely big way if this change occurs."

In hindsight, Tom *had* thought about "this thing" really, really carefully. What could've been a throw-away decision, either to allow or reject co-ed dorms, became a kind of soul searching process that envisioned a new day on the Bluff. It elevated the issue to a larger campus conversation, beyond the simple optics of genderless halls. And, in the end, Tom decided it was time. On April 2, 1987, he announced that Shipstad Hall would, starting that fall, become a co-ed dorm with men and women on alternating floors. But even before the doors of Shipstad opened to its first mixed cohort of residents, whispers abounded that one hall would not be enough. Others had nothing positive to say about the decision, waiting with bated breath to see if the experiment in Shipstad would fail. Those detractors were sorely disappointed by 1988.

Shipstad's 1987/88 cohort described their experience as "life as usual," with many praising the newfound community atmosphere in the building. That atmosphere accompanied a renewed focus on social events and student engagement in the hall, and soon student leaders were offering their thoughts on expanding co-ed living to other dorms across campus. ASUP vice president Jennifer Webber presented a proposal to the Senate in January to poll students about the idea, reporting to her colleagues that Guy Sievert had asked for help gauging student interest. If it was desired, Webber reported, Sievert would put a formal proposal before the Board of Regents by February. Quite suddenly, after more than fifteen *years* of fighting for a single co-ed dorm, it appeared a second was on course to open barely fifteen *months* after the first.

Students, with some differences of opinion, largely supported the idea. *The Beacon*, in early 1987, asked the question in its weekly poll, with responses running in the January 21 edition. Most agreed in principle, although some concerns remained—first among them giving students the option of where they wanted to live (assuming some gendered housing would remain), and ensuring women on the Bluff would have an option at all. The move to make Shipstad co-ed had deprived UP of one women's dorm where only one other existed: Mehling Hall, on the opposite end of campus. Despite a year of tight squeezes, the Board of Regents saw the value in expanding co-ed housing. Acting on Guy Sievert's proposal, the board designated Kenna Hall as co-ed on March 3. It is somewhat ironic, then, to read that Tom spoke out about dissent in the classroom that same day.

Referring to the Vatican's intervention at Catholic University of America, where Father Charles Curran was removed over his teachings about homosexuality, Tom struck out at the idea that dissent was not welcome at the Bluff. Far from it, Tom declared "We don't have to be afraid of the truth" on teaching controversial topics in the classroom. This attitude fueled his efforts to educate on AIDS, teach about human sexuality and theology, and guide the university through new chapters. By his own hand, with the start of co-ed housing on the Bluff, this attitude now also applied to campus policy.

Chapter 24

Apartheid

Since 2023, Israel's war of genocide has killed thousands of Palestinians and displaced millions more from their homes. Many were victims of American-made weapons shipped to Israel, including women, children, and babies. Prior to the war, observers on the ground and residents of the Gaza Strip called the Israeli government's treatment of the State of Palestine a form of modern Apartheid. I'd like to think that Tom would agree, but without a record of his opinion on Israeli occupation while he was alive, we can't be sure. However, we can still guess by reflecting on his reaction to this ideological cousin of Zionism. Like modern-day presidents, he dealt with the impact of the university's business interests in a pariah state committing crimes against humanity, an issue which, then, as now, emboldened a generation of student activists to fight for liberation.

The system of Apartheid, deriving from the Afrikaans word for "separateness" or "aparthood," began in South Africa in 1948. A method of social control instituted by the white minority government, it sought to categorize the country's multiracial population into four distinct racial groups and subsequently restrict their access and rights. By the 1980s, it had carved deep wounds into the national culture, fueling the rise of non-white political protest groups, and open opposition to Apartheid domestically. The growing backlash to the country's archaic social partition led to an international reassessment of relations with South Africa. Overnight, nations and entities worldwide began to consider whether to keep or divest any of their holdings tied to the country. American students were particularly energized by the ensuing campaign.

At college campuses in Portland, the issue was a hot topic, and in some cases led to direct action. In November 1985, students at nearby Reed College occupied the President's Office for three days demanding full divestiture from South Africa. At the time, the college had $6 million in direct and indirect investments in the country, and the Board of Trustees opted to not fully divest. Over 100 students responded by occupying a building in late January 1986.

Inspired by the Reed action, students at Lewis & Clark College held a fast in support of divestment the same month. Lewis & Clark's board voted instead to adhere to the "Sullivan Principles," a set of social responsibility guidelines for corporations still doing business in South Africa. The decision sent students protesting, holding vigils in front of the campus administration building. The mood nationwide was beginning to boil.

A February 2, 1986 article in the *New York Times*, "Pressure Rises on Colleges to Withdraw South Africa Interests," documented the events at Reed and similar actions around the country: Students at the University of Pennsylvania occupied the President's Office, a 24/7 operation that had lasted several weeks. At Dartmouth, protestors built structures described as "shanties" to criticize living conditions under Apartheid, only to have the structures destroyed by a right-wing student group. The article also mentioned numerous campuses that opted to fully divest, citing Bates College and University of Minnesota as leaders in the field. From 1977 to press date, the article described the growing impact of divestment:

> 70 colleges and universities in 22 states and the District of Columbia, have decided to withdraw some or all of their investments in companies doing business in South Africa, amounting to $411 million, according to the American Committee on Africa, a New York-based lobbying group. The committee said that close to 30 of the schools … made this decision since student demonstrations last April, with more than a dozen others following suit last fall.

But through much of this activity, UP remained unfazed on the topic, Tom included. At UP, the topic of divestment was one that had been previously discussed. A 1979 effort by then-faculty member Art Luther and students culminated in the ASUP passing a resolution calling for university divestment from South Africa. When no action was taken, students began demonstrating in small, but growing numbers. A handful of student picketers marched on campus during National Apartheid Day 1985, part of a larger national demonstration advocating divestment. That fall, a debate on Apartheid was held in Buckley Center: White, South African Stuart Pringle (dressed in all white) argued for the system, while one of the co-founders of the Black Panthers, Bobby Seale, argued against it. Over 200 students turned out, as interest in the topic spread.

In an April 1987 interview with *The Beacon*, Tom was asked about the divestment issue. The student journalists asked questions "on what direct or indirect financial ties the University has with companies that deal with South Africa." Tom's answer was multifaceted, and far from simple. First he explained that:

> We have no stock in any company directly in South Africa, nothing dealing with the South African government. It is a question how far you go away from the direct presence in South Africa and say that you really shouldn't have that either.

He then offered a metric, and some degrees of separation, to explain what he meant:

> Level one would be, here is a company directly dealing with the South African government. Level two is, here is a company that is in South Africa as one of a multinational corporation—they do have some operations in South Africa. (Level three is) here is a bank that lends money to some of those companies that are doing business in South Africa.

Tom said that UP, to his knowledge, had no connections at the first or second levels. Any other connections to the Apartheid government the university had were "indirect," links which were, Tom offered, "a question of how far one wants to push one's distance from what's happening in South Africa" if severed. He continued by saying there was a financially rational reason to avoid total divestment, that "there's debate within the investment field as to whether a portfolio that is totally free of all these levels of contact (in South Africa) can really be an effective financial portfolio." His interviewers moved on to other topics, but the conversation of divestment continued on the Bluff.

In September, at the beginning of the 1987/88 academic year, UP announced a debate on the subject between two experts on South Africa: Reverend Oliver Williams, CSC, a business professor from Notre Dame, and Dr. Kevin Danaher, a food activist and former political science and sociology professor from American University whose doctoral thesis covered the Apartheid boycott movement. Shortly before the debate, assistant professor Dr. Matthew Baasten wrote an op-ed for *The Beacon* titled "Apartheid—Just the Facts." Baasten, a theology faculty member, wrote of the extensive system of discrimination in South Africa, noting the arguments for and against divestment, and writing about how many in opposition to complete divestment supported the Sullivan Principles. In closing his objective overview of the arguments, Baasten urged readers to "form your own position. Maybe, you will discover that the moral issues in South Africa are simpler than they first appear."

At the September 29 debate, Father Williams argued divestment would not change the Apartheid system, while Dr. Danaher argued it would. Williams began the debate with an observation: Over one hundred American firms had pulled out of South Africa in the previous year, yet the Apartheid system remained as entrenched as ever. Corporations stood to lose out on lucrative contracts, largely due to domestic pressure, and Williams proposed that the threat of divestment was far more impactful than the act itself, comparing it to the threat of nuclear war. "The threat of use keeps bad things from happening," he said, and that "threat of disinvestment is powerful, but once we lose it, we all lose leverage."

Danaher countered with the claim that 40,000 children starved to death each day in South Africa, and that American taxpayers bore responsibility to do something. He called for total divestment, noting that while divestment alone could not solve Apartheid, it was essential to uniting the racial majority of the country against the white minority ruling class. American corporations decamping would show non-white South Africans that democracy works. "Divestment is about us," he declared, and spoke in relatively vague language about education and taking action.

Williams's rebuttal focused largely on the practicalities of divestment, the actual impact such actions had on South Africans. From his perspective, business leaving meant paid jobs leaving. He had spoken with many South Africans who had appreciated the American business presence, and who relied on the jobs those businesses offered. Prospective Black unemployment was of greater concern to Williams's arguments. Businesses that opted to stay in the country were not absolved from responsibility; he argued they should support Black South Africans fighting for their rights, but from the business perspective that equality among people meant the opening of new markets. The article concluded with the following observations:

> The speakers did not come to an agreement on the solution of Apartheid. At the very least, however, they stirred enough interest to have the audience asking questions for an hour directly after the debate and another hour at the following reception.

The debate inspired direct action by student leaders. Four weeks later, the ASUP Senate passed a resolution calling for a review of the Board of Regents' investment policies regarding South Africa, with more than two-thirds of Senators voting in favor. Nearby Willamette University's board had recently organized their own review, according to *The Oregonian*, at the recommendation of an institutional advisory committee on ethical investment.

Two days after the ASUP resolution's passage, the Board of Regents' Finance Committee responded by reviewing the university's investment policies. In a half-hour deliberation, the committee's members concurred that UP's investment policies regarding South Africa were "ethical and in accord with the University's mission statement," and opted not to take action. To complete a more thorough review, according to the committee's chairman, would've taken too long, and would not be used unless it was "vital to the school's welfare." Despite the decision, ASUP President Lisa Amato and Vice President Jennifer Webber both expressed satisfaction that the review was conducted at all.

Following the review, Tom was also quoted by *The Beacon* for his take:

> The Rev. Thomas C. Oddo, C.S.C., University president, said there is no overwhelming evidence of whether divestiture or selective investing is the answer to helping end apartheid in South Africa.
>
> "What is the best way of helping blacks in South Africa—there is back and forth debate," Oddo said. "Is it destroying the South African economy or is it strengthening those companies which are fighting for blacks' rights?"
>
> The University will continue to follow its investment policies until an effective way of exerting influence on the South African government is found, Oddo said.

In the wake of the debates and review of the university's investments, concerted action against Apartheid dimmed, though *The Beacon* would continue to cover the issue from a distance. Through fall 1989, it ran a series of four reports titled "Out of South Africa" by graduate student Ashraf Kagee, who would later become a noted author and psychology professor at Stellenbosch University in Western Cape, South Africa. The series called Apartheid and South Africa's newly-established tricameral form of government racist and antithetical to the aims of the liberation movement active in the country. In its third iteration, Kagee also declared that reform was not a suitable course; a revolution was necessary:

> The bottom line concerning the reform policy of the government, from the perspective of the oppressed majority, is that the unjust apartheid system CANNOT be reformed. It must be abolished entirely and any attempt by the ruling minority to alter the nature of apartheid is therefore purely cosmetic.

While Apartheid remained in place, the UP Board of Regents did not divest from South Africa. Abolished in the early '90s, the system had governed South Africa for over forty years, leading to thousands of deaths, tens of thousands more imprisoned, and millions displaced. Its effects are still seen today.

We can't know how Tom would've reacted to the Gaza War, or to any modern genocide. We can see, however, that in 1987, divestment was an untenable decision for him to make as president. We can assume that, in his estimation, the real amount of money potentially lost by divestment from South Africa outweighed what he believed would be the best outcomes for Black South Africans. In hindsight, it was a business decision over a moral decision, and an unfortunate decision on Tom's part. It is difficult to reconcile how, only months before the regents cleared their investment policies, he had been talking about institutions who were afraid to "stand for something."

Chapter 25

Tom Meets the Pope

Pope John Paul II was elected in the shadow of the untimely death of his predecessor. Rising to the papacy in 1978, JP2 was a young man compared to his fellow cardinals. In the subsequent decade, his fame soared to spectacular heights. Global "voyages" became a way for the Pope to interface directly with audiences on six continents. Such papal voyages were not new, but John Paul II used them extensively, and strategically, making more trips abroad than all previous popes combined.

In late 1986 and early 1987, planning began for the Pope's thirty-sixth voyage. It would follow a visit to multiple sites in Poland, his homeland. While the earlier trip that year involved the beatification of two Polish martyrs—one a bishop murdered at Dachau—and participation in the Second National Eucharistic Congress, the latter trip would involve a multi-city swing through the US and a rescheduled visit to First Nation tribes in Canada. Unlike the trip to Poland, John Paul II's voyage to the US and Canada would involve papal audiences with the general public and addresses to business executives and other notables. One such planned audience was a group of entertainment and show business invitees from the movie, music, TV, magazine, and broadcasting industries in Los Angeles. Other cities included on the Pope's route were Miami, New Orleans, and Columbia, South Carolina in the South; San Antonio and Phoenix in the Southwest; Monterey and San Francisco to round out California; and multiple stops in the Detroit metro area, including Pontiac and Hamtramck, Michigan—a major center of Polish American culture. With the itinerary publicized, the Congregation of Holy Cross prepared their own engagement with John Paul II. UP was one of over 250 Catholic institutions that sent representatives for a private audience in New Orleans, with Tom joining several other priests from Portland.

The visit came at a time of high tension within Catholic academia. Since 1971, Reverend Charles Curran had argued that homosexual relations within a committed relationship, while not optimal, were healthy for those in the relationship. Curran was an associate professor at the Catholic University of America, where he joined the faculty a few years before Tom's brief stint at the DC campus. While Curran did not endorse sexual relations between gay partners, he believed that the Catholic Church had work to do to recognize the goodness of those relationships which honored God and church teachings. He outwardly criticized the Vatican's Congregation for the Doctrine of Faith, a group based in Rome that had attempted to censor Father John J. McNeill, one of Tom's theological peers while active in Dignity. And he'd dissented on the issue of contraception, which almost lost him his job.

In 1986, the Vatican took the additional step of intervening directly in Curran's employment. It was decided that he could no longer teach while holding such views. A theology professor at the Catholic University of America since 1965, he had been temporarily removed from his position once before, for his contraception stance. This time, the ban was permanent. He was deemed unfit to teach Catholic theology within church-affiliated institutions. His dissent had become a major debate within American-Catholic academia; nevertheless, it was not a topic to discuss publicly, or even privately depending on the audience.

Many of Portland's clergy were scheduled to meet Pope John Paul II in Miami, where the pontiff would de-plane from Rome. Others planned to meet the Pope at Xavier University of Louisiana—the only Catholic HBCU in the US—over the weekend of September 11–13. These included Tom, five Black Catholic delegates from western Oregon, and six other lay delegates from across the state. Running parallel with the efforts of Dignity to expand the rights of gay people within the church, a Black Catholic Movement was growing, as calls were made by clergy for an "African American Catholic Rite."

The Pope's thirty-sixth voyage was later recounted by *Orlando Sentinel* writer Howard Means, who said that "Contradictions great and small, ludicrous and profound between the church and American life abounded during the papal visit," as many Americans discovered who Pope John Paul II was:

> —On Bourbon Street in New Orleans, the third stop on the nine-city roster, Landmark Shoppes was selling T-shirts decorated with the slogan "USA Tour / Pope John Paul II / He Comes in the Name of the Lord"

> wrapped around the benignly smiling image of a pontiff deeply troubled by the sexual mores of the Western world.
>
> Directly across the street sat a bar featuring bottomless and topless dancing, a massage parlor and a place advertising female amateur wrestling—"Anyone pinning our champ for 3 counts wins $100."
>
> —Along New Orleans' Canal Street, where the papal parade turned left toward the Superdome, John Paul II could have looked up through the bullet proof-glass roof of his popemobile and seen four billboards forming a kind of visual frame for his passage. Two pumped whiskey brands; one, a cigarette brand; and one featured Jim Palmer, the baseball pitcher turned underwear salesman, semirecumbent in nothing but his pinstriped Jockey briefs.
>
> —The pope's Superdome address to about 60,000 youths—mostly white, mostly middle class—was interrupted, by my count, 20 times by applause.
>
> The clapping came when he told the teen-agers, "There is no room in the church for selfishness. There is no room in America, in the world for selfishness. It destroys the meaning of life; it destroys the meaning of love; it reduces the human person to a subhuman level."

The visit was a time capsule for the age. "Many of the teen-agers present watched the pope," Means wrote, "on a giant TV monitor near the roof of the dome, flanked by advertisements for Budweiser beer and Marlboro cigarettes: This Bud's for you, this pope's for you; pope country, Marlboro country. For a moment, the messages seemed intertwined." On another major billboard overlooking the pontiff's motorcade route, the visit was advertised by Popeye's Chicken. An illustration of John Paul II appears to bless St. Louis Cathedral over the text "Love That City!"

Tom's interface with John Paul II in New Orleans was minimal, but still reported on by the Portland news media. Besides tangential coverage by *The Oregonian*, Tom was interviewed for an episode of AM Northwest, a morning show produced by KATU—Portland's ABC affiliate. In those days, KATU was eager to improve its ratings against competitors KGW (NBC) and KOIN (CBS). One strategy involved installing hosts that would, more or less, attract viewership through their strong personalities. Throughout 1984–1985, an upstart anchor named Bill O'Reilly had tried to do that at the network, with little success, moving on to other gigs. In other ways, KATU tried to get ahead with unique types of programming. AM Northwest was one such platform, providing current affairs commentary from local guests.

Tom's interview ran the morning of September 27. A recording of the episode has become lost media, and no mementos of the visit have survived in the UP Archive. But the episode marks a unique moment for the church in America, prior to the divulgence of systemic child sex abuse, and before the renewed social issue debates of the 1990s and 2000s, where a critical mass of believers—Catholic and not—turned out for a pope revered by the world, and seen by the faithful as a walking saint. The images from that visit live on as remarkable episodes of American pop culture across the internet.

Later footage would surface from the Pope's California visit that same month, showing the pontiff in full white garb, zucchetto hat included, taking swings in a batting cage as other priests looked on. A reporter is heard asking what position John Paul II played. "Any position he wants!" came an enthusiastic response. The footage, which was not broadcast publicly at the time, has resurfaced and gone viral several times on the Internet—although it appears faked, a left-handed actor standing in for a right-handed pope who'd never played before. But here too, we see the effects of remembered history conflating and redefining reality, as dozens of viewers have commented on the video since its upload to YouTube that they distinctly remember this visit as "the one with the Pope in the batting cage."

For Tom, it was likely a visit he remembered not for the advertising, or the gimmicks, but for the opportunity to meet God's blessed representative on Earth, one of the highest pinnacles of his religious life. A few lines from the Pope's address at the Louisiana Superdome even reminds one of Tom's ministering:

> In order, however, to accomplish this great work, to be in a condition to change the world in the name of Jesus, you yourselves must actually be living according to your own identity—*according to God's plan for your lives.* Once again it is the world of Jesus that directs your lives and tells you what that plan is. You remember how much Jesus insisted on the commandment of love, how much he insisted on living according to certain norms called the Beatitudes: "Blessed are the meek ... Blessed are the merciful ... Blessed are the clean of heart ... Blessed are the peacemakers." All of this is part of the plan.

Chapter 26

Saving AFROTC #695

In the years immediately following WWII, General Dwight Eisenhower established the Air Force's Reserve Officer Training Corps—later renamed the Air Force Reserve Officer Training Corps (AFROTC)—to build a bench of officers for future wars and periods of peace. The program was designed to layer over students' academics, providing a pathway to commissioned officer status right out of college. The program also offers a variety of two-to-four-year scholarships for eligible cadets. In this regard, AFROTC is as much a recruitment program for the US Air Force as it is a financial aid resource for college students.

University of Portland would get its own AFROTC detachment in 1951, as the armed forces navigated the Korean War and the growth of the wider Cold War. From early on, the program was a major draw for local students enrolled at UP and at other crosstown schools. The sight of cadets drilling on the campus lawn was a common one over the years, as were the speakers that AFROTC would bring in to talk to the cadets on the issues of the day, and the value of the program. By the late 1980s, Detachment #695 regularly offered about 150 scholarships annually, often awarded to the highest achieving students on the Bluff. Many of them would've been unable to complete their studies without the financial assistance provided by AFROTC. Detachment #695 was rated seventh in the nation for academic quality in September 1987, and sixty-eight freshmen enrolled as cadets that fall. Despite its recognition and strong incoming cohort, the air force was planning to strategically downsize detachments, and #695 was put on the chopping block.

In an effort to determine cost-effectiveness of AFROTC detachments, the air force created a multi-point criteria to show whether it was worth keeping certain units open. The new criteria prioritized the total number of officers commissioned from enrolled cadets and included a point on the number of minority students commissioned, to ensure a diversity of cadets enrolled in the program. Both put the UP detachment in the bottom thirty of all detachments nationwide. These thirty would be shut down, their aid programs ended regardless of students' situations. Detachment #695 just wasn't producing enough commissioned officers. It would be closed with the other detachments over an eighteen-month period.

AFROTC Commander Colonel Jack Roscoe called the decision "political" in his address to the 135 cadets of Detachment #695. He believed that, if any sort of reversal were possible, it would come "within the next two weeks or not at all." *The Beacon*'s Staff Editorial crowed "Quality is what officers are made of and UP's detachment may not have been producing 'cheap' officers, but they were well educated and well taught." Tom was furious at the news.

He announced the closure at an Academic Senate meeting. There he projected the potential impact: an $800,000–$1 million loss in tuition. It was also mentioned that detachment cadets comprised 11 percent of the School of Engineering's total enrollment. This closure was the greatest single threat to UP's student enrollment since the 1979 Iranian Revolution, which sent dozens of international students home to be with their families and effectively upset the financial state of the university. "We are very angry, and we feel the decision is unjust and uncalled for." Within hours, Tom and others in the administration were making calls to congressmen for support. It is remarkable how fervently a priest, who believed so wholly and deeply in peace and non-violence, fought for the preservation of an air force officer recruitment program. But he did, and he fought to win.

That spring, petitions were drawn up to show campus support for the program. Tom took the petitions, 1,300 total signatures, to Washington, DC, on a business trip, stopping at Oregon's congressional offices to build support for the detachment. In February, he was back on campus and photographed walking alongside Senator Bob Packwood, inspecting the cadets. A week later, Air Force Secretary Edward Aldridge declined to reverse course on closing #695. But this initial reticence did not stop Tom's efforts. While he continued to lobby for the air force to change their minds, he announced a new $2,000 scholarship designed to keep cadets on the Bluff. The measure was meant to bridge the gap in financial aid AFROTC-affiliated students might see if the detachment was shut down.

By late March, the air force blinked, and allowed Detachment #695 to continue operating until at least 1990. Secretary of Defense Frank Carlucci had issued the order himself. Behind the scenes, Oregon's other senator, Mark Hatfield, had threatened to bring air force officials before the Senate Appropriations Committee to explain their rationale for Detachment #695's closure. Assisted by Committee Chairman Senator John C. Stennis, they collectively forced the Defense Department's hand. Colonel Roscoe's successor as detachment commander Colonel Dick Frette expressed gratitude for the groundswell, saying that "[UP is] one of the few schools that has strong support for the program, all the way from Father Oddo on down."

When the detachment came up for a re-evaluation two years later, the program was renewed, and AFROTC #695 continues to operate today. Colonel Roscoe, following his stint as commander, was hired by the university as director of residence life in June 1988. The selection hinged on Tom's participation in interviews, and his final decision. Roscoe, who spent a lifelong career in the air force, had previously planned to relocate to Alaska, but decided to stay in Portland. When he was hired, he told *The Beacon*, of Tom and Guy Sievert, "They have a unique philosophy of education that I respect. They are not motivated to simply stamp out graduates, but are concerned with the growth and development of the whole person." Reflecting on the struggle to save his AFROTC unit, Roscoe later said:

> I've never seen Tom do anything where he has been more decisive. Everybody had their own reasons for wanting ROTC back, but Tom was looking at the injustice to the students. He had a very strong sense of fair play. He insisted on continuing benefits and scholarships to any cadets that decided to remain on campus. He didn't have to do that.

But anyone who knew Tom Oddo also knew he would endeavor to do right by students, and root out any injustices they suffered. A pastoral career advocating for the rights of LGBTQ+ people in the church had prepared Tom for the good fight, wherever the fight was needed. And when the fight came for AFROTC #695, Tom was front and center, refusing to back down.

Chapter 27

The Cost of Building

A friend of Tom's would recall some years later that he would get "nervous whenever there was no building going up on campus." But UP's building campaigns through the mid- to late-'80s were not free ventures. The Chapel of Christ the Teacher and the Louisiana-Pacific Tennis Center were the standout projects, relying solely on donations. Otherwise, the University was on the hook for at least some parts of the Chiles Center, renovations to Howard Hall, Pilot House, and St. Mary's, refitting of the university track, adoption of new security and residential phone systems, and the completion of the unfinished challenge par course. The university also incurred major expenses with its foray into acquiring computers and making them accesible, a major priority during Tom's presidency. These expenses existed outside of normal operating costs.

Through the 1980s, UP's cost of attendance steadily rose. The Board of Regents hiked tuition annually between 1984–1988, by rates of 8.9 percent, 8 percent, 6.5 percent, 4.2 percent, and 6 percent, respectively. Each time a hike was announced, Tom was front and center explaining the reasons for the seemingly-exponential cost of operating the university. Tuition had always, historically, been on the rise, but the '80s had turned the skew vertical.

When the 1984/85 announcement was made, Tom said a "significant portion of the raise will go directly to the financial aid program," while also offsetting other costs across departments and supporting competitive faculty salaries. Though it was "not easy to find prices rising," Tom said, he hoped students found it "relative to the kind of quality" they got in their education. "We are concerned with making tuition rates affordable, and I assure students we are doing all in our power to hold costs down." Though this may have been the central principle of the Board of Regents' forecasting, expenses kept creeping up, and students began to mentally associate the ongoing construction with higher bills. A cartoon published after the tuition hike announcement in *The Beacon*'s Editorial/Commentary section shows a student approaching an accounts payable specialist who's wearing a fancy Victorian-style dress and sitting under a sign reading PAY HERE. The student prepares to hand over a piggy bank to pay his tuition bill. Behind the specialist, a framed picture of Chiles Center is visible. It was an image conjured by students who stood in line waiting to pay their bills, wondering who actually cashed their checks.

The Beacon asked students in March 1985 what proposed tuition increases and the Reagan Administration's plan to cut financial aid would mean for their enrollment. Most said they would not be immediately impacted—aside from paying a few extra tuition dollars out of pocket. Others saw an existential threat: One freshmen student, Liz Michalek, replied that she would no longer qualify for a student loan guarantee since her parents made over $30,000 a year. Another freshman, Pam Helfrich, said the increase was enough to push her to another school, despite loving UP. Nearly everyone mentioned how the increase was to be expected, even inevitable "with all the improvements they've been doing on campus," Michalek observed.

The Beacon's Staff Editorial, gracing the opposite column, noted that the university's budget had always been a closely guarded secret. And yet, estimates were floated about the buckets that tuition dollars filled: 75–80 percent of the educational budget, 65–70 percent of the operating budget, and 55–60 percent of the capital budget. Before long, students were calling for greater transparency around the university's financials, which Tom would eventually approve for public release on *The Beacon*'s front page. Publishing such information was about both justifying the tuition hikes and defending the administration against criticism, showing that—in fact—over 45 percent of the university's operating costs were instructional, owing mostly to faculty salaries.

At the news that tuition would be raised yet again in 1986/87, Tom blamed the increasing cost of the university's liability insurance and federal financial aid hacked to size by the Reagan Department of Education. As a direct result of Reagan's policies, downward trends in enrollment added pressure on the regents to raise tuition, seeing more students leave the institution than could be replaced year over year. UP's status as a tuition-driven institution was frequently used by Tom and others to explain the need for raising rates. In 1986 alone, undergraduate enrollment fell 6.3 percent, while graduate enrollment fell another 7 percent. The drop necessitated cuts across departments, the closure of the campus gardening programs, and a gutting of the Maintenance Department's budget and staff. These cuts, like many seen throughout the Reagan administration, amounted to a form of local austerity.

Bill Cavanaugh's Commentary column, *Under Fire*, discussed the sharp rise in tuition under the headline "Skyrocketing tuition threatens students." Cavanagh lamented the trend, and worried whether the worst was yet to come:

> So while we are still fairly young and fairly vocal, we should not be so closed-minded as to ignore what is going on. While we are struggling to scrape together enough to make it through another year, we should keep in mind that we may be poised on the edge of the iceberg, and that catastrophe might wait around the corner.

That November, the university announced its latest building project: a four stage plan involving the creation of a Center for Science and Technology, the complete relocation of Columbia Hall and removal of an annex attached to the Chemistry building, and the remodeling of the Engineering and Science buildings. Though the $8 million plan would largely rely on fundraising, it was yet another reminder that tuition increases related, at least indirectly, to the constant humdrum of construction workers that visited campus each year.

1987 brought some innovation to UP's tuition model: a flat-rate for undergraduates. Announced in March, the new rate would charge all undergraduate students taking twelve or more credits $3,300 per semester, regardless of the classes they took or the program they sought. Students taking under twelve credits would pay $212 per credit, a $14 increase from the previous rate. *The Beacon* noted the new flat rate still represented a 4.2 percent tuition increase, despite Tom's assertions that it would decrease the need for students to "stretch-out" their programs of study based on what they could afford. Beside the column on the flat rate, a smaller story announced that room and board rates would also increase for the 1987/88 year, by 5.4 percent and 3.8 percent, respectively.

Tom was asked by *The Beacon*'s staff writers about the increase in tuition and adoption of a flat rate, in the same April 1987 interview where he was asked about Jack Avina's replacement and divestment from South Africa. He emphasized that UP was still a "tremendous bargain," and that the administration was keenly aware the typical student on the Bluff was not rich, but rather "basically struggling" to make their payments. On the question of "where the money from endowments and investments are spent," Tom politely jabbed back at a growing refrain among students, that the administration was somehow enriching itself:

> All of that money is spent right back into the University's program. I enjoy students who, I don't need to say they are naive, but they talk about "tuition goes up and the university makes all this profit." There is no such thing as profit in the life of the University of Portland. Any money that's there as generated income is fed right back and covers the expenses.

A discussion of the university's financial position in the 1980s would be incomplete without mentioning how Tom had saved UP money through his community outreach. The L-P Tennis Center; a multitude of campus computers; $90,000 worth of cement from Ross Island Sand and Gravel, owned by the Pamplin family, for replacing old asphalt sidewalks; among various other benefits provided by the community, all courted by Tom. His presidency saw a heavy rise in capital building projects, but not without great effort to save money and cover costs by external means. But it couldn't stop the trend altogether.

As the university entered 1989, tuition hikes were becoming an annual tradition, as sure "as death and taxes" one op-ed in *The Beacon* would complain. The year Tom assumed the presidency, 1982, university enrollment was at 2,872, and tuition was $2,175 per term ($7,141 in 2025 USD). By 1989, enrollment was down to 2,417, and tuition was $3,800 per term ($9,772 in 2025 USD), representing a 16 percent drop in students and a 74 percent increase in tuition cost—without considering the increased cost of room, board, and other campus fees. Except for 1984, every year of Tom's presidency saw a drop in student enrollment and a subsequent price hike. Even so, these numbers are an excellent gauge of long-term inflation, with UP's tuition rates now $28,400 per term. The flat-rate tuition is still in place, a lasting fixture of Tom's late presidency.

Despite the rising costs through the end of the 1980s, the campus mood was sunny. As projects wrapped up and the new decade approached, a sense of optimism prevailed over the anxieties of tuition and the growing pains of construction work. Enrollment was up again for the first time in five years, pushing the regents to study building a new residence hall to house future cohorts of undergraduates. Every day, without fail, Tom took his laps in the Howard Hall pool. It was something he did until the week he died.

Chapter 28

The Last Year, 1988–1989

Tom's last year saw the world entering a new era, and the last vestiges of the old global order disappearing. The Iran–Iraq war ends after eight years of fighting. Over 1 million are killed in the conflict, a virtual stalemate, including 8,000 civilians in the gassing of Halabja. The 1988 Summer Olympics are held in Seoul, an hour from the Demilitarized Zone with North Korea, the hermit kingdom that will become one of the last remnants of the Soviet era. Augusto Pinochet loses a referendum on his dictatorship and gives up power in Chile. NASA resumes shuttle missions for the first time since the *Challenger* disaster, as President Reagan prepares to leave office and campaigns for his successor, Vice President George H. W. Bush.

In Portland, the world felt a bit kinder: In February, an organization named Metro Catholic Broadcasting announced the groundbreaking of the "nation's only independent non-profit Catholic radio station." The station, call sign KBVM, set up shop in a small building near Mehling Hall, a space held on a $1 per year lease—the news of which prompted minor controversy among students. While not affiliated with the university, the station would take advantage of such generosity as long as the lease was valid.

Two UP seniors were married on skates in a March 1988 iteration of *Walt Disney's World on Ice* at Memorial Coliseum, to the cheers of 10,000 spectators. That same month, a special casino night was organized to fundraise for a Commons food service worker who was wounded in a drive-by shooting. The ASUP voted to donate $300 to her fund.

Meanwhile, Tom was traveling overseas in a campaign to grow the UP Alumni Association. While there, he formally established the Guam Chapter, which had raised $10,000 in the two months leading up to the visit, and was welcomed by a recent university graduate, Governor Joseph Ada, '87. He then visited high school students and spoke about Portland campus life and the experience of UP's education: He extolled the sixteen-to-one student to teacher ratio, promising students they would not be mere statistics, and called the campus a "comfortable environment" for newcomers to the mainland, a "good place to take that leap from the island life." The university's relationship with its Guamanian alumni would lead to the creation of a recurring grant for UP-bound students in 1989, a further strengthening of bonds to the Bluff. The success of the Guam outreach was typical for the later years of Tom's service, with UP's influence growing and alumni finding their way back to the university.

Colonel Jack Roscoe started as director of residential life in September, while Colonel Dick Frette took over as AFROTC Commander. Roscoe developed a proposal for a new residence hall, which Tom said could be ready within a year if the money could be found. A potential source, Metro Catholic Broadcasting, was instead weathering financial troubles of its own. Despite an enthusiastic opening announcement earlier in the year, the station reported they were $250,000 short of operating funds, and delayed the launch of KBVM until December. Meanwhile, KDUP switched its format away from commercial rock to progressive, with REM and The Smiths now dominating the Bluff's airwaves.

That fall, Angela Davis came to Portland to talk about Apartheid. Elsewhere in the city, organizers assembled the university's participation in Peace Week, a global event for world hunger awareness. UP's events included a fast that an estimated 200 people participated in. On campus, over 500 students received academic warnings based on their midterm grades, while Jay Leno played a show which brought the ASUP Major Entertainment Committee a modest profit. In Salzburg, Tom visited UP Center and inspected the facilities, his first (and last) trip to Austria as president. While he was there, the center advertised its first organized trip to the Soviet Union, planned for early 1989.

That fall, hundreds of students boarded a sternwheeler for a semi-formal dance called River Rage. Alcohol flowed freely, leading to a student falling and hurting himself so badly that paramedics met him at the dock. The ensuing commentary on alcohol abuse at school functions would remind some older students and administrators of the Coma event years prior. It prompted the ASUP to pass a resolution requiring any student club they funded to encourage responsible drinking in all promotional materials for their events, no exceptions allowed. Previous efforts by the university, with Tom's support, focused on promoting responsible decision making around drinking, and included the establishment of support groups like STAR, Students Together in Assistance in Recovery, in 1984, and SOAP, Students on Alcohol Problems, in 1987.

As the leaves turned, a new installation was erected on the Bluff: a statue of Captain William Clark alongside York, his slave, and an unnamed Indigenous guide. The Oregon Lewis & Clark Committee chose the site for the statue—depicting Clark renaming the mountain known as *Seekseekqua* by Native peoples "Mt. Jefferson"—at Tom's invitation. He was graciously thanked by the former Chairman of the committee in *The Beacon*'s Letters to the Editor section, and the Fort Clatsop National Memorial presented Tom with a heritage sign at the statue's dedication in December.

The word *Seekseekqua* is from the Sahaptin language, spoken among the Native tribes who resided along the Columbia River, and refers to the horsetail fern. The Portland metro area had, for many generations, been the ancestral home of the Chinook Nation, including the Multnomah peoples who lived on Sauvie Island by the base of the Bluff. One of the Chinooks' largest settlements was Cathlapotle, a trading village that stood close to the modern-day city of Ridgefield, Washington, where I grew up. While the Chinook tribes spoke their own language and may not have referred to the mountain as *Seekseequa*, they did meet the haggard explorers Lewis and Clark in Cathlapotle on their 1806 return trip to the east. The symbology of their exploration has, over the years, matured from a popular image of an adventurous conquest of nature to one of early American colonization of indigenous lands.

Even before more contemporary revisions of American history from Black and Indigenous perspectives in popular culture, the Lewis & Clark Committee addressed the statute's depiction of Clark's companions in the statue plaque. After first acknowledging the original names for the mountain, it read:

> This monument depicts Captain Clark pointing to Mt. Jefferson. With Clark is York, his Black slave (later freed by Clark), and an unnamed American Indian guide. These statues stand as a visual reminder that three races contributed to the success of the Lewis and Clark Expedition—symbolic of the first integrated society in the Oregon Country.

For decades, the statue stood near the edge of the Bluff, overlooking the city. It was there when I attended graduate school from 2016–2018. But in 2020, the university decided to remove it before it could be targeted or vandalized by protestors speaking out against police violence and white supremacy in American culture. Perhaps notably, York's statue was removed first.

Tom welcomed a curious new hire in December 1988: former state superintendent of public instruction Verne Duncan. A moderate Republican and a public school teacher before elected to office, Duncan was hired as dean of the UP School of Education at the end of his fourth term in office, a role he would hold through the mid-'90s, while also teaching classes. Tom still taught his human sexuality class, and planned to keep teaching as long as he could. When he wasn't teaching, running meetings, or holding court with donors, he was still just as active in campus life. In January, he was an introductory speaker and moderator for "Social Dimensions of AIDS: Sociological Analysis of the Impact of AIDS on American Society," the latest forum in the university's efforts to educate on the virus.

Seeking to replicate recent success with the Leno show, the Major Entertainment Committee booked the Sistine Chapel Choir for a campus concert over Parents Weekend. The event was a flop, instead losing the committee over $13,000. Better engagement came with UP's first Women's Awareness Week, an educational week of programming produced by the Campus Program Board that focused on addressing gender roles and stereotypes.

Soon after, the administration announced the latest tuition hike: 8.9 percent for the 1989/90 academic year. The coming fall, total undergraduate tuition, room, and board would exceed $10,000 for the first time. It required a letter from Tom to all students explaining how the increase would be spent: additional financial aid funding, paying down higher costs for regular operations, and increasing faculty pay. "Even though our tuition continues to raise," Tom reasoned, "it's not raising nearly as much as at other institutions." This may have been true of a private liberal arts school in the Portland metro area, as state schools also raised their tuition rates, but at much lower hikes: Tuition rates at institutions within the now-defunct Oregon University System went up between 18–22.5 percent from the 1982/83 and 1989/90 Academic Years. Tuition at UP, however, rose over 42 percent in the same time period.

By the end of February, KBVM was still off-air, and sought a second license extension. That month, UP welcomed business and university leaders from Jiangsu, China, who sought better business relations in Oregon. The attending representatives planned to work on new ventures with members of the Oregon Resource and Technology Development Corporation, the tech companies in the state's Silicon Forest.

Father Richard Berg, who was directly involved in the Jiangsu officials' visit, also helped organize UP's first international recruitment effort, the University of Portland Night (UPN) tour. 1989 was the fourth year of the tour, which had grown to twenty-four cities worldwide and was on track to keep growing: A single visit to Tokyo by Tom and Father Berg led to the establishment of an annual student exchange program with Sophia University, a Jesuit institution in the city.

Father Joe Corpora organized an immersion program called "Rural Plunge," which brought twenty-two students to a migrant worker farm in Cornelius, Oregon, to live and work over Spring Break. Migrant farm workers from Latin America, primarily from Mexico, have represented a major portion of Oregon's labor economy for many decades, performing tasks like fruit picking that ensure a steady flow of produce into the supply chain. Students spent their time repairing and repainting migrant shacks on the property, the first serious repair the worker's dwellings had seen in two decades.

In March, UP began a four-stage "self-study," a process that had been months in the planning. The university was preparing for reaccreditation by its regional accreditor, the Association of Northwest Schools and Colleges (ANSC), now known as the Northwest Commission on Colleges and Universities (NWCCU). As part of reaccreditation, the university was required to reflect on its institutional mission and practices. Tom and the Board of Regents used this opportunity to develop a Self-Study Steering Committee, composed of staff, faculty, and students, to engage the larger campus. The committee planned to collect responses, then report its findings at a campus-wide "convocation" in May. All of this work precipitated planned accreditor site visits in 1990, which Tom would've had in his calendar.

In spring, *The Beacon* ran its annual April Fool's edition *The Bacon*. Repeating something of a tradition, Tom was featured on the front page. Under the headline "University Sold!" staff writer "Nerf Hoop Hill" wrote that the Board of Regents had bet and lost UP in a basketball game against Notre Dame, and were now selling the campus to a familiar-named mogul:

> The University of Portland has been sold to multimillionaire Donald Rump, announced University President the Rev. Thomas C. Yoda, C.S.C., at a Thursday press conference.

> While the move to sell the University was unknown to most people, Yoda said the campus has been on the market for some time.
>
> "The Board of Regents lost a bet on the Notre Dame–UP Men's Basketball game in January," said Yoda. "To generate the funds needed to pay off the loss something had to be done and selling the University seemed like the most realistic option."

Donald Rump, it was said, planned to turn the Bluff into an amusement park: "Wally (Pilot) World." Elsewhere in *The Bacon*, Tom was referred to as "Rev. Thomas C. Odd One," in a story about updating the priestly wardrobe:

> On Monday the Vatican issued a report to all C.S.C. fathers and brothers affiliated with private colleges stating they must doff their religious garments in favor of clothing "more hip," says University President Rev. Thomas C. Odd One, C.S.C. The report quotes students at private Catholic colleges as having an "aversion" to the traditional black worn by fathers.
>
> Odd One says beginning this fall, fathers will have new wardrobes to coordinate with the four seasons. For instance, he describes the spring attire as being "lavender and chartreuse Bermuda shorts topped by a sporty polo shirt with the Holy emblem on the pocket."

The Bacon story closed by saying "Odd One admits looking forward to wearing the Vatican-approved Spandex biking pants." While Tom would not adopt a new priestly set of biking pants, he did don a set of gear for a game of Donkey Polo, the proceeds of which went to House of Light, a hospital serving children with AIDS. Tom's photo on the donkey ran in *The Beacon*'s sports section. It evokes the old adage "I can't believe they pay me to do this."

During those spring weeks, the body of a UP graduate and former AFROTC cadet came home to Portland in a flag-draped coffin. Captain Richard J. Mallon, Jr. joined the air force the same year as Colonel Jack Roscoe, both having recently left UP for service overseas. On January 28, 1970, after over 100 flights throughout Vietnam, Mallon was shot down behind enemy lines. It is speculated that Mallon survived the crash, but was captured, then held as a prisoner of war by the Viet Cong. He died in captivity around September 1975, several months after the Fall of Saigon and the final withdrawal of American forces. His name would be adopted by Detachment #695, in honor of his service and sacrifice. In the years following the war, the Vietnamese government would release the bodies of several American servicemembers, including Mallon's in late 1988. His funeral would be held in the Chapel of Christ the Teacher in April. Tom presided over the ceremony, which included the anointing of Mallon's casket and celebration of the Eucharist. A twenty-one-gun salute and a four-fighter flyover from McChord Air Force Base pierced the silence that hovered over the crowd. It was a preview of the grief to come in the fall, when another casket would rest in the chapel.

In May, Tom was elected to the Notre Dame Board of Trustees. His service on the board would regularly bring him back to South Bend, to the campus where his professional faith journey began. Tom was selected alongside the vice president of the F. W. Woolworth Company and President Reagan's Peace Corps director, who joined a swath of other business, education, and political leaders, including the president and COO of the Coca-Cola Company, as trustees.

At the Class of 1989 Commencement, Tom gave his last address in that forum. In closing, he offered a prayer for the new graduates, seen again in the looped cursive of his notes:

> May you [do] work of deep skill + care in professions that uplift the world + its people.
>
> May you raise families w/ great care as you pass on the values you've been given by your families and friends here gathered.
>
> May you serve your communities in which you live + work + worship.
>
> May you open your hearts to a God of care who will give you strength again + again to be better than you are or imagined.

Over the summer, the Board of Regents approved a new dorm for construction with a fall 1990 opening date. The four story building would include a unique mixture of multi-student suites and single-bed rooms, arranged around a landscaped courtyard. The dorm's price tag was estimated at $3 million, a figure which would be met primarily through donations. As enrollment among residential students swelled, UP's facilities crews were hard at work modifying two-person rooms to accommodate three, while rooms formerly used by dorm housekeepers were converted to provide extra single rooms. There simply wasn't enough dorm space, and the new hall would be sorely needed within two years.

With the influx of new students came the influx of new ideas for campus life, and new problems: A major proposal considered in fall 1989 involved the possible adoption of Pizza Hut stands across campus, a move seen at other institutions that had retained Marriott Food Services for their campus meal plans. There was also a wave of car thefts, ten in total that semester, whose perpetrator was never caught. In another instance of the university developing internal wellness publications, a brochure on date rape and resources associated with care and public safety was produced and distributed to the Health Center, Residence Life, and Information Center, among other high-traffic campus spots. It was an expansion of resources first offered the previous year, starting with talks on rape prevention among students. And in the residence halls, Jack Roscoe assured *The Beacon* that UP didn't have a drinking problem, but nevertheless promoted a "Party Sensibly (P.S.)" messaging approach to student alcohol consumption. Roscoe said a zero tolerance policy wasn't "realistic."

That semester the ASUP, by one vote, failed to remove a restriction on alcohol at the River Rage dance, which developed a reputation after the 1988 debacle. Meanwhile, Father Charles Schreck, CSC, who had taken over the Office of Volunteer Services from Father Joe Corpora, left his position to seek treatment for alcoholism. A candid piece involving Schreck ran in *The Beacon*, covering his decision with careful objectivity and care. These developments marked a decided change in the campus's tone toward alcohol, a more reserved and careful tone than had been seen throughout the early eighties.

In September, Tom was chosen to serve on the newly established Multnomah County Library Board of Directors alongside twelve others selected by County Commission Chair Gladys McCoy. Portland businessman Bill Naito served as an interim chairman of the board through the writing of bylaws and election of permanent officers. A few weeks later, Tom was also elected to the World Affairs Council of Oregon's Board of Trustees in its annual reorganization. He was looking forward to service on both boards, as he planned to jet back and forth to South Bend for trustee meetings.

In October, the UP Self-Study wrapped up and the Steering Committee prepared its findings and recommendations to the Board of Regents. Included were recommendations to reduce teaching workloads, the adoption of campus-wide mailboxes, revising the core curriculum, and the creation of an open forum series on campus issues. The latter sought engagement similar to the town-hall style meetings Tom held in residence halls during the first weeks of his presidency, only more issue specific. One forum Tom proposed was a discussion of the university budget, which was still a sore topic for some.

It was also that month when US News & World Report announced their ratings of colleges and universities across the country. In the Regional schools section, UP was ranked #11 out of the Top 15, the only Oregon-based institution to make the list. Tom offered his reaction to *The Oregonian*: "We're always pleased when there's external recognition of the kind of quality we know is present at the University. It then becomes a confirmation of the improvements we have been striving for (in) the past few years." He cited the university's core curriculum (largely organized around liberal arts), small class sizes, and increased faculty interface as UP's major strengths. It was in a triumphant spirit that Tom flew to South Bend for his first Notre Dame trustee meeting, attending on October 26. He would stay in Indiana two more days.

On October 28, he flew west to Santa Rosa, California, where he attended a Louisiana-Pacific board meeting, most likely a presentation on L-P's quarterly earnings report. Tom then flew north to Hillsboro, Oregon, the next morning. Since his journey had originated from Portland International Airport, he got a ride from Hillsboro to PDX to retrieve his car. That afternoon, Tom drove his Toyota back across the city, taking Columbia Boulevard as he thought about getting back to work. He reflected on his trip to South Bend, no doubt, and considered how greatly things had changed since he attended—while so much still remained the same. Perhaps the same thought occurred to him as he pictured the Bluff in twenty years, and wondered what would remain timeless against the relentless pull of time. As he drove, thinking about the future while his radio played, Norman Countryman's truck passed by.

And then, just like that, Father Tom was gone.

Part Four: This Is Death

1989–PRESENT

Something has changed. The coffee cups, the smoke, the priorities, the whining about work undone or work to do, the gossip, the expensive clothing, the "look good," the cars lined in the parking lot, and—the ghost. Sunglasses won't shade it away; wake up children; this is death.

Anonymous
The Beacon (1989)

Chapter 29

Funeral March

The news of Tom's death spread quickly, and it left the campus shell-shocked. Since his first days in Portland, he had made himself known and available to students. He was so ubiquitous to campus life that his name had been associated, at least to one student, with the very idea of a priest. A former student once counseled by Father Richard Berg, the dean of the College of Arts and Sciences, referred to a priest as "Fatheroddo Smith." When Berg asked what the student meant, he said he had thought all priests were called "Fatheroddo," not just Tom. It was like the sun had vanished, the last rays of his light, a single desk lamp, illuminating an empty office in West Hall, waiting for him to return.

As Tom's body was cut out of the wreckage of his Toyota, Father Joe Corpora went to Howard Hall to meet him for their regular Sunday swim together. When he let himself in, he found the water in the pool undisturbed. He suspected Tom had already come and gone, and thought nothing of his absence. Later, he'd go to dinner expecting to see him there. Instead, he found the other Holy Cross priests gathered, talking quietly. When they all saw Corpora, one priest turned to another and said, "Take him outside and tell him." That's how Father Joe learned his best friend had died. Not long after, the bell at St. Mary's Center chimed forty-five times, one for each year of Tom's short life.

On Sunday nights at UP, a Mass was held in the Chapel next door at 10:30 p.m. That night, it was packed with students, faculty, anyone on campus who knew Tom—which was almost everyone. Father Michael Delaney, CSC, presided over the Mass and spoke only briefly about the shared grief the campus was experiencing. He instead emphasized trusting in God and praying for Tom's surviving relatives, his mother Catherine and adopted sister Mary. That night, UP's Director of Public Relations and Information Services Paul Melhuish had nightmares about his job, and the coming days of press inquiries.

The next morning, Father Charles Sherrer, CSC, UP's academic vice president, sent an all-campus memo describing the plan for Tom's funeral. Father Richard Rutherford, the man who had coordinated the construction of Chapel of Christ the Teacher with Pietro Belluschi, was chosen to organize Tom's services. The plan was anything but simple: a three-event funeral march, spanning two states and two college campuses—a funeral service in Chiles Center on November 1, All Saints Day; then a wake, memorial service, and burial in South Bend, Indiana, on November 2, All Souls Day. It remains customary in the Holy Cross brotherhood to be interred at the South Bend Holy Cross Cemetery, necessitating the body's transport. Father Rutherford consulted a wealth of sources in planning the commemoration, to be sure that his friend's funeral was done with proper grace.

For the second time, Executive Vice President Dr. Arthur Schulte became acting president. Schulte's first term came after Brother Wilson resigned the presidency in 1981, a period defined by the possibilities of transformation in the coming years. Schulte's second term, by contrast, was defined more by the horror of Tom's death and the sudden uncertainty it left for the university. Schulte's service wasn't long term, as he never desired to be president. He was, instead, a meticulous record-keeper and financial administrator whose steady hand was called upon to provide interim leadership when situations demanded it. He would serve until the regents found a successor.

On Monday, classes were canceled and campus flags flown at half mast. Some wandered campus aimlessly. Schulte's administrative assistant Rose Marie Corah spoke to *The Beacon* about work in West Hall that day:

> It seems so empty. Every morning he would come in and get his cup of coffee. He was good about saying "good morning" every day. And, after lunch, he would come in to get his piece of candy out of the candy jar. Those are little, but important things.

Corah, whose role assisting Dr. Schulte also supported Tom, liked the young president and shared the collective shock of his death. His absence was palpable, the quiet surrounding it heavy. And, according to Corah, he left for South Bend without saying goodbye.

Tom had his own administrative assistant, a sixty-six-year-old woman named Evangeline Schopf. Asked about her impressions of the late president, she said:

> He was a very brilliant young man and his door was always open. He was a very busy man but he always had time for students and he wanted to work along with people but he did not force his authority on them.

At forty-five, Tom was still—despite greying hair—a model of youthfulness and vitality. To learn of his death created a sense of existential vertigo on the Bluff, the same feeling of imbalance when a close friend you expect to live for many years is suddenly gone. As in most of those cases, there aren't the words to explain the grief. "Ashes to ashes, dust to dust" carries new meaning when a friend dies, and yet life carries on, albeit quieter and a bit darker.

That afternoon, a silver hearse brought Tom's body to campus in a dark casket. Over 1,000 mourners stood by as local reporters took photos. Pallbearers for the initial ingress of the body into the chapel included ASUP President Bruce Patterson, two associate professors, and a member of the Board of Regents. The procession was followed by a student choir who, to flute accompaniment, sang "On Eagle's Wings." Tom's casket rested on a stretcher at the center of the chapel's worship space, where a vigil was planned through Wednesday. There, students would take hour-long shifts watching over his body. Around the clock, from sunrise to sunrise, students took their turns standing like silent guards over the remains of a fallen soldier.

The local news weekly *St. Johns Review*'s Virginia Grantier spoke to several students and priests on campus that Monday, including Father Joe Corpora. Corpora talked about how Tom lived simply and happily in his small campus apartment despite sixteen to eighteen hour work days and swimming a mile a day. He talked about Tom's cooking, a gift he shared with his friends, and his lifelong love of Italian food. "He was a very busy administrator," Corpora said, "but he remained at heart a priest."

Tom's Portland funeral service was held in the Chiles Center. Campus was closed to allow anyone who wished to mourn and process their collective grief. The Eucharist, such a seminal part of Tom's service and ministry, was not celebrated due to a Catholic custom of forgoing Communion on All Saint's Day. In attendance at Chiles, among 3,000 mourners, were several local officials: Oregon Governor Neil Goldschmidt, Multnomah County Commission Chair Gladys McCoy, Portland Mayor Bud Clark, and City Commissioner Earl Blumenauer. Father Monk Malloy flew out from South Bend to attend the service, as did ten other Pacific Northwest college presidents. Tom's mother Catherine and sister Mary both attended, sitting in the front row. Catherine wept throughout the service, and photos of the day show her composed but distraught, still caught in disbelief. It was a shared emotion. A student who wrote about the event for *The Beacon* recalled meeting Father Joe Corpora there, saying he'd "never felt more pain in another human being."

A single trumpet sounded through the arena as a choir began a solemn rendition of "Ave Maria." Father Paul Waldschmidt offered a greeting and introductory rites. A rendition of William Walsham How's hymn "For All the Saints" followed, then prayers. Father Waldschmidt gave the homily, and Portland Archbishop Father William Levada assisted with the liturgy. Waldschmidt, who became close with Tom after his assumption of the presidency, spoke from his own grief in his remarks:

> Because death carries with it such a temporal finality, there is really no adequate way to prepare for it. Even when it comes after a long and lingering illness to one who has lived a full and meaningful life—it still requires great strength of will to cope with it. When it comes to one in the prime of life, one who has so much to contribute, one so gifted as Father Tom Oddo—it is all the more difficult to accept and comprehend.

Waldschmidt said that "the University became his life," and that Tom's "seven years of service speak for themselves. His accomplishments are all around us." And while Christian scripture did not provide an easy answer for why a man with such potential and promise would be taken so soon by God, Waldschmidt affirmed that no one could argue keeping someone from the glory of God and Heaven, those things which now embraced Tom's soul.

Other speakers in the service included Bruce Patterson, chair of the Board of Regents Phillip J. Robinson, and Academic Senate Chair Dr. Steven Ward. Ward, who was also chair of the Communication Studies Department, had been a member of Tom's hiring committee and recalled how he had electrified the room with his energy. "He raised our expectations and we became better than we were." Archbishop Father William Levada said a few words, and pronounced that "One day we shall joyfully greet him again." He gave his final blessing, then circled the casket with incense. "Come to His Aid, O Saints of God" was sung as the pallbearers carried Tom's body out of Chiles Center and into a waiting hearse. Father

Joe Corpora was one of them. The arena of mourning turned inward, attendees weeping quietly as Catherine Oddo and the funeral party followed her son out the door.

Tom would be flown to South Bend that night, and Catherine would rejoin him at Notre Dame. His body would lay in a second wake there on Thursday at the Moreau Seminary Chapel, where more than 300 would attend. One of them was Father Richard Warner, the man who met Tom at Logan Airport that night in 1982, who had persuaded him to apply for the presidency. He was particularly effusive, grief stricken at the loss of one of his greatest pupils. He spoke on what Tom meant for the university:

> Tom's seven plus years as president were marvelous and memorable. They were a sign of God's grace reflected in one of God's truly holy priests, and in one of God's zealous disciples ....
>
> The seven years represented a time of confidence—an infectious optimism and trust in what could be brought about by men and women working together for common cause. This confidence mirrored Tom's approach to life and his path to holiness.

In Father Warner's opinion, Tom was a man who walked with Jesus, and whose life emulated the most immaculate of Christian lives:

> Tom was a man filled with life, and a person of faith knows that true fullness of life resides only in complete identification with the words and the actions of the life of Jesus.
>
> Tom was a man whose life was interwoven with the life of Jesus.

And while Tom's service with Dignity was hardly mentioned in his funeral liturgy, if at all, Father Warner briefly spoke to that chapter of Tom's life, saying "Tom's love and concern for others, often those seeking acceptance of self and others, and always the poor, meant that his own life combined admirably the passion of the activist and the depth of the contemplative." Father Monk Malloy, who served as the homilist—a role usually occupied by his late friend in such events—spoke about a recent conversation that he and Tom had about morality. Monk called this Tom's epitaph. At one point in the conversation, Tom declared:

> I know that I have been a sinner and I have failed many times. But my image of God is one of love and healing. I figure if I give my life in service, the God I believe in will understand about my weaknesses and celebrate the good things I was able to accomplish in my life.

On Friday afternoon, Tom was buried in Holy Cross Community Cemetery at Notre Dame, across from the plots of dozens of other Holy Cross educators. For those in the brotherhood, this is their Arlington: Among the entombed are Father Edouard Sorrin, CSC, the first Holy Cross missionary sent to the Americas (who later founded the university), and Father Ted Hesburgh, CSC, that ebullient lion of Catholic higher education. A line of mourners walked the frosty asphalt road to the gravesite, a deeply somber image captured in the dark of the Associated Press's black and white press photos. As the sun set behind the trees, and temperatures dropped to freezing, Tom's casket was lowered into the ground. Four men, Holy Cross priests, held each other and cried. Catherine Oddo wept nearby, clutching her coat against the cold as dirt was shoveled into the grave. A stillness fell over the crowd. After nearly a week of funeral services, wakes, memorials, obituaries, eulogies public and private, and the grief of two college campuses, Tom was at peace.

Chapter 30

"The grief of our great loss"

Almost immediately after the crash, remembrances of Tom poured in. Within these memories came the roots of his myth, which would only grow as those who knew him grew older themselves. In many places, most notably in the pages of *The Beacon*, there were repeated comparisons to John F. Kennedy, the Bluff becoming a modern-day Camelot. The 1990 edition of *The Log*, UP's yearbook, was dedicated to Tom's memory. The first pages include a piece on Tom's legacy, titled "One Brief Shining Moment … " which noted his growing mythos:

> to many of us Fr. Oddo seemed to be the hope of a new generation at the University—a John F. Kennedy of the Eighties. His plans to improve the University and his dream of a new Residence Hall were all cut short by his untimely death. With Fr. Oddo one felt that the age of Camelot was upon us once again, where the exchange of knowledge as well as the moulding of young minds in an international community helped put the University of Portland in the forefront among Universities throughout the United States.
>
> Long after this yearbook has come out and is lying on a dusty old shelf, Fr. Oddo's legacy will still be alive in a new generation of UP students because,
>
> *For one brief shining moment, there stood Camelot.*

The Oregonian wrote on Halloween 1989, two days after his death, that "the University of Portland loses a president who has built its academic strengths and made it a greater resource for the metropolitan area." The minor piece remarked how Oregon's strength in higher education stemmed largely from its small, independent colleges and universities, and how Tom's efforts helped build that reputation. The next day, sports columnist Terry Frei penned an article, "Oddo's death leaves one asking: Why?" which recounted his first time meeting Tom:

> Here it was, nearly midnight, and [Tom] told us he was going swimming.
>
> "That's one of the good things about this job," he said, smiling. "I get a key to the pool." …
>
> On this particular evening, he watched a UP basketball game, then attended the informal reception of the staff, boosters and a few outsiders in the old student center. He was not a particularly ebullient man, but he worked the room nonetheless.
>
> No exuberant backslaps. No pumping handshakes. Just smiles and conversation before he headed for the water.
>
> For one thing—and this is what I've nodded at every time I've heard it—Father Tom Oddo was always there, at everything, it seemed. So nobody in the UP community, or outsiders familiar with it, ever was surprised to see him.

The Beacon dedicated its November 2 edition to full-length coverage of Tom's funeral. The editorial staff included its own remembrance of Tom under the headline "Pulling through":

> Poised and articulate, sensitive and caring, charismatic and modest. Few people can claim to be even one of these, but the late Rev. Thomas C. Oddo possessed all of these attributes and more.
>
> His death has come as a shock to the students of UP, not because of what he was but, rather, who he was. Fr. Oddo could never have imagined that he would inspire such love and affection from the campus community ….
>
> He will be remembered as a man who could turn a good phrase, and draw one into his speeches. But there was more to Tom Oddo than that. He was a man who lived life for the moment, who wished only to love and be loved. It is for this reason that students continue to gather in the Chapel of Christ the Teacher to weep and to pray.

Editor-in-Chief Troy Zaboukos penned his own piece on Tom's legacy, "Oddo reached goals even by unconventional means," which ran next to a picture of Tom in his recent Donkey Basketball game. "With the energy and enthusiasm of a John F. Kennedy, Fr. Oddo not only coordinated University forces, he developed a personality for the campus." The piece discussed his moves on co-ed housing, AIDS education, and favoring dissent in the classroom—even against the express teachings of the Vatican. It spoke about how Tom made himself available, a constant visibility which previous pieces in *The Beacon* lampooned. A common refrain on campus developed among administrators that Tom never had time to meet, he was too busy chatting with the campus housekeepers. In practice, Tom tried to make time for everyone, from the newest facilities staff to the highest-level deputies in his cabinet. Students who took his Theological Problems in Human Sexuality class recalled how he insisted that his role as teacher came first, and his presidency second.

For the students and alumni who knew him, even tangentially or at a distance, the grief for Tom was palpable. The November 9 edition of *The Beacon* published multiple letters to the editor, including one from a graduate who learned about Tom's death reading *The Boston Herald*. He wrote that seeing the leaves turn on the Rhode Island shoreline as he sailed past reminded him of the fall foliage he saw on the Bluff when he first matriculated in 1982. There, Tom "showed us what participatory leadership was by being on my team in a game of extended tag."

Another letter received by *The Beacon* came from an anonymous writer, who reflected on the "body in the chapel":

> There's a body in the chapel. The boys are playing football on the leaves on the green grass in the sunshine. There's a body in the chapel. A boy kisses his girlfriend. Traffic hurries by. People are on paths they travel daily, to and fro, here and there, the same routine. The shadow, the presence; it's following, lurking behind backpacks, briefcases, lecture podiums, the buildings themselves. It's reaching, waving its transparent hand, beckoning, begging to be acknowledged, whispering, wandering, waiting. Something has changed. The coffee cups, the smoke, the priorities, the whining about work undone or work to do, the gossip, the expensive clothing, the "look good," the cars lined in the parking lot, and—the ghost. Sunglasses won't shade it away; wake up children, this is death. It's irreversible, cold, sudden, and final. It's destined—do not think otherwise. Life is unstable, ever-changing—not youthful, pretend, and free. Sift through your cloud of safety; reach through, up, into the hollow nothing that holds no

> air. Feel it. It's peaceful, empty, worry-free. Those that notice and ponder, sorrow only for yourselves. You do not understand Life. You are not free. Step back from yourselves, those that do not ponder. You are even farther from the truth. Where there is Hope, sorrow forms in the gut, for the aching of the bodies still in motion and their heart-felt sentiments, memories, regrets. Otherwise, sorrow is pointless, an emptiness that is not peaceful. Stop playing football and look up into the sky. Hold a handful of air. Watch a leaf fall. Stop your car, your work, your shopping. Feel Life. It isn't all of those things. It means more. It has always meant more; you just didn't know it. Look up into the sky; there's a body in the chapel.

Vijay Shanmugam, an infrequent contributor to *The Beacon*, commended the paper for their coverage of the tragedy, and wrote a bit about Tom's legacy:

> The Rev. Thomas C. Oddo not only touched the University as a whole, but also the lives of every individual, and your publication was very essential to the community at such a time. People and the rest of the University community will remember not only what he did but what he stood for. He had confidence in man and gave men confidence in the future. He taught mankind that the process of rediscovering the world was not over. He transformed the American spirit.

And there were the remembrances which ran in *The Beacon*, *St. Johns Review*, *The Oregonian*, *The Catholic Sentinel* and other newspapers. Each spoke to a piece of Tom's character:

> Father Oddo built this university into what it is today. He built enrollment, improved the grounds and built the Chiles Center. He was very visible to the students ... We had easier access to him. This is rare for a president of a university. I really miss him.
>
> Erin Meads, Freshman
>
> I think that he was a very beautiful person. He had an ability to draw you into his sermon and make you feel as though every word he spoke was directed at you.
>
> Allison McCormick, Sophomore
>
> He was a professor, but he was also a friend. He touched on topics that were controversial to traditional Catholic beliefs; he wasn't critical of

> things that he didn't necessarily believe in himself. He was an exceptionally nice man, very understanding. He touched the hearts of so many people on campus in different ways: as a friend, as a professor ... He was a very special person.
>
> Kellie Roche, Junior

> Father Oddo was a model to the students at the university. He was the embodiment of what the University of Portland graduate should be, in the way he could articulate himself in his speeches and when he spoke to you on a personal basis ... For me, Father Oddo was the university.
>
> Romen Bose, Junior
> Editor of *The Log* Yearbook 1989/90

> He brought a lot of life and vitality to the campus.
>
> Kelly Kryger, Senior

For Catholics who attended UP, their prior experience with the church usually involved their local priest and their region's diocese. Familiar characters were older white men ordained between the Great Depression and the end of World War II, who were now the primary religious authorities in their communities. Tom was something completely different. He was young, engaging, encouraging of dialogue, and an advocate for peace. He changed perceptions of what a priest could be for those who grew up Catholic, those of other faiths, and those without a faith at all.

Obituaries for Tom ran in dozens of newspapers nationwide, after the Associated Press printed a small blurb on his passing. Major outlets like *The New York Times* and the *New York Daily News* picked up the obit, as did regional papers like *The Salem Statesman-Journal* (Oregon), *Pacific Daily News* (Guam), and *The South Bend Tribune*, Notre Dame's local newspaper. Smaller papers throughout the western US also covered Tom's death, with obits appearing in *The Daily Herald* (Provo, UT), *The Albany Democrat-Herald* (Albany, OR), *The North County Blade-Citizen* (Oceanside, CA), *The Bremerton Sun* (Bremerton, WA), *Longview Daily News* (Longview, WA), and the *Journal and Courier* (Lafayette, IN), among others. Within the Portland metro area, *The Oregonian* devoted multiple pages and column inches to Tom's story throughout late October and November. *The Columbian*, based across the Columbia River in Vancouver, Washington, provided their own coverage of the tragedy.

In the wake of Tom's death, the Holy Cross fathers were particularly affected. Father Warner, in his eulogy at Tom's Moreau Seminary wake, said the fathers were "devastated and all but inconsolable" at the loss. A pervasive sorrow fell over the Congregation, so intense that *The Beacon* staff writers included a column titled "Can We Help?" sincerely offering whatever they could to their own grieving fathers:

> We're concerned.
>
> To members of the Holy Cross community, we are afraid many of you are trying extra hard to continue to be the forever-strong, spiritual leaders of our community during this difficult time in coping with Fr. Oddo's death.
>
> While we appreciate your example, we ask you to please not be afraid to outwardly share emotions with students of the campus community beyond the walls of The Chapel. Many of us feel close to members of your family, and we need to be needed. Just as you do.
>
> The grief of our great loss has had an equalizing effect. We are levelled.

Over the following weeks, a story emerged in *The Catholic Sentinel* and *The Oregonian* about a young farmworker named Santiago Ventura Morales. Ventura was Mixtec, born in Oaxaca, migrating to the US in the early '80s when he was fourteen. In July 1986, he was arrested for murdering another farmworker in Sandy, Oregon; he was later convicted and given a ten-year-to-life sentence in October. During the trial, he was given a Spanish interpreter, despite not regularly speaking the language. It was widely believed Ventura was innocent, framed for a crime committed by another perpetrator—purportedly another farmworker who left the migrant camp shortly after the murder. In light of new evidence, some jurors sought to reverse their decision and convince the state to drop Ventura's charges. After initial push back from the court, momentum grew for Ventura's release in 1989.

Around that time, *Catholic Sentinel* writer Donna Stepak spoke with Tom about Ventura, and explored the possibility of a scholarship for his education while incarcerated. It didn't take much to convince Tom of the need:

> Without hesitation, Father Tom expressed interest in having Santiago as a student at his institution. Instead of bureaucratic stumbling blocks, Father Tom answered my request with generous confidence in doing the right thing for a person who has been wronged.

Stepak recalled how, in 1982, Tom declared that the university should inspire in its students a value-based concern and drive for service to all people. "Clearly," she wrote, "Father Tom practiced what he preached." She would announce the scholarship offer to Morales at a press conference shortly after Tom's death. She also announced Ventura's appeal of the charges. Paul De Muniz, who would later serve as the forty-first chief justice of the Oregon Supreme Court, served as Ventura's lead defense attorney. From these efforts, Ventura was given an early release in 1991, and the charges were soon dropped for lack of evidence.

In the aftermath of his wrongful conviction and incarceration, he accepted the full-ride scholarship UP offered him, and graduated with a bachelors of social work, with a minor in political science in 1996. He worked for California Rural Legal Assistance in Fresno, and later the Oregon Law Center, providing legal resources to migrant workers. His case would eventually lead to changes in state law around court interpreters, and the creation of the Oregon Innocence Project in 2014, a legacy Tom remains a little-known part of.

Before long, university officials and students were considering how the campus should commemorate Tom's service. A proposal for a new soccer stadium would briefly carry the name "Rev. Thomas C. Oddo Stadium," but was later changed to Harry A. Merlo Field after the president of Louisiana-Pacific, a major booster of the project. The new dorm building Tom had pursued, approved by the Board of Regents, would also briefly carry his name in memoriam. That project was abandoned due to lack of funding in the early '90s, but it was not the end of plans to build a proper memorial.

A bundle of wheat tacked onto Tom's office door after his death made its way to the Shipstad Hall basement in February 1990. This symbol represented a handful of ideas, including life and resurrection, and referred to the Parable of the Wheat and Tares in the Book of Matthew: Jesus compares the kingdom of Heaven to a wheat field surreptitiously sown with weeds. The farmer tells his servants to wait until harvest time to separate the wheat from the tares. This represented the final judgment after the apocalypse, where the faithful would be separated from the wicked. The parable has a long history of interpretation that deserves more space than I can give it here. Nevertheless, the symbology is strong.

That spring, students were still discussing holding a final memorial to Tom prior to Commencement in an attempt to keep the ceremonies from becoming "a sad eulogy." Despite these intentions, the University Development Office announced the creation of the Reverend Thomas C. Oddo

Scholarship at the May event, a $100,000 endowed scholarship fund, created by donations made in the wake of his death. The scholarship continues to be awarded today.

For his successor, the regents picked Father David Tyson. Tyson was previously in the mix of curated finalists for Father Ted Hesburgh's spot at Notre Dame, a signal that he could be considered for future advancement. From the beginning of his term, Tyson had big shoes to fill, building on Tom's momentum and introducing himself to the university. So big was the learning curve that Tyson gave his first year as president a theme—The Year of Discovery: Teaching, Faith, and Service.

The Beacon was recognized in September 1990 as a "Regional Pacemaker" by the Associate Collegiate Press for its coverage of several major topics in 1989—first among them, Tom's death and funeral services. One year after the crash, October 29, 1990, a memorial Mass was held in the Chapel of Christ the Teacher. Father Tyson moderated the event, and Father Rutherford gave the homily. In spring 1991, the final funds needed to launch Tom's memorial scholarship were raised, making the awards available to students in the 1991/92 academic year. By then, the dream of a memorial residence hall had been shelved by the regents, as had the idea of a memorial fountain at the Buckley Center turnaround, first proposed by ASUP presidential candidate Mike Paluska.

In September 1992, a museum in Shipstad Hall opened, the predecessor of the present-day UP Museum and Archive. One of its first exhibits was "The Life and Times of Fr. Tom Oddo, CSC." Later in the academic year, a local sculptor named Donovan Peterson began work on what would become UP's seminal monument to Tom's legacy: "an 'interactive sculpture' of Christ the Teacher and several other figures, with space for 'people to be involved with it.'" The sculpture, which Tom had originally proposed in 1987 as a symbol of the university's dual Catholicity and openness to other faiths, would be placed between Buckley Center and the Pilot House in a triangle lot which met students on their walks across campus. The Rev. Thomas C. Oddo, CSC, Memorial Plaza was first mentioned by *The Beacon* in August 1995, as other major campus renovations concluded. Peterson's sculpture, officially titled *Christ the Teacher and Four Students*, was central to the new space. At its dedication in September, Tom's mother Catherine once again flew to Portland to attend. She had been the principal donor behind the scenes to complete the project. The sculpture and memorial remain on the Bluff today in the shadow of Franz Hall, the home of the UP School of Education.

Memorial masses for Tom continued for years after his death. The Western Orthodox Church held multiple memorials, including one in November 1993 to mark the fourth anniversary. The November 6 event was hosted by St. Paul's Western Orthodox Parish in Cambridge, Massachusetts, near where Tom cut his teeth in activism and his early ministry. Unlike other memorials to Tom, the 1993 memorial mentioned his part in co-founding Dignity/Boston, and his work with gay and lesbian Catholics. The event was meant to be "a continuation of the efforts of [Tom] to spread the Gospel within the gay and lesbian Community," according to Paul Diederich, Dignity USA's former president and Tom's longtime friend. Diederich had since joined the Western Orthodox Church as a priest, and served as organizer for the Mass.

CHAPTER 31

Journey to Your Soul

Tom's afterlife took on a strange dynamic in the decade after his death. Father Richard Berg told me a story about an anonymous woman in the 1990s who called the University of Notre Dame with a morbid inquiry: whether she could bury her miscarried child next to Tom's grave in Holy Cross Cemetery. It was quickly decided that the burial would not be possible, out of respect for the congregation and considering all of the logistics involved. It did not help that, for several months out of the year, the cemetery grounds were frozen solid, requiring a burial in warmer months. The woman never called back, and the story became a curious footnote in Tom's larger saga. It would not be the last.

In 1997, a book appeared that suggested Tom was hard at work in the afterlife, a restless soul offering insight and support from the great beyond. *Journey to Your Soul: The Angels Guide to Love and Wholeness* was marketed as, "a true experience about two women who, together with their angels, went on a spiritual journey to find their souls and the meaning of life."

The authors, Carole Marlene Sletta and Nancy Ambrose Snodgrass, channeled the spirits of two angels, "Cameron" and "Tom," whose wisdom comprised the majority of the book. "Tom" was Father Tom, who, according to the book's blurb, brought "messages of love and [showed] that the primary purpose in all of our lives is to evolve into deeper levels of loving ourselves and others." A reference to the book, then newly released, appeared in an *Oregonian* story on channeling angels through Ouija-like talking boards:

> The authors, from Tigard and Tualatin, respectively, say they relay messages from the Rev. Tom Oddo, a Holy Cross priest and late University of Portland president ....

> Sletta and Snodgrass say Oddo has definite ideas about how the church must change—including ending priestly celibacy.

Though these statements would've been easily identifiable with Tom in life, other statements attributed to him in death (and the afterlife) would give those who knew Tom great pause:

> I had grown weary of the expectations. I felt as if I had lost myself in my service to others. My love of God grew immensely as I followed my spiritual path. A deepening occurred within me and with it gratitude for the love I received from God. As I deepened spiritually, a schism began to develop between my earthly side and my spiritual side. I felt less and less connected to the people around me and to my deeper self. My soul hungered for the opportunity to be whole, but my chosen faith and path did not allow an integration of both sides of me. This saddened me and caused pain as my life progressed. I did not feel comfortable when people worshipped me. (Page 44)

In another section, "Tom" discusses a deep-seated loneliness from his presidential perch:

> I wanted to know many people around me. I wished to spend time with friends and be able to relax. However, so many respected my position that they froze when they were around me. I had only a few very close friends who were able to be themselves with me. It was as if I made others uncomfortable when I was being myself. I stopped being myself because of the discomfort it caused others. They expected a god, not a man. I understood that and it saddened me, for I was a man.
>
> Few people were brave enough to ask how I was. What was I worried about? Few expected me to worry or to have feelings. Where was the honesty and understanding that comes from sharing with friends for me? It seemed few could relate to where I was in my growth. People seemed awkward in their conversations with me. The fact that I was causing them to feel uncomfortable distressed me deeply. I felt so much love, and wanted to share it with others. My position only allowed for a relationship like that with God.

> That caused me great pain. God brought people into my life to help me grow and be my teachers. Earthly rules forbid me from accepting God's gifts. (Page 54)

The book and its suggestion that Nancy Snodgrass, the author and channeler of "Tom," knew the living Tom intimately in life are curious. In multiple places, "Tom's" transcription states that Nancy is part of a larger plan, God's plan for them both, to spread the word of life after death. In at least one part of the text, it's suggested their friendship had some forbidden undertones:

> Only on rare occasions did I connect with someone on a deeper level. Nancy was one of these people. I would look into her eyes and the feeling went deep into my soul. However, I knew I could not develop the friendship. She was married and I was a priest. The taboos prevented it. The pain I felt from not being able to develop that friendship was enormous. My soul desired the opportunity to grow. God gives us friendships so that we learn to feel. I now know that the more I feel, the closer I am to God and the wholeness I seek. I began to feel deeply for Nancy. (Page 62)
>
> Something happened to me that woke up my personal feelings. Nancy came into my life. I never spoke a word or gave her a hint at the growing feeling of love I felt. I knew it was not possible for me to express my inner feelings to her due to being a priest. But the joy she radiated was a magnet to me. I enjoyed working beside her. Even unspoken love is a magnificent thing. (Page 93)
>
> Now I am able to express my love for her and not feel shameful. You know it's shameful on earth for a priest to love a woman. How sad that is, as it destroys the soul and blocks God's intention of learning to love and feel through relationships. (Page 94)
>
> Do you know that I finally had decided, after over three years of feeling this way, that I needed to be whole and follow my soul to be complete? I was ready to give everything up and reveal my love to her. Nothing else seemed to matter. And yet, how could I leave my beloved church? I searched for an answer that would end my conflict. God allowed me to give up everything and be with Nancy, just not exactly as I thought. He wanted me to love her and heal from here and then write to you in this book. (Page 134)

It is speculative to determine exactly where Nancy and Tom would've met, as Nancy was never a UP student. Whether she was a parishioner of Tom's at St. Clement's, or a student of his at another campus, is also not known. However, a "Nancy Snodgrass" is named as associate director of United Way of Oregon in Portland, an organization of which Tom served as a board member for several years, in a 1986 *Salem Statesman-Journal* story. We should consider how, for a book written in 1997, there is a decent level of information provided about Tom's life, suggesting Nancy had access to multiple publications which told Tom's story, and that she actively researched Tom in an pre-Google era. It is likely, then, that they did know each other. What is uncertain is how she came to write observations of "Tom's" family life and boyhood that appeared to be in stark contrast to actual events:

> My childhood was quite difficult. There was little love in our home. Our existence was built on guilt and shame. Daily my mother asked forgiveness of God for our sinful ways and expected me to pray with her. I got the message early on that I was bad. From constantly hearing "Shame on you," and "We must ask for God's forgiveness," I soon came to the conclusion that I was bad. I was shameful. (Page 92)
>
> I was made to feel shameful as a child for feeling any emotion. My strict upbringing encouraged continual prayer and self sacrifice. I soon learned that my needs and feelings were not important. To express my own needs or feelings was considered a weakness. My father would say, "It's up to you to be strong and take care of your mother and sister while I am away." (Page 111)
>
> My father taught me as a child that I must be a man and not cry. My church taught me that I must sacrifice myself for God. Slowly, as I progressed along my path, and was maturing and feeling deeper, I felt my soul straining to be free of the strict confinements of the priesthood. (Page 112)

This depiction suggests "Tom" begrudgingly pursued the priesthood, and subsequently felt trapped by the customs of his vocation. "Tom" is written here in quotation marks to delineate the statements from Tom we can confirm. In more than one section, certain details are shared that seem to be out of step with how Tom would interact or speak.

For example, "Tom" refers to serving on the Notre Dame Board of Trustees, and how he believed such service would help to, in time, change the customs of the Catholic Church from within—a goal that Tom never explicitly set out to achieve. While he fought for inclusion and greater pastoral counseling for gay Catholics within the church, Tom did not dispute the Bible nor disrespect the diocesan leadership. In reference to the institution, "Tom" calls it *Notre Dame University*, rather than the *University of Notre Dame*, its proper name. A minor misstatement for the average joe, but a seemingly major error for someone who lived and breathed Catholic higher education.

In another section, "Tom" recalls a fight he had with his sister. This led to his mother shaming him and ordering him to his room. There "Tom" cried and cried, but his prayers were answered by a vision of Jesus, who told him, "Go in peace. All is as it should be. I will help and protect your sister." Experiencing the vision, and subsequent feelings of love and peace washing over him, convinced "Tom" to pursue the priesthood, the vocation he appeared trapped by less than ten pages later.

While it is very possible Nancy Snodgrass knew Tom professionally, even closely, it is unlikely that he would've shared these details with her in life or in death: Some appear to be simply untrue, fabrications of a life imagined rather than a life lived. It is unclear how well *Journey to Your Soul* sold in its initial run from White Phoenix Publishing, an independent outfit in Lake Oswego, Oregon. At least one public talk on the book was held, at the Lloyd Center Barnes & Noble in Portland in March 1998. Portions have been uploaded to the Internet Archive, an eerie entry into the record of Tom's life. No one I interviewed had anything to say about the book, and only one of them had heard of it. Despite its mystery and questionable source material, the book had an impact on its readers.

In November 1999, the *National Catholic Reporter* posted an online list of their readers' favorite books. One entry, from Marie Therese Gass in Clackamas, Oregon, references *Journey to Your Soul.* Even in a laudatory review, Gass was skeptical, but ultimately moved by the book:

> Would you read a spiritual book by someone with unusual charisma, someone you had personally met and admired? If he reminded you and others of Thomas Merton? Absolutely, so far. Now what if this man had died and was speaking through someone else? Pish-tosh and nonsense, I said—not interested in channeling, thank you very much. Then the book arrived by surprise in a package from a friend. I hesitantly peeked under the cover and, the next thing I knew, was on the last page. I wondered if I had been so absorbed in the book only because of Tom.

She spoke graciously about what "Tom" revealed through Nancy's channeling:

> Tom (in the book) says that soul and body aren't necessarily ready to go at the same moment—that his earth-soul was dying well before the accident. He says he was burning out and that, like his fellow celibate priests, he needed more human love. Now, if canonized saints have spoken through the living, why can't a young, vibrant person who dies do the same?

She ended the brief review reflecting on the larger message of the book, and Tom's words, even with skepticism toward the methods used by its authors:

> But leaving out any acceptance of channeling or attraction to Tom's messages, does this book have other values? By its end, I was caught up in optimism and hope for my life and the life of the world. The old memorized phrases about God being all-knowing, infinite, etc., took on new life. This book's repeated chorus is that God is love—not judgment or preachiness.

Regardless of whether the "Tom" of *Journey to Your Soul* was the spirit of Father Tom, or an idealized version used for the book's narrative, the idea that "God is love" full stop was foundational to Tom in life and followed his memory in death. The book is now out of print, though used copies can still be found online.

Chapter 32

Beyond Camelot

The Bluff was full of life as I walked to the Pilot House in September 2023. Students lounged on the lawn and sat at tables studying, while others filed in ahead of me for lunch. A few broke off to the left to get drinks at the bar inside, which looks more like an upscale sports bar and grill than a campus common area. On the TVs, various games were shown on ESPN and ESPN2 while *Talladega Nights: The Ballad of Ricky Bobby* played silently on the largest screen. Sitting in front of it, I found an older man in a polo shirt, wearing a large Holy Cross necklace. Father Richard Berg is nearly as energetic as when he was dean of the College of Arts and Sciences, perhaps even more so. He greeted me with a big smile and a firm handshake. Our excitement was palpable. To Father Dick, the story of Tom Oddo is as much a part of his life's story as his current work, the book *Scars*—a novel about PTSD that will soon be adapted into a film. But to most people, Tom's story is almost completely unknown. That's where I came in.

My first question to Father Dick was "Which word best describes Tom Oddo?" In my head, I had a preconceived notion that it would be something like "leader," "charismatic," or "bold." Without thinking, he said "Tom Oddo is my friend." *Is*, not was. For many decades, Tom still spoke to Dick, and in many of life's trials Dick would seek out Tom for the answer. After all these years, their bond was still strong, and it seems that Dick is not alone. The more I researched, the more I interviewed, and the more I wrote, Tom's presence became clearer and clearer.

Tom Oddo was a stranger to me before that summer, as I finished work on another book, a non-fiction leadership study profiling seven controversial college presidents in the Pacific Northwest. As I researched, Tom's story popped up. It was the curious story of a priest who, at a young age, took the reins of a college adrift and revitalized it for a new kind of a student, and for a new millenium. It was also the story of a foundational, if underappreciated, leader in the early gay rights movement, who believed in the decency of all people and sought to make his church understand the plight of his flock, and of LGBTQ+ people of no religious affiliation.

And what a timely story: While writing this book, I have witnessed a world in the grip of pandemics, runaway technology, the abridgement of civil rights, and the proliferation of genocide and war. Such topics were nothing new to Tom's era, if only more contained by the lack of the internet. Perhaps the reason Tom's story is so timeless is because he was always looking toward the future: Whenever he spoke of peace, he thought of those future generations not yet born. Whenever the topics of computers and computer access, or co-ed housing were broached, he thought of the ways in which society was changing. Whenever he thought about AIDS, he thought about how his university would treat every student from admission to graduation, no matter their health status, and participate in public education about the virus. And whenever Tom thought about God's love, it was universal and belonged to everyone, a notion that continues to draw controversy in the church. No matter the issue, Tom focused on what tomorrow would bring. His board appointments in the weeks prior to his death show his eye was on the future, always looking to build bridges, always trying to weave his campus and city communities together.

Tom was, for most of his life, devoted to teaching. Beyond the call of priesthood, Tom was called to be an educator, and he fully embraced the role no matter what his official job title was. As president, he made a point of teaching undergraduate classes through most of his term, including Theological Problems in Human Sexuality, and planned to keep teaching into retirement. A sign which hung in Shipstad Hall for years included a quote from Tom about the importance of the work to the world and the university:

> Of all the great work that mankind does, none is as important—or as taken for granted—as teaching. At the University of Portland, however, it is our reason for being. In the daily exchange on our campus, in the classroom and the residence hall, on our playing fields and in meeting rooms, minds are molded, hearts are opened, and young lives are shaped. That is a tricky and often difficult business. To do it well requires a scientist's commitment to technique, an artist's gift of passion, and a parent's sense

> of love and devotion. Not everyone is so fully blessed, but those who are are those who teach.

When I asked what Tom's greatest accomplishment was on the Bluff, those that knew him had different, but equally important answers: Father Dick believed Tom's fundraising, contributions to student recruitment, and reforms to the Board of Regents were his greatest achievements. To Father Joe Corpora, it was getting UP to think of itself as "more than a little school" and effectively establishing the university's national reputation. Beyond the academic, Joe firmly believes Tom's work in Dignity created the momentum which led to the partial blessing of same-sex couples by the Vatican under Pope Francis.

Without the work of priests like Tom, he contends, such topics would not have captured the Vatican's attention, and would not have evolved to places of greater acceptance liturgically. And so long as the progress remains fragile, the work remains important: At the time of this writing, the United States Conference of Catholic Bishops, the conglomerated successor of the NCCB and the Conference of Catholic Bishops, has openly agreed with the Trump Administration's endorsement of the gender binary—the erasure of transgender people—in federal policy, after Pope Francis advised American Catholics to choose the "lesser of two evils" in the 2024 election. Progress won can be just as easily lost, withered over time by the currents of the past.

To Father Monk Malloy, Tom was the first in a wave of transformative Holy Cross presidents, innovators who used their positions and brought their campuses closer to their communities. When he became president of Notre Dame, Malloy says he "inherited something that wouldn't have existed otherwise," that wouldn't have developed without Tom. Father Richard Rutherford says that co-ed dorms were Tom's greatest challenge, and subsequently his greatest achievement. Despite their difference in opinion, they all described Tom in the warmest terms possible: "a dynamo," "a healer," and always "a good friend." Ed Oddo, Tom's cousin, says that "Tom would've made a great apostle," a description he feels adequately describes the work he did and the impact he made, and would've continued to make.

The Bluff has changed significantly since Tom was alive, but its foundation wouldn't exist without his presidency: The Chapel of Christ the Teacher continues to provide unique worship spaces to thousands of students, staff, and faculty each year, including the university's confession booth. The Chiles Center has hosted visits by President George W. Bush,

Bob Dylan, Stephen Hawking, and the Dalai Lama, in addition to Pilots basketball games and annual Commencement ceremonies (including the May 2018 iteration, when I walked across the stage to receive a master's degree). The L-P Tennis Center still operates, providing tennis, pickleball, badminton, and volleyball courts to students each week, and remains the home of UP Women's and Men's Division I tennis.

Housing on the Bluff remains co-ed, and now offers gender inclusive housing for all students, but primarily for the LGBTQ+ community. And as Franz Hall was completed, the interior of the previously open-ended campus was closed in, creating UP's academic quad and completing the vision of Tom and his successors to develop a world-class university. If the afterlife gives the ability, Tom would no doubt look on the modern Bluff with great pride and accomplishment. The University of Portland has become an internationally renowned institution of higher education, whose success can be directly traced to the work of its seventeenth president. *The Beacon*'s memorial edition published on November 2, 1989, ended a segment on the issue, titled "The First 24 Hours: How UP community reacts to its tragic loss," with this summation of Tom's legacy:

> Behind the Chapel doors, each decorated with a twig wreath tied with a purple ribbon, Fr. Oddo's body is at rest in familiar surroundings. Soon, his body will be taken away from the University of Portland for good.
>
> Yet, like the ever-visiting pink that lingers in an evening sky, and like the sense of unity that lingers in the hearts of members of this particular UP generation, so, too, will Fr. Oddo's spirit linger. And his legacy will remain unmatched.

In many ways, his legacy is one of building, of growing, and of evolving, but it is also still deeply rooted in his Catholicity, his morals, and his warm embrace of people. His was a life that, while concerned with personal questions about sin and repentance, prioritized the physical and spiritual well-being of others. Perhaps that's why, even today—some four decades after his death—flowers regularly appear on his South Bend grave, each bud a silent reminder of Tom's impact on the lives of those who knew him, and those that never did.

Chapter 33

The Shadow

The Lord is my Shepherd, I shall not want. He maketh me to lie down in green pastures: he leadeth me beside the still waters. He restoreth my soul: he leadeth me in the paths of righteousness for his name's sake. Yea, though I walk through the valley of the shadow of death, I will fear no evil. Thou preparest a table before me in the presence of mine enemies: thou anointest my head with oil; my cup runneth over. Surely goodness and mercy shall follow me all the days of my life: and I will dwell in the house of the Lord for ever.

Psalm 23

According to Ed Oddo, Tom's favorite verses were the Psalms. Psalm 23 has a particular resonance. The shadow of his death hung over the Bluff for years after the accident, something Norman Countryman dealt with every day. Cleared of wrongdoing by Portland Police, and with the county opting not to press charges, he was a free man—but one weighed down by the guilt of October 29. In the research and writing of this book, the one person I hesitated to meet was Norman. Whether it was self-trepidation over resurfacing bad memories, or the belief he would be repulsed by the idea of his name appearing in print, I hesitated for months. Finally, as the manuscript neared its conclusion, I decided I needed to meet him.

My initial message to Norman stated my goal: to create a biographical mosaic of Tom's life and times, something that should include him if only tangentially. His involvement felt like something Tom would've wanted. I offered to change details of his story, or provide a pseudonym to protect his identity as best I could. But to my surprise, the response I got was warm, receptive, surprisingly eager, and altogether reflective:

> A lot of time has passed since the accident and I would be lying if I say it was not traumatic, followed by a long period of redefining my purpose of being alive in this human body. On one hand I could try and develop a logical explanation for all of the circumstances but ultimately it is not for me to know the why but to trust that it was part of higher purpose for both of us that continues to this very day . . .
>
> I welcome the opportunity to get to know Tom more intimately through your writing and that part of my soul that accepts an unknown destiny and to offer my heart and being to become aware of what is to be revealed in the process.

Soon, I was connected with Jeremie, Norman's son, and the three of us made plans to get together in Portland on Labor Day Weekend 2024. That Sunday, September 1, we met at a Mexican restaurant less than two miles from the site of the accident three and a half decades prior. In all that time, Norman and Jeremie had never discussed it.

At seventy-five, Norman still sports a long beard, no longer a reddish-brown but snow white. As we wait for Jeremie, he tells me about his life and upbringing on a dairy farm in Spokane. Life was about work, and it was all he knew from a young age. Following his high school graduation, Norman enrolled in a machine-processing program at Oregon Technical Institute, and was soon working at Hyster Company in Portland. In 1971, Jeremie was born, the second of three children Norman had with his first wife. Shortly after, Norman was drafted into the US Army, the second to last draft call of the Vietnam War. With his technical education, he avoided deployment to Vietnam and shipped off instead to Fort Hood, Texas. Jeremie, who found himself there many years later, called it "the sphincter of the United States." While Tom protested the war over a thousand miles away in New England, Norman was helping men get out of the conflict.

Starting as a legal clerk, he quickly found a niche for himself helping discharge soldiers with what would later be called post-traumatic stress disorder. After helping over fifty men leave the service, the commanding officer left the post, and Norman wrote his own reassignment. Fort Hood at the time was, according to him, filled with drugs. Infantrymen, COs, nearly everyone used them recreationally—weed, LSD, and worse. They were less about euphoria and more about escape, the tools with which men of war used to cope with the horrors they had committed overseas. Seeking more stable work, Norman spent a year in a machinist shop making swagger sticks for the officers and metal flag stands for the rest—army accoutrement.

Discharged in 1975, he went back to work at his old job at Hyster, and soon bought the house he owned on Calvert Street in St. Johns, in the far northwest corner of the city. It was a three bedroom house on a gravel road that he paid $15,000 for—still something he considers "the best deal [he] ever made." St. Johns, now a quaint neighborhood at the edge of Portland, was once a rougher place: The house across the street was derelict, the property next door a wrecking yard with over thirty truck bodies in various states of decay. But Norman loved his house. He continually made improvements, adding a concrete pad to the backyard for car repairs, and when an electrician's shoddy work caused the roof to catch fire, Norman patched it up himself. But the house became a home when Jeremie came to live with him in 1986. By then, Norman had left Hyster, longing for the outdoor work he used to do while farming, and started his own landscaping business.

Having lived with his mother in Spokane all his life, Jeremie began to build a relationship with his father over homemade race cars. Other members of the family raced in Washington, and Portland Speedway was a short drive from St. Johns. In time, Norman and Jeremie were fixing up old Chevy Novas, preparing them to race. By 1989, they had moved out of the Calvert Street house and were living with Norman's girlfriend. The house was rented out to various tenants, supplementing Norman's landscaping income. That October, the latest renter requested the property be cleaned up and the Nova on the backyard pad removed. The Sunday before Halloween, October 29, Norman and Jeremie arrived at the house to take the car away.

That afternoon, neither Norman or Jeremie knew who Tom was, even as *The Oregonian* reporters arrived. Once the scene was cleared, the beleaguered Countrymans towed the Nova to their storeyard. That night, they arrived to find company waiting at Norman's girlfriend's house, whom they politely asked to leave. Without so much as a word shared between them, they both went to bed. The next morning, Monday, October 30, Jeremie took the bus to Centennial High School like he always did. Not long after arriving, he was called to the office. The Principal and school counselor were waiting. One of them asked Jeremie, "What are you doing here?"

"It's Monday," Jeremie had said. "It's a school day."

"Don't you know what's happened?" they asked. One of them pulled out that morning's copy of *The Oregonian.* Brent Wojahn's photo of the blue Corolla was on the front page, under the bolded headline Crash Kills UP President. Taking the paper, Jeremie read Don Hamilton's story. The gravity of the moment set in. The person their trailer killed was a national figure; someone with international recognition; someone whose demise was soon known around the world, and mourned by thousands.

Norman rarely got out of bed for a month afterward. He "quit life" as they both recall. It took even longer until he was capable of visiting the Bluff, despite living only a few miles away. He described those months as "a living death," and Jeremie's life, once balanced by the yin/yang partnership he had with his father, soon frayed. He took care of Norman, but the stress grated him. For seven months, Norman kept away from the university, unable to control his emotions and unsure of what to do.

In April 1990, he found the strength to visit UP and gave his only news interview on the crash to Amy Boothe at *The Beacon*. While he spoke with her, Norman felt a vibration form across his body. To this day, he says that Tom's spirit connected with his, and assured him everything was okay. That everything was at it should be. In that brief moment recounting the worst day of his life, Norman Countryman found a shred of peace.

While Norman had been cleared of criminal negligence, his car insurance was set to balloon if he chose to renew his policy. For the cost he expected to pay the next three years, he said he'd rather get an education, and let the insurance lapse. He didn't mind taking the bus. And he did go back to school, in fall 1990. Through it all, he kept thinking about Catherine and Mary, Tom's sister, and how he wished he could change the past. The guilt of the accident would follow him for many years afterward.

They eventually moved back into the Calvert House, although Jerermie wouldn't stay for long. His relationship with his father worsened, and he was let go from his job at Montgomery Ward's for misbehavior. Now a student at Mt. Hood Community College, school was his only refuge. Norman also found safe harbor going back to school, attending Portland Community College for a degree in manufacturing. From seven in the morning to four in the afternoon, Norman worked on machining projects—something that allowed him an escape from the shattering grief that accompanied his memories of the accident. By 1991, Jeremie felt rudderless, and met with a Marine recruiter to discuss his future. That summer, he enlisted and shipped out, first to Japan, then to San Diego where he eventually met the woman he would marry.

Through the '90s, Jeremie served multiple deployments in the Marine Corps. His job involved the loading and unloading of ships carrying supplies abroad. Norman kept a low profile at home, eventually moving into a trailer and taking a job at Precision Castparts, an aerospace manufacturer. In 1998, Jeremie left the marines and settled in Utah after a short return to Portland. By 2003, looking at his bank account and wanting for something purposeful, he told his wife he was thinking about joining the national guard, where his son had recently enlisted. That year, the guard was mobilized and sent to the Middle East. For another seven years, Jeremie served multiple deployments in Afghanistan and Iraq, moving his growing family twenty-three times to three continents. Three times, he was injured by IEDs while driving supply trucks. Despite assurances from his unit that he was physically healthy and eligible for re-enlistment, Jeremie opted to retire from the military in 2010. Back stateside, x-rays showed multiple vertebrae in his back had fused together, and six different surgeries were required to fix his body. Just as Jeremie had been by his father after the accident, Norman was there for his son as he recovered in the hospital.

Though they kept in touch with monthly phone calls, Norman and Jeremie's relationship was still far from whole. For most of the 2010s, they had no relationship to speak of. They now say it was for stupid reasons, but that keeping the relationship was impossible for both of them. Jeremie finally decided to break the ice once more, and found his father's address, now in Molalla, Oregon—a town about forty-five minutes from Portland. One day, Jeremie drove to his house, found him working in the front yard, and there they made up again, like no time was lost.

By now, Norman had developed prostate cancer. At its worst, Norman's prostate-specific antigen (PSA) levels, which hover from zero to four in a healthy person, spiked to 125. Jeremie's wife once dealt with thyroid cancer while he was deployed, he told me, and the chemo treatments she received were particularly harsh. Norman wanted no part of it, and instead insisted on alternatives. He researched medicinal cannabis and the effects it can have on cancer reduction and elimination, and later started his own cannabis grow. Soon he was taking highly-concentrated super doses to ease the cancer's spread. Swapping roles once more, Jeremie cared for Norman as he fought his cancer, just as Norman had for Jeremie in surgery, and Jeremie had for Norman in the aftermath of the accident. As we talk, Norman is proud to report his PSA levels have dropped to 1.5, something he considers a medical miracle in the face of surely-fatal cancer.

Today, Norman and Jeremie think about October 29, and about Tom often. In our conversation, they repeatedly theorized what would've happened had even one second differed in their respective timelines: What if Tom had taken a second longer to get in his car? What if they had taken longer to load the Nova and check the trailer hitch? What if neither vehicle had been on Columbia Boulevard? What could have been if 3:42 pm that Sunday thirty-five years ago had been any different? But such thoughts are fleeting.

Norman tells me "We don't have the past, we don't have the future. We just have now." Jeremie agrees. Having fought in multiple combat zones, having killed for the US flag and nearly dying for it, he firmly believes, "When it's your time to go, there's nothing you can do about it." In this sense, they both think that Tom's death, while tragic and regrettable, was as perfect as it could've been—instant, without pain, at a marvelous climax of a life that had impacted so many and would continue to affect generations of people who would never know his name.

Our conversation that afternoon was one of the most impactful moments of *my* life, even as an outsider, a stranger contributing little besides a listening ear. The questions of life and death are ones that haunt me every day of my adulthood, the dread you may experience when you start to consider the meaning of life—let alone the meaning of *your* life. But here, among the three of us, there seemed no need for answers, only an appreciation for the questions. Norman and Jeremie were incredibly kind, generous with their time, and thankful that we talked. I was in return. As we concluded our time together, I recalled a line Kurt Vonnegut would use at the end of his lauded lectures: "And I urge you to please notice when you are happy, and exclaim or murmur or think at some point, 'If this isn't nice, I don't know what is.'"

Norman and Jeremie don't talk politics, as a rule. But they do talk about their faith. Both find solace in a higher power: Norman follows the teachings of Eastern spiritual practitioners, while Jeremie belongs to the Mormon Church. Both see the impact of people like Tom on faith communities worldwide. As they have picked up the pieces of their lives and relationships, they have come to a place of mutual understanding: That life is about being content in our short existence, that money and prejudices are mere hindrances to finding joy. And there is the word we all came to: *joy*. Tom's was a gospel of joy. Of joyous celebration of life, of joyful remembrance of those we've lost, and of joy in the everyday, the mundane, even the sadness, that we should be blessed to feel anything at all. And it was a gospel of peace. Of peace on Earth, and peace toward one another.

It is a miracle someone like Tom would risk his career, swimming against the current, to promote this message in a world that became increasingly darker and more hostile, and in a church that had begun to turn against the reforms of Vatican II, and against the ideas of the "New American Catholic." It is, perhaps, also a miracle and a curse that such a message resonates with audiences today. That with it, the church has a roadmap to a future that is more inclusive, more diverse, and more Christ-like (in Tom's eyes). That without it, the doors to the House of the Lord would remain closed, forever, to the people needing it most.

Today, his final resting place is quiet and picturesque, a testament to the beauty of the Earth. Holy Cross Community Cemetery lies between two lakes on the Notre Dame campus, St. Mary's to the south and St. Joseph's to the east, and sits under a thick cover of trees with a single roadway running through it. Inside the cemetery fences, hundreds of stone crosses stand in neat, long rows. Follow the signage to Section 3, Row G, Grave 14, and you'll find him. A brief inscription, customary for these men, makes a simple marker to his legacy:

R.I.P.

Rev.

Thomas C. Oddo, C.S.C.

June 12, 1944

October 29, 1989

In April 2025, after advance copies of this book were sent to reviewers and contributors, I received an urgent message from Brian McNaught. His husband of 49 years, Ray Struble, also read the book and felt strongly that more context was needed in Part One, on the early days of Dignity-USA. Ray had been an activist himself, and having known many of Dignity's national officers was keenly aware of things behind the scenes. He told me that, while some may have known about Paul Shanley's crimes, many did not, and most were only made aware of them when the laicized priest was arrested and charged in 2002. Tom, who Ray says worked closely with Shanley, nevertheless was completely unaware of his double life, and was unlikely to have taken his confession. While my research suggested they were only professional acquaintances, Ray's memory could mean they were more like friends. For what it's worth, they were *not* confidants.

Ray also told me about living with Tom in the late '60s and early '70s, ending this memory with a curious observation:

> I was a CSC Seminarian from the fall of 1969 to June of 1972 whereupon I became a housemate with Tom, my new partner, [Brother] Bill Maudlin, CSC, and a few others in Belmont, Massachusetts. I shared the basement with Tom which had two beds separated by a curtain. This was after my partner and I left the CSC [Novitiate] in Bennington, Vermont. Tom was still at Harvard finishing his PhD in Theology. I moved out with my partner in August of 1972 after we each had secured jobs and were able to pay rent. Tom moved out to an apartment of his own in Back Bay shortly after defending his thesis. In knowing Tom all those years I'd have to say I never knew him. He kept everything very close to the vest.

Alex Frisbie is a former TV media producer and director. He worked at WNAC-TV for many years, and still resides in Boston.

Brian McNaught has worked as a diversity coach for businesses and business leaders since the 1980s. His memoir, *A Prince of a Boy: How One Gay Catholic Helped Change the World*, is available now from Cascade Books.

Cardinal Humberto Meideros served as archbishop of Boston from 1970 until his death in September 1983. Later, reports surfaced that he shuffled pedophile priest John Geoghan between multiple parishes, and was aware of sexual abuse claims against Paul Shanley.

Catherine Oddo lived the rest of her life in Florida, where she had settled with her late husband Dominick. She passed away in 2012 at the age of 94.

Ed Oddo graduated from Siena College in 1966. He worked at IBM for over 30 years. He is retired and lives happily in southern California with his wife.

Elaine Noble won two consecutive terms in the Massachusetts House of Representatives. She ran for US Senate in 1978, and later worked for Boston Mayor Kevin White. She is retired and lives in Florida.

Father Edward "Monk" Malloy, CSC retired from the presidency of Notre Dame in 2005. He has written several books about his life, career, and tenure, and continues to advise university presidents and corporate executives.

Father Jeff Schneibel, CSC has been UP's university archivist since 2012. He was previously a philosophy professor and director of the UP Salzburg program. He is notable on the Bluff for his "edgy humor" and "thought-provoking homilies."

Father Joe Corpora, CSC left UP to become assistant superior of the Holy Cross Congregation, later serving as lead pastor of churches in Portland and Goodyear, Arizona. He currently serves the University of Notre

Dame as a priest-in-residence and associate director of the Transformational Leaders Program.

Father Paul Waldschmidt, CSC served as auxiliary bishop until 1990, and carried an emeritus title until his death in 1994. West Hall, UP's administrative building, was renamed Waldschmidt Hall in his honor.

Father Richard "Dick" Berg, CSC served as dean of the College of Arts and Sciences until 1991. He then became lead minister at St. Andre Besette Chapel in downtown Portland. He wrote the book *Scars*, which was later adapted into a feature film. He continues to serve students on the Bluff as a priest-in-residence.

Father Richard Rutherford, CSC received multitudes of praise for his work planning and coordinating Tom's memorial. He taught in the Theology Department from 1976–2012. He still works with Father Dick as an emeritus faculty member and priest-in-residence.

Jeremie Countryman left Portland in 1991 for the marine corps, and later served in the army national guard. He retired from the armed forces in 2010 and has returned to building and refurbishing race cars. He plans to spend his retirement with his best friends—his wife, his son, and his father Norman.

Norman Countryman went back to college shortly after Tom's death. He would go on to receive a bachelors in film production from Portland State University. Before he retired, he worked as technical director of PSU-TV and as a producer for Portland Community Media.

Pat McArron served as DignityUSA's first director of the Pacific Region from 1977–1979. He later served as vice president, then president of DignityUSA from 1999–2002. He worked for the US Postal Service for 33 years and is now retired.

Patti Brown worked in UP dining services for over 40 years, serving thousands of students and six presidents. She retired from the Bauccio Commons in 2024.

Paul Diederich stayed active in the Dignity orbit for many years, eventually marrying and settling down in Boston with his husband. He retired from his customhouse brokerage work in 2012. He passed away in October 2023, as this book was being written.

Sister Jeannine Gramick, SL was banned from pastoring to gay people by the Washington Archdiocese in 1984, and was the subject of a Vatican investigation in 1988, but continued her advocacy through New Ways Ministry. She continues to speak out for change in the church.

Acknowledgements

I have many people to thank for their support, encouragement, guidance, and prayers throughout the process of writing this book. It would not have been possible without them. First, the following individuals who spoke with me about Father Tom:

Alex Frisbie, director of the *All God's Children?* 1981 TV broadcast; Brian McNaught and Ray Struble, DignityUSA activists (married in 1976) who worked, demonstrated, and lived with Tom; Ed Oddo, Tom's cousin and close friend through high school; Father Richard Berg, CSC, former dean of the College of Arts and Sciences at the University of Portland (UP) during Tom's presidency; Father Joseph Corpora, CSC, Tom's close friend and former UP director of the Office of Volunteer Services; Father Edward "Monk" Malloy, CSC, president of the University of Notre Dame (1987–2005) and Tom's friend in seminary; Father Richard Rutherford, CSC, longtime UP theology professor who led the construction of Chapel of Christ the Teacher and later coordinated Tom's funeral services; Father Jeff Schneibel, CSC, UP's university archivist; Norman and Jeremie Countryman, a loving father and son entwined by fate with Tom's death; Pat McArron, a gay Catholic activist who helped start Dignity/San Diego, and later hosted a major Dignity conference there; Patti Brown, a UP food service worker who had known Tom throughout his presidency; and Sister Jeannine Grammick, SL, co-founder of New Ways Ministry and a colleague and co-author of Tom's in the 1970s.

Additional thanks to Scott Daniels and the folks at the Oregon Historical Society Research Library, who provided support in finding additional materials related to Dignity/Portland and UP.

To the University of Portland Clark Library, whose digital archive of *The Beacon* student newspaper was the backbone of this project. It is an amazing resource and a model for online archives everywhere. To generations of editors, writers, and contributors to *The Beacon*, a publication that has provided excellent student journalism and commentary for over a century.

To Jill Uhacz, Cathy Falk, and Kurt Vonnegut, three people who taught me how to write. To Charley Praither, Peter Khalil, and my loving family for pushing me to write, no matter what, and for listening to every detail of this story. To Daisy for the endless hours spent next to me as this book came together.

Special thanks to the Unencumbered Press team: to Stephanie Johnson Lawson for believing in the power of this story; to Luis Ramos, for designing a beautiful book and being incredibly patient with my many edits; to Alexa Schmidt for providing great support in the drafting and editing of the manuscript; to Bailey Harrington for her careful proofreading and fact-checking that strengthened the text; and to Megan Jessop for helping share this story with new readers.

Finally, to Mary Lynn Gonzales—Tom's sister. I hope this book does his memory justice.

Concelebration: A collective celebration of the Eucharist involving multiple priests.

CSC: Abbreviation for Congregation of Holy Cross, a denomination within the Catholic Church.

Ecumenicalism: The concept of unity between Christian denominations.

Eucharist: A sacrament in Catholicism commemorating the Last Supper which involves various practices, including the blessing of bread and wine, Communion, and prayers. A central point of Catholic Mass.

Good Friday: The sixth day of Holy Week, commemorating the crucifixion and death of Jesus.

Hail Mary: A prayer common among Catholics; see: Part One.

High Church: Church services and worship that rely on priestly authority, sacraments, and ritual symbology. Catholicism is often considered "high church," compared to Protestantism, which is often considered "low church" for the lack of these practices.

Holy Communion: A portion of the Eucharist, a practice where Catholic parishioners pray and receive bread and wine to symbolize Jesus Christ giving his body and blood for mankind. The presentation of the bread and wine is Communion.

Homophile: Referring to the Homophile movement, the organization of gay people into clubs and social groups and the creation of gay-specific media in the 1950s and '60s. A forerunner to the era of activism born from the Stonewall riots of 1969.

Laicized: The defrocking, or removal of vestments and title, of a priest.

Laity: Non-ordained Catholic parishioners (or non-Catholics). Singular: layperson.

Liturgy: The importance of church service and worship.

Mariology: The study of Mother Mary in Christian Theology.

Maundy (Holy) Thursday: The fifth day of Holy Week, the days leading up to Easter, commemorating the washing of feet by Jesus (the action is called "Maundy") and the Last Supper.

Novitiate: A strict period of religious study and training in a restricted environment prior to taking vows, i.e., as a priest.

Ordination: The conferring of Holy Orders, the last step in becoming a priest.

OSCO: Abbreviation for the Order of the Cistercians of the Strict Observance, also referred to as the *Trappists*, a religious order within the Catholic Church.

Pontiff: Another word for pope.

Rosary: A spoken, Scripture-based prayer using prayer beads.

SJ: Abbreviation for Society of Jesus, also referred to as the *Jesuits*, a religious order within the Catholic Church.

SL: Abbreviation for Sisters of Loretto, a women's religious institute within the Catholic Church.

** Photograph or includes photograph of Tom Oddo*

^ Pseudonym used by author (i.e., The Beacon publishing as "The Bacon")

An updated, living bibliography can be found at unencumberedpress.com/against-the-current-bibliography.

Prologue

Boothe, Amy and Scott Thompson. 1990. "Previous Accident Embellished," *The Beacon*, University of Portland, 12 Apr: 1, 5.

Boothe, Amy. 1990. "Owner of Run-Away Trailer, Countryman Seeks Inner-Resolve," *The Beacon*, 5 Apr: 1, 5.

Brown, Patti. 2023. Personal interview with Tyler Bieber, 23 Sept.

Hamilton, Don. 1989. "Crash Kills UP President," *The Oregonian,* 30 Oct: 1. Photo by Brent Wojahn.*

Soma, Tom. 1989. "On the Bluff: The Goodness of Seven," *Portland Magazine*, University of Portland, Vol. 8, Autumn: 3–7.*

Part One: Hail Mary, Full of Grace
1944–1982

Chapter 1: *Queens*

Bureau of the Census. 1920. "Fourteenth Census of the United States: 1920—Population," US Department of Commerce, 24 Jan: 29a. Accessed 5 Sept 2023.

"Catherine Anna Oddo," Ancestry.com. Accessed 5 Sept 2023.

"Dominick C Oddo," Ancestry.com. Accessed 5 Sept 2023.

Evening Star. 1938. "Principals at Georgetown Graduation," New York, 14 June.

Everett Press. 1944 "Wounded in Action," 8 Dec.

Kravif, Hy. 1935. *The Telephone and Telegraph Workers.* International Pamphlets, No. 44.

New York Daily News. 1957. "250 Physicians Expected to Turn Out for Assembly," 7 Apr.

New York Daily News. 1957. "Medics Select '58, '59 Chiefs," 3 Dec.

New York Daily News. 1958 "MDs to Review Medical Uses of Hypnosis," 6 Apr.

New York State Census. 1915. "Enumeration of the Inhabitants," State of New York, 1 June: 10. Accessed 5 Sept 2023.

New York State Census. 1925. "Enumeration of the Inhabitants," State of New York, 1 June: 19–20. Accessed 5 Sept 2023.

Oddo, Edward. 2024. Personal interview with Tyler Bieber, 22 Jan.

Oddo, Thomas. Untitled autobiographical sketch, cir. 1987.Accessed from University of Portland Archives, 2 Aug 2023.

The Brooklyn Daily Eagle. 1939. "Amen Sifts Death of Informant: Hints Ex-Cop Poisoned for Charging Plot," 14 Aug: 1.

The Cross, 1958–1959. Holy Cross High School (New York).*

The Cross, 1959–1960. Holy Cross High School (New York).*

The Cross, 1960–1961. Holy Cross High School (New York).*

The Tablet. 1939 "Graduation Held At Mary Immaculate," 27 May.

United States Local Exemption Board. 1918. Registration Card for Jacob Anthony Arthen, serial #4120, issued 12 Sept.

US Commissioner of Immigration. 1897. "List or Manifest of Alien Immigrants for the Commissioner of Immigration," US Department of the Treasury, 1 June: 141. Accessed 5 Sept 2023.

Chapter 2: *Indiana*

Baker, Father. 1963. "Are You in the Swim?," *Religious Bulletin*, University of Notre Dame, Vol. XLIII, No. 15, 12 Nov: 4.

Chicago Tribune. 1965. "Irish Swim Team Beats Canadians," 24 Jan: 44.

O'Connell, Jack. 2013. "The Day JFK Died," *Notre Dame Magazine,* 22 Nov. https://magazine.nd.edu/stories/the-day-jfk-died/. Accessed 31 Jan 2024.

Scheuble, Bob. 1965. "Stay Hall Plans Proceed," *The Scholastic*, University of Notre Dame, 12 May: 1,6.

Siegwald, Pete. 1965. "President's Medallion Selections," *The Scholastic*, University of Notre Dame, 5 March: 15.

Student Directory, 1961–1962. University of Notre Dame: 80. Accessed 28 Apr 2023.

Swim Roster, 1961–1962. University of Notre Dame. Accessed 28 Apr 2023.

The Dome, 1961–1962. Yearbook. University of Notre Dame.*

The Dome, 1962–1963. Yearbook. University of Notre Dame.*

The Dome, 1963–1964. Yearbook. University of Notre Dame.*

The Dome, 1964–1965. Yearbook. University of Notre Dame.*

The Scholastic. 1964. "Don't Choose the Mug," University of Notre Dame, 15 May: 14–15.

The Scholastic. 1964. "Hall Presidents' President," University of Notre Dame, 1 May: 15.

The Scholastic. 1964. "Soaring Spirit," University of Notre Dame, 30 Oct: 14.

The Scholastic. 1965. "A Salute to the Seniors … ," University of Notre Dame, 28 May: 5.

The South Bend Tribune. 1963. "N.D. Swimmers Topple Kent: Blanchard Sets Pool Record for Irish," 24 Feb: 38.

The Voice of Notre Dame. 1964. "Sophomore Named Queen, Badin, SMC Win in Contests," University of Notre Dame, 3 May.*

The Voice. 1963. "Junior Weekend March 6–8," University of Notre Dame, 5 Dec: 1.

University of Notre Dame. 1965. "Last Visit of The Class of 1965 to Sacred Heart Church," 5 June. Includes handwritten passages by Tom Oddo.

Chapter 3: *The New American Catholic*

Alumnus Magazine. 1970. "CSC Ordinations," University of Notre Dame, May–June: 31.

Anello, Robert L. 2014. "Priestly Celibacy and Identity: The Rocky Reception of Vatican II's 'Presbyterorum Ordinis,'" After Vatican II: Implementation and Responses, *US Catholic Historian*, Vol. 32, Issue 4: 27–53.

Bianchi, Eugene C. 1970. "John XXIII, Vatican II, and American Catholicism," The Sixties: Radical Change in American Religion, *The Annals of the American Academy of Political and Social Science,* Vol. 387, Jan: 30–40.

Malloy, Edward A. "Monk", CSC. 2023. Personal interview with Tyler Bieber, 18 Sept.

Pogorelc, Anthony J. and James D. Davidson. 2000. "American Catholics: One Church, Two Cultures?," *Review of Religious Research*, Vol. 42, Issue 2, Dec: 146–158.

Pontius, Gertrude. 1969. "Catholic Churches Mark Good Friday: At Notre Dame," *The South Bend Tribune* (Indiana), 4 Apr: 16.

President's Newsletter. 1970. "The University at Large," University of Notre Dame, Vol. XIII, No. 5, March: 4.

The Beacon. 1963. University of Portland, Vol. 62, No. 9, 23 Nov: 1–3. Multiple articles on the JFK assassination.

The New American Catholic. 1968. Directed by Stuart Schulberg. NBC.

Chapter 4: *"The Maturing Years"*

Boehme, Christopher. "The Oddo Chronicles," *Portland Magazine*, University of Portland, Vol. 8, Autumn 1989, 10–16.*

Malloy, Edward A. "Monk," CSC. 2009. *Monk's Tale: The Pilgrimage Begins, 1941–1975*. University of Notre Dame Press.

Sullivan, Fr. Patrick, CSC. "Remarks at Memorial Mass for Tom Oddo, CSC, Stonehill College, October 31, 1989."Accessed from Stonehill College Archives, 11 May 2023.

The South Bend Tribune. 1970. "Holy Cross Sisters Take Final Vows," 17 Aug: 8.

The South Bend Tribune. 1970. "Mass Planned at St. Mary's," 17 April: 26.

The South Bend Tribune. 1970. "Vigil Masses Are Added in Most Catholic Parishes," 27 Mar: 22.

The South Bend Tribune. 1970. Grove–Krueper Wedding Notice. 9 Aug: 65.

The South Bend Tribune. 1971. "Holy Cross Nuns Make Final Vows," 16 Aug: 29.

Chapter 5: *Dignity*

Diederich, Paul, Hart, Jack, and Oddo, Fr. Tom. 1974. "Report on Constitution Vote," *Dignity*, Vol. V, No. 1, Jan: 8–10.

Diederich, Paul, Hart, Jack, and Oddo, Rev. Thomas C., CSC. 1974. "Letter to Fr. Ramon Wagner and Members of the Gay Ministry Task Force," *Dignity*, Vol. V, No. 5, May: 5. (Letter dated 1 Apr 1974.)

Dignity. 1974. "Quickies," Vol. V, No. 6–7, June–July: 8.

Gay Community News. 1973. "Catholic Gays Celebrate," Vol. I, Issue 25, 8 Dec: 2.

HUB Newsletter. HUB Newsletter, Vol. 3, No. 2, March–April. Archives of Sexuality and Gender, link.gale.com/apps/doc/JYYJAS785070727/AHSI?u=-multnomah_main&

sid=bookmark-AHSI. Accessed 12 Dec. 2023.

LaBriola, Carrie. 1974. "Priest Explains Catholic Views on Homosexuals," *The Journal Herald* (Dayton, Ohio), 7 June: 11.

Longcope, Kay. 1973. "The Homosexual, the Catholic Church and Dignity," *Boston Globe Magazine*, 22 July: 22–25. Photo by Paul Connell.*

Longcope, Kay. 1974. "2 priests Attack church Rules on Homosexuals," *The Boston Globe*, 10 Mar: 43.

Longcope, Kay. 1974. "Case for Homosexuals: Civil Rights vs. Morality," *The Boston Globe,* 19 June: 47.

McNaught, Brian. 2024. Personal interview with Tyler Bieber, 5 Dec.

McNeill, Fr. John J., S.J. 1974. "The Spirit Is Calling Us! Part III: Tradition and Homosexuality," *Dignity*, Vol. V, No. 1, Jan: 4–5.

McNeill, Fr. John J., S.J. 1974. "The Spirit Is Calling Us! Part IV: Human Nature and Human Freedom," *Dignity*, Vol. V, No. 2, Feb: 6–9.

Medsger, Betty. 1973. "Berrigan, McAlister Reveal Marriage," *National Catholic Reporter*, 8 June: 3.

NC News Service. 1974. News release on New England Clergy Institute. 9 July: 21.

Oddo, Rev. Thomas C, CSC. 1973. "Hall Praised for Stand," editorial, *The Fitchburg Sentinel*, 7 June: 4.

Oddo, Rev. Thomas C, CSC. 1974. "Homily," *Dignity*, Vol. V, No. 2, Feb: 4–5.

Spaulding, Jack. 1973. "Catholic Homosexuals Hold First Convention," *National Catholic Reporter*, 14 Sept: 1, 16.

The Boston Globe. 1973. "Corporations, Sexuality, Prayer, Paulist Topics," 2 Oct: 28.

The Greenfield Recorder. 1973. "Homosexual," Greenfield, Massachusetts, 2 Feb: 20. Originally published by *Associated Press*.

The Homosexuals (1967). Produced by William Peters. CBS.

The Observer. 1974. "Homosexuality to Be Discussed," University of Notre Dame, 17 Oct: 7.

Parker, Robert J. (1973). "The End of the Beginning: A Report on the State House hearing on Bills to End Discrimination due to Sexual Preference." *Boston Gayline*, Vol. 3, No. 2, March–April: 4–9.

Vatican Congregation for Catholic Education. 1974. "A Guide to Formation in Priestly Celibacy," *Origins*, NC Documentary Service, Vol. 4, No. 5, June 27.

Wallace, Mike. 1967. *CBS Reports: The Homosexuals*. Documentary.

White, Diane. 1974. "Gays in 4th Festival at UMass," *The Boston Globe,* 6 May: 18.*

Chapter 6: *Happy Warrior*

Adams, James E. 1976. "Catholic Homosexual Meeting," *St. Louis Post-Dispatch*, 12 Feb: 4C.

Being Gay and Catholic with Dignity. 1977. Directed by James C. Fleck. Jeskor Creative Services.

Blau, Eleanor. 1976. "Vatican Disputed By Homosexuals," *The New York Times*, 22 Feb: 26.

Breig, Joseph A. 1975. "Care of 'Gays.'" *Pittsburgh Catholic,* 7 Nov: 4.

Certification of Results, Gay Rights National Lobby, 3 Aug 1976.

Daily Evening Item. 1974. "Single Parents," Lynn, Massachusetts, 17 May: 12.

Dignity of San Diego. 1976. "Gay Ministry: A Workshop for Priests in the San Diego Roman Catholic Diocese," June 18.

Dignity website, www.dignityusa.org. Accessed 14 July 2023.

Gay Community News. 1974. "Massachusetts Gay Rights Bills: Spring 1974," Vol. 1, No. 37, 9 Mar: 4.

Gay Community News. 1974. "State Hearings on Gay Rights Bills," Vol. 1, No. 37, 9 Mar: 1–2.

Gay Community News. 1974. Ad in favor of S.B. 1585. Vol. 1, Issue 50, 8 June: 5.

Gill, Alan. 1975. "Homosexuals to hold convention," *The Sydney Morning Herald*, 25 Apr: 7.

Gill, Alan. 1982. "Can homosexuals still be Christians?," *The Sydney Morning Herald*, 7 Apr: 14.

Girard, Fred. 1974. "Catholic Church Criticized: 100 Demonstrate for Pro-Gay Columnist," *Detroit Free Press,* 3 Sept: 3.

Grammick, Sr. Jeannine, Nugent, Fr. Robert, and Oddo, Fr. Thomas. 1975. *Homosexual Catholics: A Primer for Discussion*. Dignity.

Lake Shore Visitor. 1976. "Dignity Group Seeks 'Justice' for Homosexuals," Erie, Pennsylvania, 13 Aug: 19.

LGBTQ Religious Archives Network. n.d. "Brian McNaught | Profile." https://lgbtqreligiousarchives.org/profiles/brian-mcnaught. Accessed 7 Feb 2024.

Longcope, Kay. 1975. "American Catholic Bishops Urged to Establish Office on Women's Issues," *The Boston Globe*, 19 Nov: 60.

Longcope, Kay. 1975. "Catholic Bishops Soften Hard Line on Social Issues," *The Boston Globe*, 23 Nov: 56.

Longcope, Kay. 1975. "Hub Catholics Work to Turn Political Clout Myth into Reality," *The Boston Globe*, 30 June: 1, 12.

Longcope, Kay. 1976 "Vatican Affirms Traditional Sex Teaching," *The Boston Globe*, 15 Jan: 6.

Longcope, Kay. 1976. "Catholic Sex Edict—Reaction," *The Boston Globe*, 16 Jan: 25.

McArron, Pat. 2024. Personal interview withTyler Bieber, 6 Aug.

McGirr, Kevin J. 1975. "Dignity Convention," *Gay Community News*, Vol. 3, No. 11, 13 Sept: 1.*

McNaught, Brian. "Brian McNaught: Biography." https://brian-mcnaught.com/biography. Accessed 3 July 2024.

McNaught, Brian. 1975. "An Open Letter to the Dignity Community," *Dignity*, Vol. VI, No. 8, Aug: 6.

Mixner, David and Bailey, Dennis. 2000. *Brave Journeys: Profiles in Gay and Lesbian Courage*. Random House Publishing Group: 81.

National Conference of Catholic Bishops. 1976. "To Live in Christ Jesus: A Pastoral Reflection on the Moral Life," United States Catholic Conference, 11 Nov: 19.

NC News Service. 1974. "Rome Asks Jesuit to State Views on Homosexuality," 24 Jan: 1–2.

Oddo, Fr. Tom. 1974. "The Spirit Calls Us Anew—Labor Day Weekend, 1974," *Dignity,* Vol. V, No. 9, Sept: 2–4.

Petoskey News Review. 1974. "Protestors Support Gay Writer," Petoskey, Michigan. 3 Sept: 21. UPI news release.

Russell, John F. 1976. "Hate the Sin but Love the Sinner. Sin? What Sin??," *The Linacre Quarterly*, Vol. 43, No. 3, Article 7.

Sabo, Corinne. 1992. "Claiming Our Untold Herstory," *Woman Space*, Women's Community of San Antonio, Vol. 4, No. 8, June: 2.

The Boston Globe. 1977. "Quotes from Our Readers," 26 Sept: 21.

The National Office of Dignity. 1975. "Press Release," *Dignity*, Vol. VI, No. 8, Aug: 1.

The New York Times. 1974. "Paper Is Assailed by a Homosexual," 11 Aug: 27.

The New York Times. 1974."A Parade Closes Gay Pride Week," 1 July: 33. Photo by John Muravcki.*

The New York Times. 1975. "Homosexual Rights Backed by Parley," 3 Sept: 50.

Chapter 7: *The Monk and the Activist*

Braude, Ann. 2005. "A Short Half-Century: Fifty Years of Women at Harvard Divinity School," Convocation address,Harvard University, 19 Sept.

Brown, Susan K. 1979. "A Lama on Wheels," *The Harvard Crimson*, 20 Oct. https://www.thecrimson.com/article/1979/10/20/a-lama-on-wheels-pyou-dont/. Accessed online, 12 July 2023.

Jordan, Mark. 2020. "Recalling the 'Brave Spaces' for LGBTQ+ History Month." Interview by Jordan Venditelli. Harvard Divinity School News Archive, 27 Oct.

Oddo, Thomas Charles. 1979 (March). "The Monk and the Activist: A Comparative Study of the Spirituality of Thomas Merton and Daniel Berrigan." PhD thesis, Harvard University.

Oldham, Olivia G. 2018. "When 'He' Isn't God Anymore," *The Harvard Crimson*, 18 Oct. https://www.thecrimson.com/article/2018/10/18/pronoun-noisemakers-god/. Accessed online, 12 July 2023.

Sacred Congregation for the Doctrine of the Faith. 1975. *Persona Humana: Declaration on Certain Questions Concerning Sexual Ethics.* 29 Dec.

The Harvard Gazette. 2008. "Krister Stendahl, 86, Was HDS Dean from 1968–1979," 17 Apr. https://news.harvard.edu/gazette/story/2008/04/krister-stendahl-86-was-hds-dean-from-1968-1979/. Accessed online, 12 July 2023.

The New York Times. 1970. "Rabbi Martin Katzenstein dies; Acting Dean of Harvard Divinity," 6 Sept: 51.

Chapter 8: *Stonehill College*

All God's Children? 1981. Directed by Alex Frisbie, featuring Thomas C. Oddo. WNAC-TV Boston, March 31.

Athol Daily News. 1979. "Cardinal Says Gay Acts Cannot Be Approved," Athol, Massachusetts, 7 July: 14. Originally published by *Associated Press.*

Franklin, James L. 1979. "Cardinal Reaffirms Stand on Homosexuality," *The Boston Globe*, 6 July: 1.

Oddo, Thomas, CSC. 1978. "Stonehill Commemorates Thomas Merton," *The Summit*, 6 Dec: 7.

Oddo, Thomas, CSC. Undated. "Gay People Within the Church." Essay written ca. 1981–1982. Accessed from University of Portland Archives, 20 Jan 2025.

Oddo, Tom, CSC. 1981. "Tempering the Myth of Gay Ministry." In *Theological Pastoral Resources: A Collection of Articles on Homosexuality from a Pastoral*

Perspective, edited by Kathleen Leopold, HM and Thomas Orians. Sixth Edition. Dignity, Inc.

Oddo, Tom, CSC. 1981. "The Minister's Challenge to Guilt." In *Theological Pastoral Resources: A Collection of Articles on Homosexuality from a Pastoral Perspective*, edited by Kathleen Leopold, HM and Thomas Orians. Sixth Edition. Dignity, Inc.

Owens, Steve. 1981. "We Are God's Children Too," *Gay Community News*, 4 Apr: 10.

Sipress, Alan. 1982. "Catholic Gays Claim Diocese Ignores Them," *The Boston Globe*, 29 Aug: 21, 25.

Stonehill College News Bureau. 1974. Media Release. July.

Stonehill College News Bureau. 1977. "Priest Fights for Homosexual Rights," 20 Oct.

The Boston Globe. 1975. "Other editorial comment … ," 23 Apr: 14.

The Lexington Leader. 1979. "Cardinal Repeats Catholic Church's Condemnation of Homosexual Acts," Lexington, Kentucky, 6 July: A14. Originally published by *Associated Press*.

The Summit. 1981. Stonehill College, 18 Nov: 4.*

Part Two: Challenger
1982–1986

Chapter 9: *Portland in the 1980s*

Baldwin, Kent. 1981. "Philosophy Prof Leaving U of P," *The Beacon*, University of Portland, Vol. 82, No. 16, 15 Jan: 1.

Connelly, James T, CSC. 2001. *A Century of Teaching, Faith, and Service: The University of Portland 1901–2001: A Prose and Photographic Review of the First Hundred years of Oregon's Catholic University*. University of Portland Press.

Lauer, John. 1981. "Students End Hunger Strike," *The Beacon*, University of Portland, Vol. 82, No. 29, 23 Apr: 1.

Medlin, Mark. 1982. "Academic Year Exciting, Eventful," *The Alpha*, University of Portland, 6 Aug: 3.

Price, Larry W., et al. 1987. *Portland's Changing Landscape*. Occasional Papers in Geography No. 4.

Scott, Katie Collins. 2018. "Former University of Portland President Listed in Grand Jury Abuse Report," *National Catholic Reporter*, 25 Sept. Originally published by *Catholic News Service*.

The Beacon. 1980. "Faculty Pay Increases," University of Portland, Vol. 81, No. 19, 28 Feb: 1.

The Beacon. 1980. "Tuition to Increase," University of Portland, Vol. 81, No. 19, 28 Feb: 1.

The Beacon. 1981. "Letters to the Editor," University of Portland, Vol. 82, No. 16, 15 Jan: 2–3.

The Beacon. 1981. "Letters to the Editor," University of Portland, Vol. 82, No. 18, 29 Jan: 2.

The Beacon. 1981. "Letters to the Editor," University of Portland, Vol. 82, No. 23, 5 Mar: 2.

The Beacon. 1989. "Top Stories of the 1980's," University of Portland, 7 Dec: 6–7.*

Weber, Mark. 1981. "Bro. Wilson Resigns Presidency," *The Beacon*, University of Portland, Vol. 83, No. 1, 3 Sept: 1.

Wilson, Brother Raphael. 1981. "Bro. Wilson Acknowledges Concerns," *The Beacon*, University of Portland, Vol. 82, No. 25, 26 Mar: 3.

Chapter 10: *New Man On Campus*

Berg, Richard. 2023. Personal interview with Tyler Bieber, 7 Sept.

Boehme, Christopher. 1987. "The President as Pastor," *Portland*, University of Portland, Vol. 6, No. 4: 14–17.

Carman, Diane. 1982. "5 U of P Presidential Finalists Revealed," *Oregon Journal*, 9 Apr: 23.

Colby, Richard. 1982. "UP Chief Outlines Main Goals," *The Oregonian*, 21 May: 33.*

Johnson, Pat. 1982. "Racquet Center Plans Move Ahead," *The Beacon,* University of Portland, Vol. 84, No. 4, 23 Sept: 1.

NC News Service. 1982. "New President Wants to Involve University with City, Church," 25 May: 13.

Oddo, Thomas C, CSC. 1982. "New President; Oddo Excited About Year," *The Alpha*, University of Portland, 6 Aug: 2.*

Raffanti, Michael. 1982. "New President Stresses Visibility," *The Beacon,* University of Portland, Vol. 84, No. 1, 2 Sept: 4.*

Raffanti, Michael. 1982. "Oddo Assumes Presidential Position," *The Beacon,* University of Portland, Vol. 84, No. 1, 2 Sept: 1.*

Raffanti, Michael. 1982. "Oddo Relates Views on Campus Concerns," *The Beacon,* University of Portland, Vol. 84, No. 2, 9 Sept:6.

Schreck, Rev. Charles, CSC. 1982. "School Faces New Directions," *The Beacon,* University of Portland, Vol. 84, No. 6, 7 Oct: 2.

The Beacon. 1982. "For President: Committee Narrows Candidates to Five," University of Portland, Vol. 83, No. 25, 1 Apr: 1.

The Beacon. 1982. "Funds Aid Sports," editorial, University of Portland, Vol. 84, No. 2, 9 Sept: 2.

The Beacon. 1982. "Oddo Addresses Senators, Extends Invitation," University of Portland, Vol. 84, No. 5, 30 Sept: 1.

The Beacon. 1982."Administration Rearranges Organization," University of Portland, Vol. 84, No. 1, 2 Sept: 4.

The Columbian. 1982. "Priest Named President of University of Portland," Vancouver, Washington, 20 May: 3. Originally published by *Associated Press.*

The Oregonian. 1982. "5 Finalists Named for UP's Top Post," 9 Apr: 31.

The Oregonian. 1982. "UP Names Oddo Chief," 20 May: 33.

Chapter 11: *Inauguration*

Johnson, Pat. 1982. "Oddo Visits Dorms," *The Beacon*, University of Portland, Vol. 84, No. 8, 21 Oct: 3.

Miller, Alison. 1982. "University Honors Oddo During Inauguration," *The Beacon*, University of Portland, Vol. 84, No. 7, 14 Oct: 6–7.*

Miller, Alison. 1982. "Week Offers Abundant Activities," *The Beacon*, University of Portland, Vol. 84, No. 6, 7 Oct: 1.*

Oddo, Rev. Thomas C, CSC. 1982. *Inauguration Address.* Delivered 10 Oct.

Raffanti, Michael. 1982. "Berle Show Disappoints Critic," *The Beacon*, University of Portland, Vol. 84, No. 7, 14 Oct: 8.

Raffanti, Michael. 1982. "Hesburgh Shares Presidential Insights," *The Beacon*, University of Portland, Vol. 84, No. 7, 14 Oct: 7.

Whitney, David. 1982. "New UP President to Promote Social Justice, Values," *The Sunday Oregonian*, 10 Oct: D4.*

Chapter 12: *The First Year, 1982–1983*

Butterworth, Beverly H. 1983. "Party Follows Final Curtain Call for Operatic Cast," *The Sunday Oregonian*, 20 Mar: 135.

Corpora, Joseph. 2023. Personal interview with Tyler Bieber, 28 Dec.

Lageson, Anna. 1983. "Dundore Organizes Lifeyard Exhibit," *The Beacon*, Vol. 84, No. 29, 28 Apr: 11.

Miller, Alison. 1982. "Campaign Aids Development," *The Beacon*, University of Portland, Vol. 84, No. 9, 28 Oct: 1.

Miller, Alison. 1982. "Oddo Explains Capital Fund Drive," *The Beacon*, University of Portland, Vol. 84, No. 10, 4 Nov: 3.

Miller, Alison. 1983. "Dean Schoeck Resigns Position," *The Beacon*, University of Portland, Vol. 84, No. 16, 20 Jan: 1.

Miller, Alison. 1983. "Oddo Announces Open Search," *The Beacon*, University of Portland, Vol. 84, No. 25, 31 Mar: 1.

Miller, Alison. 1983. "Task Force Completes First Meeting," *The Beacon*, University of Portland, Vol. 84, No. 18, 3 Feb: 1.

Nellor, Dan. 1983. "Specific Skills Increase Desirability," *The Beacon*, University of Portland, Vol. 84, No. 20, 17 Feb: 7.

Nellor, Dan. 1983. "Students May Lack Training for Future Technology," *The Beacon*, University of Portland, Vol. 84, No. 19, 10 Feb: 6.

Nellor, Dan. 1983. "Students Need Computers," *The Beacon*, University of Portland, Vol. 84, No. 21, 24 Feb: 5.

Nellor, Dan. 1983. "Two Departments Face Conflict over Classes," *The Beacon*, University of Portland, Vol. 84, No. 22, 3 Mar: 10.

Nudo, Mario. 1983. "Forces to Meet, Discuss Future," *The Beacon*, University of Portland, Vol. 84, No. 17, 27 Jan: 1.

Oddo, Thomas C. 1982. "Letters to the Editor: Oddo Corrects," *The Beacon*, University of Portland, Vol. 84, No. 9, 28 Oct: 2.

Portland Magazine. 2014. "Class Notes," Vol. 33, Spring: 41.*

Starbuck, Scoop.^ 1983. "Oddo Becomes AC," *The Bacon*, University of Portland, Vol. 84, No. 25.5, 1 Jan: 4.*

The Beacon. 1982. "Thanksgiving Canned Food Drive Continues," University of Portland, Vol. 84, No. 12, 18 Nov: 10. Photo by John Dougherty.*

The Beacon. 1983. "Circle K Sponsors 'Kiss-a-Pig' Contest," University of Portland, Vol. 84, No. 17, 27 Jan: 3.

The Beacon. 1983. "Mourning Continues," University of Portland, Vol. 84, No. 21, 24 Feb: 1.

The Columbian. 1983. "Art Exhibit's Theme Is Life in Nuclear Age," Vancouver, Washington, 26 Apr: 40.

The Oregonian. 1983. "Charity Officers Set," 12 Feb: 21.

The Sunday Oregonian. 1982. "Solutions to the Nuclear Arms Race," Convocation Announcement, Portland State University, 7 Nov: 14.

The World. 1983. "Computers and Religious Values Will Meet Head on at Conference," Coos Bay, Oregon, 25 Aug: p. 6.

Chapter 13: *Talking Peace and Ethics*

Oddo, Rev. Thomas C, CSC. 1983. "The Religious Challenge for Peace," Delivered 23 Nov.

Oddo, Rev. Thomas C, CSC. 1984. "Priorities and Mission of the University of Portland." Delivered 2 June.

Oddo, Rev. Thomas C, CSC. 1984. "Reflections at the Province Assembly," 10–14 June.

Smeback, Kym. 1984. "Oddo Elaborates on Education," *The Beacon*, Vol. 85, No. 21, 23 Feb: 3.

The Oregonian. 1983. "Thanksgiving Services Slated," 19 Nov: 36.

The Oregonian. 1984. "Serendipity: Ideas," 11 May: 80.

The Oregonian. 1984. "Students Get Involved in Projects for Peace," 10 May: 109.

Chapter 14: *Chiles Center*

Badolato, Diana. 1983. "Construction Proceeds on Schedule," *The Beacon*, University of Portland, Vol. 85, No. 1, 1 Sept: 5.

Braxton, Brenda. 1984. "Center Opens Window to U of P," *The Beacon*, University of Portland, Vol. 86, No. 1, 6 Sept: 1.

Cluff, Carl. 1982. "Multipurpose Complex Unveiled for Pilots," *The Oregonian*, 26 Oct: 79. Photo by Greg Lawler.*

DeBuse, Nikki. 1986. "The Dream Come True," *The Beacon*, University of Portland, Vol. 88, No. 5, 2 Oct: 8.

Drew, Jacque. 1984. "Student Use of Chiles Center Examined," *The Beacon*, University of Portland, Vol. 86, No. 7, 18 Oct: 1.

Dunevant, Ron. 1983. "Frame Completed as Fund Raising Continues," *The Beacon*, University of Portland, Vol. 85, No. 5, 29 Sept: 1, 6.

Ehlinger, Rebecca. 1984. "Use of Earle A. Chiles Center Studied," *The Beacon,* University of Portland, Vol. 85, No. 29, 26 Apr: 1.

Johnson, Pat. 1983. "Neighbors Discuss Development," *The Beacon*, University of Portland, Vol. 84, No. 16, 20 Jan: 3. Photo by Andy Arnold.*

Lovell, Fred. 1984. "Louisiana Pacific Donates Tennis Area," *The Beacon*, University of Portland, Vol. 86, No. 6, 11 Oct: 1.

Miller, Alison. 1982. "Oddo Explains Capital Fund Drive," *The Beacon*, Vol. 84, No. 10, 4 Nov: 3.

Miller, Alison. 1983. "Ground-Breaking Slated, Dome Construction Begins," *The Beacon*, University of Portland, Vol. 84, No. 29, 28 Apr: 1.

Nicholas, Jonathan. 1984. "Having the Bite Stuff: They're Off," *The Oregonian*, 29 June: 15.

Oddo, Rev. Thomas C, CSC. 1983. "Remarks, University of Portland Ground Breaking: Earle A. Chiles Center," Delivered 18 May. Accessed from University of Portland Archives, 2 Aug 2023.

Pasero, George. "Pilots' Dome Rises to Take Its Place Among Autumn Splendor," *The Sunday Oregonian*, 30 Oct: 41.

Schneidermann, Floyd. 1984. "Wide Use Ahead for Pilots' New Facility," *The Sunday Oregonian*, 21 Oct: 126.

The Oregonian. 1983. "UP Ceremony Signals Start," 19 May: 60.

University of Portland. 1984. "Tennis Center to Be Built," Press Release, 2 Oct.

Viall, Lesli. 1986. "Oddo Addresses University Issues at Convocation," *The Beacon*, University of Portland, Vol. 88, No. 3, 18 Sept: 1, 5.

Wilmes, James. 1986. "New Phone System Purchased," *The Beacon*, Vol. 88, No. 1, 4 Sept: 3.

Woodward, Nadine. 1984. "Chiles Center Dedicated Before Crowd of 1,700," *The Beacon*, University of Portland, Vol. 86, No. 8, 25 Oct: 1.*

Chapter 15: *The Gipper Visits the Bluff*

Connolly, Carolyn. 2016. "Campaign Trail: President Ronald Reagan, 1984," PortLog, University of Portland, Nov 1. https://sites.up.edu/museum/campaign-trail-president-ronald-reagan-1984/. Accessed 27 Apr 2023.

Drew, Jacque. 1984. "Political Rally, U of P Clash," *The Beacon*, University of Portland, Vol. 86, No. 9, 1 Nov: 5.

Manley, Paul. 1984. "Band Plays on, but Not for Reagan," *The Oregonian*, 20 Oct: 1.

Perry, Douglas. "Liar, Liar, Pants on Fire': Remembering Ronald Reagan's 'Shocking' 1984 Visit to Portland," *The Oregonian/OregonLIVE,* 20 Feb. https://www.oregonlive.com/today/2016/02/liar_liar_pants_on_fire_rememb.html. Accessed online, 21 Sept 2013.

Piatz, Judy. 1984. "Reagan Blasts Mondale Policies," *The Beacon*, University of Portland, Vol. 86, No. 8, 25 Oct: 1.

Piatz, Judy. 1984. "Reagan Speaks in 'Dome' Tuesday," *The Beacon*, University of Portland, Vol. 86, No. 7, 18 Oct: 1.

Reagan, Ronald. 1984. "Remarks at a Reagan–Bush Rally in Portland, Oregon." Delivered 23 Oct. Available from: https://www.reaganlibrary.gov/archives/speech/remarks-reagan-bush-rally-portland-oregon.

Shen, Fern. 1984. "Fans Strain for Glimpse of Reagan," *The Oregonian*, 23 Oct: 15.

The Oregonian. 1984. "'Joke' No Laughing Matter," 31 Oct: 62.

Van House, Teri. 1984. "Reagan Plays to Mixed Reviews," *The Beacon*, University of Portland, Vol. 86, No. 8, 25 Oct: 5.

White House Television Office. 1984. "President Reagan's Remarks at a Reagan-Bush Rally in Portland, Oregon on October 23, 1984." Courtesy of Ronald Reagan Presidential Library. YouTube video, uploaded 27 Aug. 2018. Accessed from https://youtu.be/yH1zDlASkhM?si=dQqs6RtqZmWexHEv.

Chapter 16: *Apathy*

Braxton, Brenda. 1985. "Asbestos Insulation Investigation Slated," *The Beacon*, University of Portland, Vol. 86, No. 22, 28 Feb: 1, 4.

Braxton, Brenda. 1985. "Design Errors Prompt Dome Lawsuit," *The Beacon*, University of Portland, Vol. 86, No. 15, 10 Jan: 1.

Braxton, Brenda. 1985. "KDUP's Cable Debut Delayed Again," *The Beacon*, University of Portland, Vol. 86, No. 16, 17 Jan: 1, 4.

Clohessy, Craig. 1985. "Simple Meal Receives Nationwide Recognition," *The Beacon*, University of Portland, Vol. 87, No. 12, 21 Nov: 4.

Drew, Jacque. 1984. "Ticket Handlers Cut Back, Voice Disapproval," *The Beacon*, University of Portland, Vol. 86, No. 14, 13 Dec: 1.

Drew, Jacque. 1985. "Union Urges L-P Donation Dropped," *The Beacon*, University of Portland, Vol. 86, No. 18, 31 Jan: 1.

Fundingsland, Brian. 1985. "Campus Thief Steals Money From Offices," *The Beacon*, Vol. 87, No. 3, 19 Sept: 3.

Gamaunt, Roger. 1986. "No Major Entertainment Scheduled," *The Beacon,* University of Portland, Vol. 87, No. 18, 30 Jan: 4.

Lamberty, Ruth. 1985. "ICC OKs Toga Dance, Passes Two Allocations," *The Beacon*, University of Portland, Vol. 87, No. 14, 12 Dec: 4.

Lovell, Fred. 1984. "University Ad-Hoc Committee Studied," *The Beacon*, Vol. 85, No. 28, 19 Apr: 1, 4.

Piatz, Judy. 1985. "Villa R.A.s Fired After Mehling Prank," *The Beacon*, University of Portland, Vol. 86, No. 21, 21 Feb: 1, 4.

Rubenstein, Sura. 1985. "Catholic Labor Leader Voices Barb," *The Oregonian*, 17 Jan: 63.

Schmitke, David Rex. 1984. "Controversy Continues over KDUP," *The Beacon*, University of Portland, Vol. 85, No. 24, 15 Mar: 1, 3.

Schmitke, David Rex. 1985. "'Self-Seriousology,' Lack of Fun Invades Campus," *The Beacon*, University of Portland, Vol. 86, No. 16, 17 Jan: 3.

The Beacon. 1984. "Administration's Policy Ignores Good Friday," editorial, University of Portland, Vol. 85, No. 28, 19 Apr: 2.

The Beacon. 1984. Untitled editorial cartoon (Good Friday), University of Portland, Vol. 85, No. 28, 19 Apr: 2.

The Beacon. 1985. "Apathy Expressed Through Stagnation," University of Portland, Vol. 86, No. 22, 28 Feb: 3.

The Beacon. 1985. "Concert Fails to Attract Crowd," University of Portland, Vol. 87, No. 3, 19 Sept: 3.

The Beacon. 1985. "Father Anderson Dies of Cardiac Arrest," University of Portland, Vol. 86, No. 24, 14 Mar: 4.

The Beacon. 1985. "McCoy Dies of Heart Attack," University of Portland, Vol. 87, No. 11, 14 Nov: 1.

The Beacon. 1985. "Promises, Promises," editorial, University of Portland, Vol. 86, No. 16, 17 Jan: 2.

Winpenny, Karen. 1985. "Senators to Decide Toga Fate," *The Beacon*, University of Portland, Vol. 87, No. 13, 5 Dec: 1.

Chapter 17: *The Coaches*

Avina, Jack. 1987. "Avina Discusses Resignation." Interview by Dan Christopherson. *The Beacon*, University of Portland, Vol. 88, No. 23, 19 Mar: 15.

Belanger, Paul. 1985. "Harriers Win National Title," *The Beacon*, University of Portland, Vol. 87, No. 12, 21 Nov: 1.

Christopherson, Dan. 1985. "Women's Athletics Commits to NCAA," *The Beacon*, University of Portland, Vol. 87, No. 13, 5 Dec: 1, 4.

Christopherson, Dan. 1987. "Avina Resigns Pilot Helm," *The Beacon*, University of Portland, Vol. 88, No. 22, 12 Mar: 1, 11.

Frei, Terry. 1987. "Pilots Should Widen Search," *The Oregonian*, 27 May: 21.

Kahn, David. 1985. "Season Puzzling to Avina," *The Oregonian*, 8 Feb: 165, 169.

Los Angeles Times. 1987. "Ex-Trail Blazer Becomes a Coach," 31 May. Originally published by *Associated Press*.

Mulfur, Bill. 1986. "Olmsted Philosophical About Losing Lady Pilots Coaching Job," *The Oregonian,* 1 Mar: 48.

Oddo, Rev. Thomas C, CSC. 1987. "An Interview with the President." Interview by the *Beacon* interview team, *The Beacon*, University of Portland, Vol. 88, No. 28, 23 Apr: 7.

Wheeler, Ken. 1987. "Avina Steps Down as Pilots' Coach," *The Oregonian*, 11 Mar: 47, 54.

Wheeler, Ken. 1987. "Steele Hired to Coach Pilots," *The Oregonian*, 28 May: 41.

Chapter 18: *Chapel of Christ the Teacher*

Buhler, Cathy. 1986. "Chapel to House Yearbook, Paper Offices," *The Beacon*, University of Portland, Vol. 87, No. 25, 27 Mar: 4.

Christopherson, Dan. 1986. "Chapel Dedication Oct. 5," *The Beacon*, University of Portland, Vol. 88, No. 2, 11 Sept: 1.

Farris, Michael. 1986. "Dome Traffic Angers Residents," *The Beacon*, University of Portland, Vol. 87, No. 25, 27 Mar: 5.

Farris, Michael. 1986. "University Officials Discuss Plans for St. Mary's, Pilot House," *The Beacon*, University of Portland, Vol. 87, No. 23, 6 Mar: 1.

Gaussoin, Lori. "Chapel Brings Changes, New Beginnings," *The Beacon*, University of Portland, Vol. 88, No. 25, 2 Apr: 12.

Hayakawa, Alan R. 1986. "New Chapel to Be Dedicated at University of Portland," *The Oregonian*, 5 Oct: 26.

Kapitanovich, Michelle. 1986. "Mass, Festivities Celebrate Dedication," *The Beacon*, University of Portland, Vol. 88, No. 5, 2 Oct: 1.

Nellor, Dan. 1983. "Students, Faculty Express Need for Union," *The Beacon*, University of Portland, Vol. 85, No. 3, 15 Sept: 1.

Rutherford, Richard. 2023. Personal interview with Tyler Bieber, 9 Sept.

The Beacon. 1986. "Fenced In," University of Portland, Vol. 87, No. 19, 6 Feb: 4. Photograph by Mary Nittinger.*

The Beacon. 1986. "Grand Event," University of Portland, Vol. 88, No. 6, 9 Oct: 1. Photograph by Joe Brockert.*

The Beacon. 1986. "Scissors Please!," University of Portland, Vol. 88, No. 2, 11 Sept: 1. Photograph by Joe Brockert.*

The Oregonian. 1985. "Metro Roundup: Projects Approved," 19 Nov: 55.

The Oregonian. 1985. "Permits for Chapel, Subdivision Gain OK," 19 Nov: 66.

Viall, Lesli. 1986. "New Telephone System Proposed," *The Beacon*, University of Portland, Vol. 87, No. 29, 24 Apr: 1.

Viall, Lesli. 1986. "St. Mary's Lounge Project Underway," *The Beacon*, University of Portland, Vol. 88, No. 2, 11 Sept: 1.

Vogel, Greg. 1986. "Dorm Ceiling Caves in at Christie Hall," *The Beacon*, University of Portland, Vol. 87, No. 19, 6 Feb: 1.

Wilmes, James. 1985. "Chapel Permit Granted," *The Beacon*, University of Portland, Vol. 87, No. 12, 21 Nov: 1.

Wilmes, James. 1986. "Pilot House, Chapel Facilities on Schedule for Completion," *The Alpha*, University of Portland: 4.

Part Three: Camelot
1986–1989

Chapter 19: *Campus Life*

Anctil, Rick. 1988. "'Outfield' Loss Final at $17,000," *The Beacon*, University of Portland, Vol. 89, No. 19, 11 Feb: 6.

Austin, Christina. 1987. "John Denver Directs Music to Social Issues," *The Beacon*, University of Portland, Vol. 89, No. 6, 8 Oct: 9.

Badolato, Diana. 1984. "Black History Week Begins," *The Beacon*, University of Portland, Vol. 85, No. 20, 16 Feb: 1.

Church, Foster. 1985. "Charitable Organizations Seek Relief From Sales Tax," *The Oregonian*, 5 Mar: 33.

Corrado, Andrew. 1987. "Voyager Astronauts to Speak," *The Beacon*, University of Portland, Vol. 88, No. 22, 12 Mar: 5.

Davison, Ty. 1987. "Concert Losses Result in Doubt of Major Entertainment Feasibility," *The Beacon*, University of Portland, Vol. 89, No. 13, 3 Dec: 4.

Emter, Robert. 1987. "Club Aids Recovering Alcoholics," *The Beacon*, University of Portland, Vol. 88, No. 18, 5 Feb: 9.

Enberg, Laurie. 1986. "Program Offers Assistance," *The Beacon*, University of Portland, Vol. 88, No. 4, 25 Sept: 3.

Enberg, Laurie. 1986. "Williams Show Profits $10,000," *The Beacon*, University of Portland, University of Portland, Vol. 88, No. 9, 30 Oct: 5.

Fisher, Mary Kaye. 1988. "Hatfield to Address Graduates," *The Beacon*, University of Portland, Vol. 89, No. 28, 21 Apr: B.

Fisher, Mary Kaye. 1988. "Ursula Le Guin Shares Her Views on Literature," *The Beacon*, University of Portland, Vol. 89, No. 22, 3 Mar: 6.

Gaussoin, Lori. 1987. "BC Computer Lab Completed," *The Beacon*, University of Portland, Vol. 88, No. 18, 5 Feb: 4.

Green, Ashbel S. 1987. "Scholars Take Plunge into Realities of Street Life," *The Oregonian*, 3 Aug: 11. Photo by Kraig Scattarella.*

Idler, Constance. 1987. "Catholic Radio to Be Broadcast from UP," *The Beacon*, University of Portland, Vol. 89, No. 2, 10 Sept: 1.

Kinnicutt, Abigale. 1986. "Computer Agreement Negotiations Continue," *The Beacon*, University of Portland, Vol. 88, No. 7, 16 Oct: 1.

Lawrence, Mitch. 1986. "NCAA Convention to Settle Proposition 48 With Cooler Heads," *Clarion-Ledger*, Jackson, Mississippi, 13 Jan: 31.

Oddo, Thomas C, CSC. 1984. "University of Portland Victory March." Music by Phillip Cansler.

Ott, Heidi. 1985. "Prizes Provide Incentive for Faculty, Staff Activity," *The Beacon*, University of Portland, Vol. 87, No. 11, 14 Nov: 11.

Ott, Heidi. 1986. "Comic Humors Sell-Out Crowd," *The Beacon*, University of Portland, Vol. 88, No. 8, 23 Oct: 8.

Poush, Michelle. 1988. "Senate Votes $300 to Rudolph Fundraiser," *The Beacon*, University of Portland, Vol. 89, No. 24, 24 Mar: 4.

Schmitke, David Rex. 1984. "Committee Suggests Regent Change," *The Beacon*, University of Portland, Vol. 85, No. 21, 23 Feb: 1, 3.

Schmitke, David Rex. 1984. "U of P Celebrates Women's Week," *The Beacon*, University of Portland, Vol. 85, No. 23, 8 Mar: 3.

Seigneur, Cornelia Becker. 2009. *West Linn*. Arcadia Publishing.

Stupur, Danette. 1985. "Music Damage Reported to ICC," *The Beacon*, University of Portland, Vol. 87, No. 7, 17 Oct: 4.

The Beacon. 1986. "A Home Away from Home," University of Portland, Vol. 88, No. 4, 25 Sept: 3. Photograph by Joe Brockert.*

The Beacon. 1987. "Celebrities," University of Portland, Vol. 88, No. 21, 26 Feb: 1. Photograph by Tina Wager.*

The Beacon. 1987. "CPB Speaker to Discuss Subliminal Advertising," University of Portland, Vol. 88, No. 20, 19 Feb: 7.

The Beacon. 1987. "Current Issues Vital to Oddo Presidency," editorial, University of Portland, Vol. 88, No. 28, 23 Apr: 2.

The Beacon. 1987. "Say What?," University of Portland, Vol. 88, No. 18, 5 Feb: 9. Photograph by Christian Bayer.*

The Beacon. 1988. "Rudolph Still in Serious Condition," University of Portland, Vol. 89, No. 24, 24 Mar: 4.

The Oregonian. 1984. "How Multnomah County Voted,", table of election results, 8 Nov: 40.

The Oregonian. 1987. "Business Digest: The Region," 4 Aug: 36.

Viall, Lesli L. 1987. "Campus Beautification Day Planned," *The Beacon*, University of Portland, Vol. 88, No. 23, 19 Mar: 5.

Wager, Tina. 1987. "Manila Archbishop to Speak at Graduation," *The Beacon*, University of Portland, Vol. 88, No. 27, 16 Apr: 1.

Wilmes, James. 1986. "Officials Discuss Student Issues," *The Beacon,* University of Portland, Vol. 88, No. 7, 16 Oct: 1. Photograph by Christian Bayer.*

Woodward, Nadine. 1984. "ABC-TV Correspondent to Speak," *The Beacon*, University of Portland, Vol. 86, No. 4, 27 Sept: 1.

Chapter 20: *Dark Horse*

Johnson, Dirk. 1987. "University of Notre Dame: After 35 Years as President, Hesburgh Retires," *The New York Times*, 18 May: 6.

Malloy, Edward A. "Monk," CSC. 2016. *Monk's Tale: The Presidential Years, 1987–2005*. University of Notre Dame Press.

McCluskey, Neil et al. 1967. "Land O'Lakes Statement: The Nature of the Contemporary Catholic University," International Federation of Catholic Universities.

Mouasher, Maher. 1986. "The New Guard," *The Scholastic*, University of Notre Dame, Vol. 128, No. 4, 2 Oct: 7–9.

Notre Dame Report. 1986. "Corporate Grants Committee Named," Number 8 (86/87), 19 Dec: 153.

Oddo, Thomas C, CSC. 1987. "Inaugural Mass Homily," *Notre Dame Report*, Number 5 (87/88), 6 Nov: 170–172. Delivered 23 Sept.

Pankowski, Mark. 1986. "Officials Discount Story Saying Malloy Next ND President," *The Observer*, University of Notre Dame, 3 Nov: 1, 3.

The Idea of the Catholic University. 1967. "Land O'Lakes Statement," Land O'Lakes, Wisconsin, 23 Jul: 1.

The New York Times. 1986. "Notre Dame President Trying Again to Retire," 13 June: 14. Originally published by *Associated Press*.

Chapter 21: *A Value-Centered Education*

Connelly, James T. "The University of Portland: A Catholic University?" American Catholic Studies (American Catholic Historic Society), Vol. 116, No. 1, Spring 2005, pp. 29-41.

Fox, Tim. 1986. "Speakers Face Topics in Conference," *The Beacon*, University of Portland, Vol. 88, No. 4, 25 Sept: 3.

Oddo, Rev. Thomas, CSC. 1985. "A Perspective on Catholic Higher Education." Delivered Aug 1985. Accessed from University of Portland Archives, 20 Jan 2025.

Oddo, Thomas C, CSC. 1986. "Value-Centered Education and Freedom of Inquiry: Some Perspectives on the Delicate Balance." Remarks delivered 9 Dec to the Northwest Association of Schools and Colleges. Accessed from University of Portland Archives, 20 Jan 2025.

Oddo, Thomas. 1985. "Service with (Com)passion." Accessed from University of Portland Archives, 2 Aug 2023.

The Rotarian. 1985. "Ethics: The Discipline of Right and Wrong," Oct: 34.

Chapter 22: *AIDS*

Austin, Christina. 1987. "AIDS Prevention Begins on College Level," *The Beacon*, University of Portland, Vol. 88, No. 23, 19 Mar: 11.

Harvey, Lori. 1986. "Speakers Address AIDS," *The Beacon*, University of Portland, Vol. 87, No. 23, 6 Mar: 4.

Harvey, Lori. 1986. "Speakers to Discuss AIDS at Presentation," *The Beacon*, University of Portland, Vol. 87, No. 21, 20 Feb: 4.

Hoover, Nancy. 1987. "'Safe Sex' Brochure Prepared," *The Beacon*, University of Portland, Vol. 89, No. 6, 8 Oct: 1.

McCarthy, Justin. 2019. "Gallup Vault: Fear and Anxiety During the 1980s AIDS Crisis," Gallup, 28 Jun.

Padilla, Catherine. 1988. "AIDS Brochure Completed," *The Beacon,* University of Portland, Vol. 89, No. 25, 31 Mar: 4.

The Beacon. 1987. "AIDS Brochure Responsible Move," editorial, University of Portland, Vol. 89, No. 6, 8 Oct: 2.

The Beacon. 1988. "AIDS Brochure Balances Issues," editorial, University of Portland, Vol. 89, No. 25, 31 Mar: 2.

The Beacon. 1986. "Opinion Poll," University of Portland, Vol. 87, No. 17, 23 Jan: 2.

The Beacon. 1988. "Views on Campus," University of Portland, Vol. 89, No. 24, 24 Mar: 2.

Chapter 23: *Co-Ed Housing*

Anctil, Rick. 1988. "Second Coed Hall Proposed to Senate," *The Beacon*, University of Portland, Vol. 89, No. 16, 21 Jan: 4.

Christopherson, Dan. 1987. "Shipstad to Become a Co-Ed Hall," *The Beacon*, University of Portland, Vol. 88, No. 25, 2 Apr: 1.

Davidson, Ty-dye. 1987. "Surprise! Ohno Says No More Intervisitation!!!," *The Bacon*, University of Portland, 1 Apr: 1.^

DeBuse, Nikki. 1988. "Oddo Supports Dissent in Classroom," *The Beacon*, University of Portland, Vol. 89, No. 22, 3 Mar: 3.

Fogel, Lynn. 1987. "Greiner Discusses Rally for Coed Residence Halls," *The Beacon*, University of Portland, Vol. 88, No. 24, 26 Mar: 4.

Jenck, Martin J., et al. 1984. "Letters to the Editor: Coed Housing a Change for Progress," *The Beacon*, University of Portland, Vol 85, No. 18, 2 Feb: 2.

Nellor, Dan. 1983. "Co-Ed Dorms a Progressive Step," *The Beacon*, University of Portland, Vol. 85, No. 1, 1 Sept: 3.

Phillips, Katherine. 1987. "Students Favor Coed Dorms, Open Lounge," *The Beacon*, University of Portland, Vol. 88, No. 20, 19 Feb: 1, 5.

Poush, Michelle. 1987. "Students Claim 'Life as Usual' in Coed Hall," *The Beacon,* University of Portland, Vol. 89, No. 3, 17 Sept: 8.

Poush, Michelle. 1988. "Regents Approve Second Coed Residence Hall," *The Beacon*, University of Portland, Vol. 89, No. 22, 3 Mar: 1.

The Beacon. 1987. "Coed Housing Needs Consideration," editorial, University of Portland, Vol. 88, No. 20, 19 Feb: 2.

The Beacon. 1987."Coed Dorm Reality, Thanks to Oddo," editorial, University of Portland, Vol. 88, No. 26, 9 Apr: 2.

Viall, Lesli L. "Coed Proposal May Go to Committee," *The Beacon*, University of Portland, Vol. 88, No. 23, 19 Mar: 1, 5.

Yocum, Jennifer. 1984. "Growing Population Forces Dorm Swap," *The Beacon*, University of Portland, Vol. 85, No. 16, 19 Jan: 1, 3.

Chapter 24: *Apartheid*

Baasten, Matthew. 1987. "Apartheid—Just the Facts," *The Beacon*, University of Portland, Vol. 89, No. 4, 24 Sept: 3.

Corvallis Gazette-Times. 1984. "Experts Say Selling S. Africa–Related Investments Unwise," *Corvallis Gazette-Times,* 2 Dec: 12. Originally published by *Associated Press.*

Idler, Constance. 1987. "Coma Party Ruled Illegal by OLCC," *The Beacon*, University of Portland, Vol. 89, No. 13, 3 Dec: 1.

Idler, Constance. 1987. "Senate Calls for Investment Review by Board of Regents," *The Beacon*, University of Portland, Vol. 89, No. 8, 22 Oct: 4.

Kagee, Ashraf. 1989. "South African Government in No Hurry for Reform," *The Beacon*, University of Portland, Vol. 91, No. 7, 12 Oct: 4.

Kapitanovich, Michelle. 1987. "Regents Respond to Divestment Review," *The Beacon*, University of Portland, Vol. 89, No. 11, 12 Nov: 1, 3.

Oddo, Thomas C, CSC. 1986. "Value-Centered Education and Freedom of Inquiry: Some Perspectives on the Delicate Balance." Remarks delivered 9 Dec to the Northwest Association of Schools and Colleges. Accessed from University of Portland Archives, 20 Jan 2025.

Oddo, Rev. Thomas C, CSC. 1987. "An Interview with the President." Interview by *The Beacon* interview team, *The Beacon*, University of Portland, Vol. 88, No. 28, 23 Apr: 7.

Phillips, Katherine. 1987. "Divestment Issues Debated," *The Beacon*, University of Portland, Vol. 89, No. 5, 1 Oct: 1.

Richards, Ken. 1985. "South African Apartheid Best Dissolved Slowly," *The Beacon,* University of Portland, Vol. 87, No. 10, 7 Nov: 3.

The Africa Fund. 1988. "Divestment Action on South Africa by US and Canadian Colleges and Universities," Aug.

The Beacon. 1985. "Apartheid Protests," University of Portland, Vol. 87, No. 7, 17 Oct: 4. Photograph by Brad Newgard.*

The Beacon. 1985."City Bits: Reed Students Protest South African Investments," University of Portland, Vol. 87, No. 10, 7 Nov: 6.

The Beacon. 1986. "City Bits: Reed Students Occupy Building in Protest," University of Portland, Vol. 87, No. 18, 30 Jan: 6.

The Beacon. 1988. "Openness Adds to Students' Trust," editorial, University of Portland, Vol. 89, No. 28, 21 Apr: 2.

Williams, Lena. 1986. "Pressure Rises on Colleges to Withdraw South Africa Interests," *The New York Times*, 2 Feb: 14.

Chapter 25: *Tom Meets the Pope*

John Paul II. 1987. "Address of His Holiness John Paul II," 12 Sept: Part I, Sect. 5, Para. 1.

Means, Howard. 1987. "Is Pope Out of Touch?," *The Orlando Sentinel*, 20 Sept: 107.

Rubenstein, Sura. 1987. "Oregon Catholic Representatives to Take Part in Papal Meetings," *The Oregonian*, 7 Sept: 27.

The Oregonian. 1987. "Daytime Highlights," 28 Sept: 27.

Viall, Lesli. 1986. "Catholic Teaching Roles Discussed," *The Beacon*, University of Portland, Vol. 88, No. 8, 23 Oct: 1, 5.

Chapter 26: *Saving AFROTC #695*

Baxter, Ray. 1988. "Cadets' Future Still Uncertain," *The Beacon*, University of Portland, Vol. 90, No. 6, 6 Oct: 1, 4.

Boothe, Amy. 1988. "Roscoe Joins Student Services," *The Beacon*, University of Portland, Vol. 90, No. 1, 1 Sept: 10.

Fisher, Mary Kaye. 1988. "Roscoe's Leadership Pushes ROTC to Top," *The Beacon,* University of Portland, Vol. 89, No. 27, 14 Apr: 10.

MacKay, Deana. 1988. "Cadets Keep Fighting for UP Detachment's Survival," *The Beacon*, University of Portland, Vol. 89, No. 19, 11 Feb: 1.

The Beacon. 1988. "AFROTC Will Need Continued Support," editorial, University of Portland, Vol. 89, No. 17, 28 Jan: 2.

The Beacon. 1988. "Congressional Visit," University of Portland, Vol. 89, No. 20, 18 Feb: 1. Photograph by Roger Bighouse.*

The Beacon. 1988. "Fate of UP's ROTC Unknown," University of Portland, Vol. 89, No. 20, 18 Feb: 4.

The Beacon. 1988. "ROTC Detachments Remain Open," University of Portland, Vol. 89, No. 27, 14 Apr: 1.

The Beacon. 1988. "ROTC Receives New Hope," University of Portland, Vol. 89, No. 23, 17 Mar: 4.

The Beacon. 1988. "UP's Air Force Detachment to Reopen," University of Portland, Vol. 89, No. 25, 31 Mar: 1.

Viall, Lesli L. 1988. "Cadets, Oddo Work to Reverse AFROTC Detachment Closure," *The Beacon*, University of Portland, Vol. 89, No. 18, 4 Feb: 1.

Viall, Lesli L. 1988. "Packwood to Visit ROTC Cadets Friday," *The Beacon*, University of Portland, Vol. 89, No. 19, 11 Feb: 1.

Viall, Lesli. 1988. "Air Force to Close ROTC Detachment," *The Beacon*, University of Portland, Vol. 89, No. 17, 28 Jan: 1, 4.

Viall, Lesli. 1988. "ROTC Closed at UP; U of M Remains Open," *The Beacon*, University of Portland, Vol. 89, No. 21, 25 Feb: 1.

Chapter 27: *The Cost of Building*

Becker, Charlotte. 1985. "Administration Releases President's Report," *The Beacon*, University of Portland, Vol. 87, No. 9, 31 Oct: 1.

Buhler, Cathy. 1986. "Funding Sought for New Technology Center," *The Beacon*, University of Portland, Vol. 88, No. 12, 20 Nov: 1.

Cavanagh, Bill. 1986. "Skyrocketing Tuition Threatens Students," *The Beacon*, University of Portland, Vol. 87, No. 24, 13 Mar: 3.

Clohessy, Craig. 1986. "Room and Board Rates to Increase," *The Beacon*, University of Portland, Vol. 87, No. 23, 6 Mar: 1.

Courtney, Matt. 1986. "Par Course Under Repair," *The Beacon*, University of Portland, Vol. 88, No. 10, 6 Nov: 4.

Hill, David. 1988. "Donation Saves UP More Than $90,000," *The Beacon*, University of Portland, Vol. 90, No. 1, 1 Sept: 1, 4.

Idler, Constance. 1988. "1988–89 tuition rate increases 6 percent," *The Beacon*, University of Portland, Vol. 89, No. 23, 17 Mar: 1, 4.

Kinnicutt, Abigale. 1986. "PC Discount Plan Discussed," *The Beacon*, University of Portland, Vol. 88, No. 3, 18 Sept: 1.

Kinnicutt, Abigale. 1986. "Tuition Revenue Increases," *The Beacon*, University of Portland, Vol. 88, No. 9, 30 Oct: 1.

Lovell, Fred. 1984. "Tuition Increase Scheduled," *The Beacon*, University of Portland, Vol. 85, No. 23, 8 Mar: 1.

Nellor, Nancy. 1985. "Tuition, Room and Board Rates Rise," *The Beacon*, University of Portland, Vol. 86, No. 23, 7 Mar: 1.

Oddo, Fr. Tom, CSC. 1988. "1988–89 Tuition and Room/Board Rates," Advertising Supplement, *The Beacon*, University of Portland, Vol. 89, No. 23, 17 Mar: 12.

Phillips, Katherine. 1987. "Enrollment Down 6.6% from Fall," *The Beacon*, University of Portland, Vol. 88, No. 19, 12 Feb: 1.

Ripp, Corrie. 1983. "Enrollment Figures In," *The Beacon*, University of Portland, Vol. 85, No. 5, 29 Sept: 4.

The Beacon. 1983. "Tuition Increases," University of Portland, Vol. 84, No. 23, 10 Mar: 1.

The Beacon. 1984. "Tuition Increase Hits Hard at U of P," editorial cartoon, University of Portland, Vol. 85, No. 23, 8 Mar: 2.

The Beacon. 1985. "University's Budget Remains a Secret," editorial, University of Portland, Vol. 86, No. 24, 14 Mar: 2.

Viall, Lesli L. 1987. "Flat Tuition Rate to Be Adopted," University of Portland, Vol. 88, No. 22, 12 Mar: 1, 5.

Viall, Lesli L. 1987. "Flat-Rate Tuition Being Considered for Fall Semester," *The Beacon*, University of Portland, Vol. 88, No. 18, 5 Feb: 1, 4.

Viall, Lesli. 1986. "Tuition Rates to Rise 6.5 Percent This Fall," *The Beacon*, University of Portland, Vol. 87, No. 26, 3 Apr: 1.

Viall, Lesli. 1986. "Undergraduate Enrollment Falls 6.3 Percent," *The Beacon*, University of Portland, Vol. 88, No. 5, 2 Oct: 1, 4.

Chapter 28: *The Last Year, 1988–1989*

Baxter, Ray. 1988. "Fasting, Introspection Common Experiences This Week at UP," *The Beacon,* University of Portland, Vol. 90, No. 12, 17 Nov: 1, 4.

Baxter, Ray. 1988. "New Residence Awaits Funding, Formal Approval," *The Beacon*, University of Portland, Vol. 90, No. 13, 1 Dec: 1, 3.

Beegle, Donna, Smith, Karen, and Zaboukos, Troy. 1989. "Residence Staff Follows P.S. Approach to Drinking," *The Beacon*, Vol. 91, No. 8, 19 Oct: 6, 10.

Boothe, Amy. 1988. "Roscoe Joins Student Services," *The Beacon*, University of Portland, Vol. 90, No. 1, 1 Sept: 10.

Carlson, Ragnar. 1988. "Black Activist to Speak at PSU on Apartheid," *The Beacon*, University of Portland, Vol. 90, No. 5, 29 Sept: 1.

Chuinard, EG. 1989. "Letters to the Editor: University Applauded for Statue," *The Beacon*, University of Portland, Vol. 90, No. 16, 19 Jan: 3.

Connor, Helen. 1989. "Redirecting the University of Portland," *The Beacon*, University of Portland, Vol. 90, No. 23, 16 Mar: 8–9.

Connor, Helen. 1989. "State Superintendent Hired by Education School," *The Beacon*, University of Portland, Vol. 90, No. 15, 12 Jan: 1.

Forsberg, Holly. 1988. "New Air Force ROTC Commander Lands at UP," *The Beacon*, University of Portland, Vol. 90, No. 5, 29 Sept: 4.

Hart, Mary. 1989. "KBVM Still Off the Air, Acquires Second License Extension," *The Beacon*, University of Portland, Vol. 90, No. 21, 23 Feb: 4.

Hart, Mary. 1989. "UP Students Experience Life on Migrant Farm," *The Beacon*, University of Portland, Vol. 90, No. 25, 30 Mar: 1.

Haytas, Helana. 1989. "KDUP Acquires Funding for Broadcasting Board," *The Beacon*, University of Portland, Vol. 90, No. 22, 2 Mar: 1, 5.

Haytas, Helana. 1989. "Sistine Concert Results in $13,025 Loss for CPB," *The Beacon*, University of Portland, Vol. 90, No. 20, 16 Feb: 1, 4.

Hill, Jim. 1989. "3 Private Oregon Colleges Rank Among the Best in Report," *The Oregonian*, 7 Oct: 20.

Hill, Nerf Hoop. 1989. "University Sold!," *The Bacon*, University of Portland, Vol. ∞, No. √33, 1 Apr: 1.^

Kapitanovich, Michelle. 1986. "Week of Events Focus on Alcohol Awareness," *The Beacon*, University of Portland, Vol. 88, No. 7, 16 Oct: 1.

Metscham, Suzanne. 1989. "Self Study Points Toward Change," *The Beacon*, University of Portland, Vol. 91, No. 6, 5 Oct: 1.

Moore, Elizabeth. 1989. "Library Commission Attends Orientation," *The Oregonian*, 18 Sept: 18.

Nuxoli, Karen. 1988. "Radio Station Breaks Ground," *The Beacon*, University of Portland, Vol. 89, No. 20, 18 Feb: 1.

Oddo, Rev. Thomas, CSC. 1988. "A President's Welcome," *The Alpha*, University of Portland: 2.

Oddo, Rev. Thomas, CSC. 1989. "Commencement Address." Remarks delivered at the 1989 UP Commencement. Accessed from University of Portland Archives, 12 Aug 2024.

Oregon Statesman-Journal. 1989. "World Affairs Council Chooses New Officers," Salem, Oregon, 30 Sept: 19.

Oregon University System. "Annual Tuition and Fee Rates for Full-Time Students 1973–74 through 1992–93." In *Academic Year Fee Book, 1982–83 through 2011–12*. Published by Oregon University System Budget Operations Division.

Postrel, Dan. 1988. "State School Chief Takes University of Portland Job," *Oregon Statesman-Journal*, Salem, Oregon, 23 Dec: 1–2.

Rambo, K. 2023, 2023. "University of Portland Takes Down Statue of Lewis & Clark Slave York," *The Oregonian/OregonLIVE,* 17 Jun 2020. Updated 22 Feb 2023. https://www.oregonlive.com/news/2020/06/university-of-portland-takes-down-statue-of-lewis-clark-slave-york.html. Accessed 2 Jan 2024.

Rubenstein, Sura. 1989. "Pilot, Missing in Asia Since 1970, Laid to Rest," *The Oregonian*, 25 Apr: 13.

San Nicolas, Claudine. 1988. "Portland Alumni Welcome Oddo," *Pacific Daily News*, Agana Heights, Guam, 6 Mar: 3.

San Nicolas, Claudine. 1988. "Portland U. Seeks Students," *Pacific Daily News*, Agana Heights, Guam, 10 Mar: 7.

Shankle, Michele. 1988. "KBVM: $250,000 Shortfall Delays Broadcast," *The Beacon*, University of Portland, Vol. 90, No. 3, 15 Sept: 1.

Stumbo, Stacy D. 1989. "Campus Struck by Seven Car Thefts," *The Beacon*, University of Portland, Vol. 91, No. 3, 14 Sept: 1.

Stumbo, Stacy D. 1989. "UP Ranked in National Magazine," *The Beacon*, University of Portland, Vol. 91, No. 8, 19 Oct: 1.

Symonds, Darryl. 1988. "KDUP Turns on New Sound," *The Beacon*, University of Portland, Vol. 90, No. 5, 29 Sept: 4.

The Beacon. 1989. "Alcoholism Prompts Schreck to Leave UP," University of Portland, Vol. 91, No. 5, 28 Sept: 1, 3.

The Beacon. 1989. "Tuition Increase: Sign of Things to Come?," editorial, University of Portland, Vol. 90, No. 21, 23 Feb: 2.

The Beacon. 1989. University of Portland, Vol. 90, No. 27, 13 Apr: 12. Photograph by Mike McDougall.*

The Man, Scott. 1989. "C.S.C. Fashions to Change," *The Bacon*, University of Portland, Vol. ∞, No. √33, 1 Apr: 3.^

The Observer. 1989. "Lewis, Oddo, Ruppe Elected to ND Board of Trustees," University of Notre Dame, 19 May: 4.Special to *The Observer*.

The South Bend Tribune. 1989. "Rev. Oddo Elected Notre Dame Trustee," 24 May: 22.

Van Tilburg, Christopher. 1988. "Alumnus Makes Reminiscent Journey Back to the Sparkle of Europe—Salzburg," *The Beacon*, University of Portland, Vol. 90, No. 13, 1 Dec: 6–7.

We Proceeded On. 1989. "Captain Clark Monument Dedicated at University of Portland," Vol. 15, No. 1, Feb: 28.

Zaboukos, Troy. 1989. "'Alternative-Style' Dorm Approved for Fall '90," *The Beacon*, University of Portland, Vol. 91, No. 1, 31 Aug: 1, 3.

Zaboukos, Troy. 1989. "AIDS Conference Educates Students," *The Beacon*, University of Portland, Vol. 90, No. 18, 2 Feb: 1, 5.

Zaboukos, Troy. 1989. "Tuition Expenses Raise 8.6%, Largest Jump in Five Years," *The Beacon*, University of Portland, Vol. 90, No. 21, 23 Feb: 1, 4.

Zaboukos, Troy. 1989. "UP Alumnus Identified After 19 Years," *The Beacon*, University of Portland, Vol. 90, No. 28, 20 Apr: 1.

Zaboukos, Troy. 1989. "UPN Tour Marks First International Visit," *The Beacon*, University of Portland, Vol. 90, No. 25, 30 Mar: 1, 5.

Part Four: This Is Death
1989–PRESENT

Chapter 29: *Funeral March*

—. 1989. "Vigil Service and Final Commendation for Reverend Thomas C. Oddo, C.S.C., President of the University of Portland," 1 Nov. Pamphlet.

Albany Democrat-Herald. 1989. "Memorials Begin for Scholar Killed in Car Accident," Albany, Oregon, 31 Oct: 5. Originally published by *Associated Press*.

Albany Democrat-Herald. 1989. "University of Portland President Killed in Crash," Albany, Oregon, 30 Oct: 5. Originally published by *Associated Press*.

Anonymous. 1989. "Letters to the Editor: A Reflective Essay," *The Beacon*, Vol. 91, Issue 11, 9 Nov: 2.

Boothe, Amy. 1989. "The First 24 Hours: How UP Community Reacts to Its Tragic Loss," *The Beacon*, Vol. 91, No. 10, 2 Nov: 4–5.

Boothe, Amy. 1989. "UP President Dies in Auto Accident," *The Beacon* Special Edition, University of Portland, 30 Oct: 1.

Bose, Romen. 1989. "Friends, Peers Pay Tribute to Oddo," *The Beacon*, Vol. 91, No. 10, 2 Nov: 1, 7.

Davison, Ty. (1990). "The Rev. Thomas Oddo CSC: A year after his death." *The Beacon*, University of Portland, Vol. 93, No. 10, 1 Nov: 2.

Dunham, Courtney. 1989. "Family, Friends Pay Respects to Oddo," *The Beacon*, University of Portland, Vol. 91, No. 11, 9 Nov: 1, 7.

Eldh, Wendi. 1989. "Mass Planned for UOP's Oddo," *Pacific Daily News*, Agana Heights, Guam, 6 Nov: 10.

Grantier, Virginia. 1989. "Sad Day at the U of P," *St. Johns Review*, Vol. 85, Issue 52, 2 Nov: 1, 3.*

Hamilton, Don. (1989). "Hundreds mourn at Oddo's burial in Notre Dame cemetery." *The Oregonian*, 4 Nov: 20.

Journal and Courier. 1989. "Deaths: Rev. Thomas Oddo," Lafayette, Indiana, 31 Oct: 16.

Longview Daily News. 1989. "Oddo Remembered as Dedicated Teacher," Longview, Washington, 2 Nov: 19. Originally published by *Associated Press*.

Masson, Louis. "Remember Always the Swimmer," *Portland Magazine*, University of Portland, Vol. 8, Autumn: 8–9.

Oregon Statesman-Journal. 1989. "Portland School Mourns President," Salem, Oregon, 31 Oct: 5. Originally published by *Associated Press*.*

Peynet, Paulette. 1989. "University's Father Oddo Laid to Rest," *Catholic Sentinel*, 10 Nov: 18–19.

Rutherford, Richard with Barr, Tony.1990. *The Death of a Christian: The Order of Christian Funerals*. Liturgical Press: 265–266.

Sherrer, Charles D, CSC. 1989. "Funeral Services for Father Oddo," University of Portland, Office of the Academic Vice President, 30 Oct.

Soma, Tom. 1989. "On the Bluff: The Goodness of Seven," *Portland Magazine*, University of Portland, Vol. 8, Autumn: 3–7.

Spokane Chronicle. 1989. "U of Portland Chief Killed in Car Wreck," Spokane, Washington, 30 Oct: 5. Originally published by *Associated Press*.

The Beacon Special Edition. 1989. "Oddo Funeral Set for Wednesday," University of Portland, 30 Oct: 2.

The New York Times. 1989. "Father Thomas Oddo, Catholic Educator, 45," Obituaries, 31 Oct: 38. Originally published by *Associated Press*.

The Observer. 1989. "Notre Dame Trustee Killed in Auto Accident," University of Notre Dame, 31 Oct: 3.Special to *The Observer*.

The Oregonian. 1989. "Host of Dignitaries to Attend Funeral for University of Portland President," 1 Nov: 22.

The Oregonian. 1989. "Oddo Contribution Cut Short," 31 Oct: 18.

The South Bend Tribune. 1989. "Oddo, Formerly of N.D., Killed in Auto Accident," South Bend, Indiana, 30 Oct: 30.*

The Sun. 1989. "Church Scholar Remembered," Bremerton, Washington, 31 Oct: 10. Originally published by *Associated Press*.

Wahpepah, Wilda. 1989. "Stunned Students Say They Related to Father Tom," *The Oregonian*, 31 Oct: 11.

Wahpepah, Wilda. 1989. "UP Pays Homage to President," *The Oregonian*, 2 Nov: 21, 26.

Waldschmidt, Most Rev. Paul E, CSC. 1989. "Office of the Dead for Rev. Thomas C. Oddo, CSC." Originally delivered 1 Nov. Accessed from private document collection of Fr. Richard Rutherford, 9 Sept 2023.

Warner, Richard V, CSC. 1989. "Eulogy for Thomas C. Oddo, C.S.C.," Originally delivered 2 Nov 1989.

Chapter 30: *"The grief of our great loss"*

Boothe, Amy. 1990. "Hear campus issues," *The Beacon*, University of Portland, Vol. 91, No. 27, 19 Apr: 2.

Boothe, Amy. 1990. "The First 24 Hours," *The Log*, yearbook, University of Portland, Vol. 56, Spring: 124–127.

Catholic Sentinel. 1989. "UP Community Grieves Over Father Oddo's Death," Vol. 120, No. 45, 3 Nov: 1, 10–11.

Corvallis Gazette-Times. 1989. "Oregon Briefs: Driver Cleared in Fatal Crash," Corvallis, Oregon, 9 Dec: 4.

Davison, Ty. 1990. "The Rev. Thomas Oddo C.S.C.: A Year After His Death," *The Beacon*, University of Portland, Vol. 93, No. 10, 1 Nov: 2.

Frei, Terry. 1989. "Oddo's Death Leaves One Asking: Why?," *The Oregonian*, 1 Nov: 23.

Grantier, Virginia. 1989. "Sad Day at the U of P," *St. Johns Review*, Vol. 85, Issue 52, 2 Nov.

Hamilton, Don. (1989). "Hundreds mourn at Oddo's burial in Notre Dame cemetery." *The Oregonian*, 4 Nov: 20.

Nilles, Nancy. (1993). "Campus Art." *The Beacon*, University of Portland, Vol. 95, No. 20, 25 Feb: 7.

Nip, Melissa. 2009. "Art, Hidden and in Plain Sight," *The Beacon*, University of Portland, Vol. 111, No. 8, 29 Oct: 7.

Slepak, Donna. 1989. "Santiago Morales' Story Moved Father Tom Oddo," *Catholic Sentinel*, 10 Nov.

St. Louis Review. 1992. "Wronged Oregon Migrant Worker Accepts University's Scholarship," 20 Mar: 4.

Stumbo, Stacy. 1989. "UP Students Mourn Loss of 'Our President,'" *Catholic Sentinel*, Vol. 120, No. 45, 3 Nov: 10.

The Beacon. 1989. "Can We Help?," editorial, University of Portland, Vol. 91, No. 11, 9 Nov: p 2.

The Beacon. 1989. "Pulling Through," editorial, University of Portland, Vol. 91, No. 10, 2 Nov: 2.

The Beacon. 1990. "Give Paluska a Shot," editorial, University of Portland, Vol. 91, No. 21, 1 Mar: 2.

The Beacon. 1992. "Newsbriefs: New Museum to Open in Shipstad," University of Portland, Vol. 95, No. 4, 24 Sept: 4.

The Beacon. 1993."Newsbriefs: Mass to Honor Memory of Fr. Thomas Oddo," University of Portland, Vol. 96, No. 9, 4 Nov: 6.

The Boston Globe. 1989. "Western Orthodox Church in America: Memorial Mass for Fr. Tom Oddo, C.S.C.," advertisement, 4 Nov: 27.

The Log. 1990. "One Brief Shining Moment," yearbook, University of Portland, Vol. 56, Spring.*

The Oregonian. 1989. "Oddo Contribution Cut Short," 31 Oct: 18.

The Oregonian. 1989. "Pilots Hoping to Score Goal: New Stadium," 13 Nov: 21.

Tyson, Father David. 1990. "An Interview With Father Tyson." Interviewed by Scott Brutocao. *The Scholastic*, University of Notre Dame, 26 Apr : 8–10.

Zaboukos, Troy. 1989. "Plan for Dorm Construction Rests on Donation," *The Beacon*, University of Portland, Vol. 91, No. 12, 16 Nov: 1, 4.